New Families, Old Scripts

by the same authors

Trauma, Attachment and Family Permanence
Fear Can Stop You Loving
Edited by Caroline Archer and Alan Burnell for Family Futures
Foreword by Daniel A. Hughes
ISBN 1 84310 021 5

First Steps in Parenting the Child Who Hurts
Tiddlers and Toddlers, Second Edition
Caroline Archer
Adoption UK
ISBN 1 85302 801 0

Next Steps in Parenting the Child Who Hurts
Tykes and Teens
Caroline Archer
Adoption UK
ISBN 1 85302 802 9

of related interest

Reaching the Vulnerable Child
Therapy with Traumatized Children
Janie Rymaszewska and Terry Philpot
Foreword by Mary Walsh, Co-founder and Chief Executive of SACCS
ISBN 1 84310 329 X

The Child's Own Story
Life Story Work with Traumatized Children
Richard Rose and Terry Philpot
Foreword by Mary Walsh, Co-founder and Chief Executive of SACCS
ISBN 1 84310 287 0

Fostering Now
Messages from Research
Ian Sinclair
Foreword by Tom Jeffreys, Director General, Children, Families and Young People Directorate, DfES
ISBN 1 84310 362 1

Connecting with Kids through Stories
Using Narratives to Facilitate Attachment in Adopted Children
Denise B. Lacher, Todd Nichols and Joanne C. May
ISBN 1 84310 797 X

A Safe Place for Caleb
An Interactive Book for Kids, Teens, and Adults with Issues of Attachment, Grief and Loss, or Early Trauma
Kathleen A. Chara and Paul J. Chara, Jr.
Illustrations by J.M. Berns
ISBN 1 84310 799 6

New Families, Old Scripts

A Guide to the Language of Trauma and Attachment in Adoptive Families

Caroline Archer and Christine Gordon

Foreword by Alan Burnell

Jessica Kingsley Publishers
London and Philadelphia

First published in 2006
by Jessica Kingsley Publishers
116 Pentonville Road
London N1 9JB, UK
and
400 Market Street, Suite 400
Philadelphia, PA 19106, USA

www.jkp.com

Library of Congress Cataloging in Publication Data
A CIP catalog record for this book is available from the Library of Congress
Archer, Caroline, 1948-
New families, old scripts : a guide to the language of trauma and attachment in adoptive families / Caroline Archer and Christine Gordon, foreword by Alan Burnell.
    p. cm.
Includes bibliographical references and index.
ISBN-13: 978-1-84310-258-8 (pbk. : alk. paper)
ISBN-10: 1-84310-258-7 (pbk. : alk. paper) 1. Adoptive parents--Handbooks, manuals, etc. 2. Parenting--Handbooks, manuals, etc. 3. Problem children--Handbooks, manuals, etc. I. Gordon, Christine. II. Title.
 HV875.A682 2006
 649'.145--dc22

2005035139

British Library Cataloguing in Publication Data
A CIP catalogue record for this book is available from the British Library

ISBN-13: 978 1 84310 258 8
ISBN-10: 1 84310 258 7

Printed and bound in Great Britain by
Athenaeum Press, Gateshead, Tyne and Wear

Caroline Archer:
I dedicate this work to my husband whose quiet, rock-like
character allowed me to experience a truly 'secure base' and learn
to explore; and subsequently to my four adopted children, for
allowing me to share their early hurts and ongoing struggles.
Between them they have shown me most of
what I needed to know.

Christine Gordon:
Dedicated to my mum, who gave me the security and stability that
she never had in her childhood. Mum, in doing so you taught me
the power of love and also that change is possible.

Acknowledgments

We are grateful to Alan Burnell and Jay Vaughan, co-directors at Family Futures Consortium, for their encouragement in developing this guide from planning stage through to completion. Their belief and support has been invaluable. Our thanks, too, go to Griselda Kellie-Smith (also of Family Futures) for reading and commenting on our efforts so cogently and to Charlotte Chan (now part of Family Futures' support team for families) for painstakingly untangling many of our last-minute manuscript knots. In addition, we thank Steve Jones, commissioning editor at Jessica Kingsley Publishers, for believing in us and sticking with us over 'the long haul' and 'the shorter overhaul'.

Special mention must be made of all the friends, colleagues, parents and children who have contributed so much to our understanding over the years. We have gained immeasurably from the persistence, courage, humour and determination of so many adoptive families: they have certainly been our best teachers! We are also indebted to Adoption UK (formerly PPIAS) whose backing initially enabled us to attend training events on attachment and trauma, both at home and abroad, and set us on track. Finally, we owe a great debt of gratitude to Dr Daniel Hughes for his openness and groundbreaking approach to psychotherapeutic work with troubled children and families. Dan is now training consultant to Family Futures, flying in regularly from Maine to keep us on our toes!

This has been, and continues to be, an exciting and collaborative journey: we hope readers will join us as we meander through some of the complex byways of adoptive family life. Please don't rush to complete the journey in one go. Use our guide as you would any travel guide: choosing the areas you'd most like to visit and sharing them with colleagues, family or friends. Take time to rest and reflect along the way, remembering that it's the journey that's important, not the final destination.

Contents

Foreword

Currently, great emphasis is placed on recruiting adoptive parents, in order to increase the number of children, at present accommodated, who would benefit from the permanency of adoption. This is an important and worthy direction for social policy to take. Perhaps the most important lesson we have learned at Family Futures, both from experience and from adoption literature, is that post-adoption support is *the* vital determinant of placement outcome. Recent adoption support agency legislation represents recognition at governmental level of the importance of supporting adoptive families into the future. Since children placed for adoption today are older and more challenging, with a wider range of attachment difficulties and unresolved early traumas than previously, parenting these youngsters requires more than endless love, good intentions and commitment.

That 'something else', I believe, is specific parent education and support for adopters from experienced adoptive parents who can empathise and identify with their struggles. Parents are not only the most precious resource society has for adopted children, they can make the difference between lives overshadowed by crime, prostitution, drug addiction or mental illness and the integration of vulnerable children into society as healthily functioning adults. In my view the role of parent mentor as 'guide and interpreter' for adopters is the key to the future of a successful and effective adoption service in the twenty-first century.

The model for today's adoption service is an integrated, multi-disciplinary pre- and post-adoption specialist service. Children being placed for adoption today have multiple needs: neurophysiological, socio-emotional and psychological: their parents need access to expert services to help address these issues. However, parents remain the primary agents of change for their youngsters. The 'structure, nurture, engagement and challenge' (Jernberg and Booth 2001) they offer to their adopted children is the vital conduit for repair, re-learning and healthy development. To sustain this, parents also need to be nurtured, supported and guided. In my experience it is other experienced parents who have the greatest understanding, compassion and wisdom to provide this.

This book is drawn from the experience and understanding gained by a generation of adopters who have pioneered reparenting work with older adopted children. Caroline Archer and Christine Gordon have led this movement and in writing this book have attempted to encapsulate the experience of those pioneers. The approach and strategies they outline here describe very clearly the style of parenting that 'challenging children' require. This very practical, yet theoretically-based, approach is what parents often crave, as it is those day-to-day struggles that can make or break adoptive placements.

As an agency, Family Futures has pioneered an integrated multi-disciplinary approach, working with experienced parents as co-workers and in partnership with adoptive parents seeking our help. Without adopters as part of the team, and without parent mentors' collaboration, our service to children and families would not be as effective as it is today. I believe that all adoption agencies should consider recruiting trained parent mentors as an integral part of their adoption service.

I hope this book will be a valuable guide for parent mentors and adoptive parents alike and will also enhance the skills adoption professionals bring to the families with whom they work.

Alan Burnell
Co-director of Family Futures Consortium

An introduction to the language of trauma and parent mentoring

The lives of children and their adoptive families are complex and multi-faceted. The majority of children now placed for adoption have experienced damaging levels of traumatic separation, loss, neglect, abuse or chronically inconsistent care that falls well short of Bowlby's concept of 'good enough' parenting. Their attachment patterns are insecure and disorganised: a variety of therapeutic inputs are frequently needed, for child, parents and family, over the lifetime of the placement, and beyond. In the authors' experience these needs are best met through packages of integrated, attachment-based, multi-disciplinary support that actively promote the role of parents as the prime 'movers and shakers' in their children's journey towards greater physical, social, emotional, intellectual and spiritual health. Below are some useful definitions of trauma and attachment (see also Figure 1).

Trauma:

- is 'a wound or injury to mind or body that implies the need for repair' (Waites 1993)
- is 'a disorganization, or failure of organization, of the system' (Waites 1993)
- creates a profound sense of helplessness and isolation
- involves neurobiological responses (fight, flight and freeze) that are initially adaptive to survival.

Attachment:

- is 'an enduring affective bond characterized by a tendency to seek and maintain proximity to a specific person, particularly when under stress ... which profoundly influences every component of the human condition' (Levy and Orlans 1998)

- is 'a relationship that develops between two or more organisms as their behavioural and physiological systems become attuned' (Field 1985)
- is an ongoing relational process involving two individuals promoting reciprocity and co-regulation and protecting against trauma.

Attachment disorganisation:

- 'disorganized attachment behavior (reflects) a profound failure to integrate attachment-related behavior, feelings and thoughts' (Solomon and George 1999)
- 'across the lifespan, the disorganized attachment category is characterized by contradictory behavioural strategies' (Lyons-Ruth, Bronfman and Atwood 1999)
- attachment disorganisation is closely associated with neurobiological disorganisation in infancy due to maltreatment or repeated trauma.

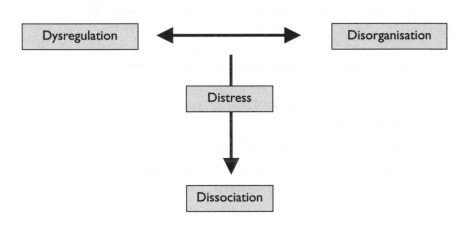

Figure 1: Trauma: the four 'D's

Adoptive parents living with maltreated and traumatised youngsters often experience high levels of stress themselves as they struggle to understand, contain, nurture and educate their troubled children. Whilst the support needs of their families are now being recognised, the means of meeting them has been less comprehensively addressed. It is for this reason that the innovative developments made by the authors, initially through Family Futures Consortium but now extending into local agency provision, are discussed here. Just as families' support requirements are complex and multi-faceted, so too are the therapeutic responses that have been introduced to provide 'best fit, best practice' for individual families. Within this context the role of the parent mentor evolved to foster relationships with adopters built on trust and mutual respect and to nurture the family support networks that are essential to this most challenging of parenting tasks. A two-year, part-time training programme offered by Family Futures Consortium provides ideal preparation for experienced adoptive parents wishing to undertake the mentoring role in their local communities.

Role of the parent mentor

A significant part of the parent mentor's remit is to provide support and coping strategies for adopters who are struggling to understand and deal with their children's puzzling behaviour. Mentors, experienced adopters themselves, spend a good deal of time with parents, getting to know them and gaining their trust. The many hours spent discussing individual difficulties with adopters face to face are supplemented by telephone calls and extended follow-up letters. The latter allow mentors time to reflect on the family's current situation and to expand the understanding and range of intervention strategies offered to parents. Mentors can also supplement their ongoing interpretations of the behavioural 'language of trauma' children unconsciously use to let parents know of their difficulties.

Over time these letters have proved invaluable, both in reinforcing adopters' memories of discussions and in providing a permanent record and reminder of the complex behaviours they face with their children. As their number grew it became obvious that, although each letter was written with a specific family in mind, they formed universal templates that could be tailored to fit other families facing similar difficulties. In doing so it is important to strike the right balance between 'bespoke' and 'off the peg' solutions. Tailors have specific areas of individual measurement that are superimposed onto basic templates, to create individual patterns that best fit the 'bumps and bulges' of the individual. So too, the unique 'bumps and bulges' of adoptive families are best covered by practitioners who apply a 'made-to-measure' approach, rather than 'one size fits all'.

All the letters set out in the Alphabet of Issues in this book are drawn from actual letters written for individual families over the past five years by the authors. Identifying features have been removed and names changed to preserve families' anonymity; in some cases additional material has been added to the originals, to further extend their scope. It is the authors' hope that reproducing these letters for a wider audience, of adoptive parents and their supporters, will bring additional insights and confidence that reflect their approach to traumatised children. Readers are invited to 'pick and mix' the issues addressed to suit their individual needs, whilst remaining mindful that the best solutions will be sensitively tailored for 'goodness of fit'. Here parents, as 'the experts' on their own youngsters, should feel particularly well placed to come up with the most appropriate and effective strategies to suit their unique situations.

Learning the language of trauma and hurt

Parent mentors can be pivotal in enabling adopters to 'get on the same wavelength' as their troubled children, to begin to make sense of their behavioural 'language' and thinking patterns, through familiarising them with the 'language of trauma'. If a child is born into a family where fear, unpredictable behaviour and maltreatment are common features, his body, brain and nervous system develop to maximise his capacity to survive. He develops insecure, often disorganised, patterns of attachment. In the face of ongoing insecurity and unpredictability his neurobiological systems repeatedly go on 'red alert', priming his body to respond through physical and psychological 'fight, flight or freeze': major heart and respiration rate changes are observable. Although young children may be completely helpless to fight back or run away, these physical changes still occur, leading to overwhelming feelings of fear, panic and distress.

Consider more closely what this means for developing children, where the senses and emotions predominate and language is mostly pre- or non-verbal. Youngsters draw most of the information about their internal world from their inner senses and about the outside world from the more familiar external senses of touch, taste, smell, sight, hearing and movement. Bathed in a stream of sensory and emotional information from 'good enough' caregivers they derive increasing order and meaning. With parents' ongoing support, they gradually become more fluent in the 'language' of their bodies and increasingly competent in expressing themselves to others, primarily through non-verbal means, such as facial expressions, gesture, posture, muscle tone, and rudimentary play.

Figure 2: Attachment security

Simultaneously, sensitive caregivers learn to make sense of these communications and 'talk back' to their children, nurturing their connections with them and the children's connections with and within themselves. Over time neurobiological information pathways are established, forming part of the internal system of feedback loops through which they learn to manage and process incoming information. Provided with repeated opportunities to practise self-regulation, social interactions, to feel 'heard' and to 'read' other people, children develop secure attachment relationships (see Figure 2). Through the continuous process of feedback from their parents they derive perceptions of themselves as valued members of the family. They learn to rely on caregivers to take good care of them and that their world is predictable and to a growing extent influenced by them, as they gain understanding of, and control over, their internal and external environment.

In contrast, traumatised and maltreated children are exposed to very different patterns of attachment experience and acquire a very different 'script' within their original family environment. Since the interactive socio-emotional language of their caregivers is impoverished or garbled, these youngsters do not receive appropriate recognition of, or feedback from, their rudimentary communications. Their chances of acquiring healthy attachments and sensory and emotional literacy are compromised; their perceptions of themselves and their world are distorted (see Figure 3). These youngsters cannot create sufficient order out of their unpredictable or terrifying

Figure 3: Attachment insecurity

environments to develop a positive sense of self, trust in their caregivers, or gain realistic views of their own capacities. Like all children they are immersed in the language of their families and their communication skills develop to facilitate their survival within this environment. Sadly their first language, their 'mother tongue', is the language of trauma and hurt, based on models of an unsafe and unpredictable world. Since their thinking and internal feedback loops are distorted or poorly developed, this is a language where the potential for misunderstanding is great and the capacity for self-knowledge and self-expression limited. Moreover, since the 'mother tongue' is the one on which individuals continue to rely, particularly in stressful circumstances, traumatised children are likely to go on experiencing communication and relationship difficulties, even in new, healthier environments. Understanding the language of trauma allows adopters to talk to traumatised and maltreated children in more meaningful ways and gradually introduce them to a newer language: the language of security and love.

Behaviour as children's first language

For young children, the primary means of relating to, and interacting with, their world is through behaviour and body language. It is in the things they do, or do not do, that they 'speak' to us of their thoughts and needs and recount their experiences and difficulties. Since, developmentally, actions precede words, if children's early attachment experiences are not 'good enough', they get stuck in 'acting out', or 'acting in' what they cannot put into words. Indeed, maltreated children can be highly articulate at expressing themselves through their behavioural conversations: the language of trauma is predominantly the language of 'doing' (or 'not doing'). These communications are primarily unconscious and frequently remain in discrete feedback loops that become self-perpetuating. On an internal level ('talking to themselves'), they do not interconnect sufficiently with other internal feedback systems to be influenced by them. On an external level ('talking to others') children may continue acting in ways that elicit angry or hurtful responses from caregivers, or that fail to elicit 'answers'. These patterns are evident in the way some traumatised youngsters engage in repetitious behaviours, without gaining comfort (due to 'internal road blocks'), or in how many appear not to learn from their mistakes, even with the support and guidance of their parents ('external road blocks').

Since adoptive parents often feel isolated and alone with their troubled children, a key role for parent mentors is to help them establish better attachment connections within their family through strengthening links within their local community. The wisdom of the saying 'it takes a community to raise a child' is perhaps nowhere better demonstrated than in 'instant' families, where children are suddenly transplanted from one environment to another and parents, thrust into unfamiliar roles, need all the help they can muster.

In addition to fostering sound external support networks, mentors strive to develop close relationships with adoptive parents, and their families, modelling the positive regard, understanding, availability, dependability and healthy boundaries that form the basis of all good attachment relationships. By nurturing these close connections (see Figure 4), empathically exploring and containing parents' anxieties and doubts and actively encouraging their belief in themselves as 'good enough' caregivers, they enable adopters to gain the security and confidence to become highly effective 'Jemima Crackit' attachment figures for their children and to play an invaluable role in healing the hurts of early developmental attachment trauma. This process can be qualitatively and quantitatively demanding of energy and time but leads to long-term improvements for all members of the adoptive family: as 'Panicchio' learns to let go of his 'knee-jerk' stress responses and gradually becomes a 'real-live child' (see pp.29–31 for a description of the Jemima Crackit and Panicchio characters).

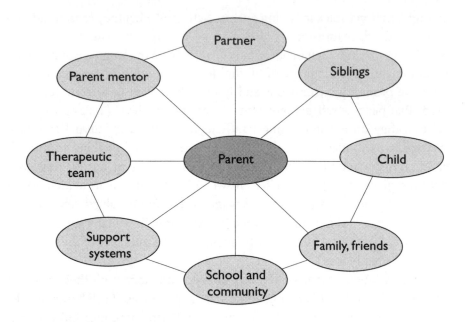

Figure 4: Making connections

Introducing the families

The families outlined briefly below reflect adoptive family life in the twenty-first century and form the basis for our 'worked examples' in the Alphabet of Issues. These letters are the backbone of this book and are drawn from real-life letters written by parent mentors for individual parents and children, to supplement ongoing therapeutic support work. They have been adapted to fit our anonymised families and to cover specific issues in greater detail. They are intended to provide basic patterns from which mentors and parents, working together, can create individual, attachment-based reparenting programmes for their families.

The youngsters described range from four to twelve years: teenagers often need additional strategies that take account not only of their traumatic histories but also acknowledge the extensive practice they have had in the 'language of trauma' and the negative feedback loops that can evolve in adoptive families who receive insufficient effective support early on. We begin the Alphabet of Issues with an explanation of two of our main characters that help readers to understand the language of trauma followed by a lengthy discussion that reflects the significance of aggressive and angry behaviour in many adoptive families. Since children rarely demonstrate a single behaviour in isolation, readers are also cross-referenced to other related areas within the book.

The Ponting family

Justin and **Juliet** live with **Grace** and **Peter** Ponting. Justin was placed with his adoptive family aged three years after suffering abuse and neglect in his birth family. Justin seemed to be managing well in his adoptive family until the family were approached to adopt his birth sister, then aged three years herself. Juliet, too, had experienced abuse and neglect, despite increased social work support to her birth family. From the start Juliet displayed major behavioural problems which dominated family life and left Justin feeling left out and resentful. Four years down the line Grace and Peter are seeking help with both children's aggressive and angry behaviour.

Grace and Peter are very caring parents: excellent at providing nurturing experiences for both children. However, they struggle with establishing boundaries and structure in the family and with helping Justin (now eight years) manage his anger towards Juliet. Justin often says he hates his sister. Rather than giving Justin opportunities to explore these feelings, Grace tells Justin he does not really mean it and he, in fact, loves Juliet. Having no real way of expressing his feelings verbally, Justin's angry outbursts increase, both at home and school, making home life difficult and resulting in loss of friendships. Justin is now very unhappy and blames his sister for all his difficulties.

Work with Grace and Peter is aimed at helping them examine their parenting styles, emphasising how talented they are in nurturing their children while endeavouring to help them lay down firm boundaries and develop their skills in hearing what Justin has to say, allowing him to express his anger with, and jealousy of, his sister, and offering Justin (and Juliet) sufficient opportunities to express their anger more appropriately.

The Warne family

Elaine and **Sam** Warne find **Mic** and **Sara**'s sexualised behaviours, attention seeking and tendency to 'space out' (dissociate) difficult to handle. Mic (eight years) and Sara (five years) had been sexually abused by birth family members and associates on a prolonged and organised basis. Neglect and unpredictable parenting added to their distress. At ages five and three years the children were the subject of Child Protection Orders and, following two short foster placements, joined their adoptive family two years later.

Intense therapeutic work was supplemented by regular mentoring support to the family. An attachment-based, developmental reparenting approach formed the foundation for strategies developed in partnership with Elaine and Sam to help them understand and manage the traumatic legacy of the children's histories and the challenges they posed.

The McGrath family

Matt (aged five years) came to his adoptive family one year ago, joining Ceri (12 years, placed at age three years), two older birth children of Josie and Freddy McGrath, and Lucy, their young granddaughter. Matt's history is explored in some depth in the'"F" is for feelings' section. Matt suffered emotional and physical neglect, including malnutrition, whilst living with his birth mother. Subsequently, with his maternal aunt, he was exposed to serious neglect, physical abuse and, probably, sexual abuse from casual visitors to her home. At four years, following failed rehabilitation attempts and several short foster placements, Matt joined Freddy and Josie's family.

Matt's behaviour proved problematic, even to his experienced adopters: including prolonged periods of screaming, 'control issues', 'going slow' and not responding to his caregivers yet chatting away to acquaintances and strangers. The family were supported over an extended period. Their mentor was a regular caller for some time, helping Josie, Freddy and their two eldest children make sense of Matt's puzzling responses and devising ways of 'getting in touch' with Matt using 'Think Toddler Think' and developmentally-based strategies.

Ceri had by this time been part of the adoptive family for almost eight years. He too had experienced serious neglect in his birth family. Currently his persistent stealing cried out for individual and family therapeutic work, with ongoing home support from the mentor.

The Lee family

Sharon (six years) and nine-year-old Carrie's adoptive placement with Gill and James Lee followed early birth family experiences of global neglect and repeated physical restraint (Sharon). Several brief foster placements followed, causing added disruption to Carrie's schooling and compounding both girls' distorted world-views. Whilst Sharon 'acted out' her distress through non-compliance, aggression and acting with little recognition of danger, Carrie 'acted in', frequently shutting down and resisting closeness. In the main Carrie exhibited protective 'parentified' behaviour towards Sharon yet sometimes displayed unexpected outbursts and loss of control and had also been seen to threaten Sharon verbally and physically.

The parent mentor's work focused on addressing Sharon's dangerous behaviour, helping Carrie get in touch with her 'little girl inside' and making sense of both girls' puzzling responses to pain. Their parents were introduced to the concept of attachment reparenting and helped to create appropriate strategies using their newly identified 'Jemima Crackit' skills.

The Katich family

As a baby, **Anthea** experienced neglect and abuse at the hands of her birth parents. When accommodated, she had several changes of carer prior to being placed with her adoptive parents, **Jackie** and **Simon** Katich, at five years of age. Anthea has a limited emotional repertoire, tending to respond to situations with rage that masks other overwhelming emotions: primarily terror and grief.

Now, aged 12 years, Anthea has recently transferred to secondary school and is having major difficulties adjusting to changes in classroom routine, taking greater responsibility for herself, and maintaining friendships. Frequently when she returns home from school, she has intense outbursts, during which she swears, shouts and defies parental requests. She has, at times, resorted to physical attacks on her adoptive mother. The family was referred for therapeutic help when the placement was at breaking point. The initial work focused on helping Anthea and her parents get in touch with Anthea's painful history and to recognise the impact this continues to have on her. She continues to struggle in school. Her parents receive regular support from their parent mentor to help them, and school staff, manage Anthea's distressing behaviours more effectively.

The Tait-Pritchard family

Kirsty is the eldest of four siblings accommodated after serious concerns about their welfare within their birth family. All four children were neglected emotionally and physically over a prolonged period. On placement in their first foster home Kirsty was six years old, **Josh** four years, **Alex** three years and **Danny** eighteen months old. Kirsty had demonstrated some overtly sexualised behaviour, whilst within her birth family, suggestive of sexual abuse. She had also been described as rude and aggressive, with a tendency to overeat and with poor personal hygiene. The youngsters were often found barely clad, unwashed, smelly and riddled with head lice.

After some months in care the children moved to two separate families. Josh and Alex were placed for adoption together; Kirsty and Danny, now eight years and three years respectively, moved in with a lesbian couple. Kirsty's adoptive family was immediately referred for therapy. Initially it was

Danny whose difficulties relating to his new parents, **Mel** and **Rae**, caused the greatest anxiety. He would 'go to anyone', and was generally a busy and demanding youngster. Whilst Kirsty was described by outsiders as 'smiley, helpful, good mannered, sociable' and 'doing well in school', her adopters often experienced her as 'distant' or 'like a lodger' at home. Here she avoided intimacy, was over-compliant and behaved in 'strange and sneaky' ways, behind adults backs. Kirsty also spent periods alone 'staring into space', or masturbating, and occasionally exhibited inappropriate, sexualised behaviour towards her adoptive parents.

Whilst therapeutic family work with Danny focused on developmental reparenting to establish security and boundaries and to encourage greater self-regulation, work with Kirsty needed to be more gradual, as she frequently dissociated in 'difficult' situations. At home, the mentor focused on support-ing Mel and Rae alter their perspective on 'being good', in light of Kirsty's early history, and actively engaging in 'wicked' and fun ways with her. Her parents were also encouraged to help Kirsty recognise and express her feelings and needs more openly.

The Kasprowicz family

At the age of four years, **Luke** has been living in his adoptive family for almost 12 months. Luke's birth mother was a habitual drug user who worked as a prostitute to support her habit. This meant she often left Luke alone, scared, cold and hungry, whilst she went out for long periods. When at home she was often 'too spaced out' to identify or meet his basic needs; her lifestyle provided Luke with little consistency, predictability or emotional security.

During his first year, Luke was accommodated. Following an unsuccessful attempt at rehabilitation with his birth mother, Luke experienced several further foster care moves and began to display some worrying behaviours indicating attachment insecurity. **Maria** and **Anthony** Kasprowicz, Luke's adoptive parents, were determined to overcome his difficulties, supported by their extensive family and friendship networks. Therapeutic family work and mentoring was undertaken and Luke's adopters began to take on board the serious effects of Luke's early traumatic history. They are now eager to help Luke feel safe with them and to challenge his beliefs that they will let him down and that he will soon be moving on.

The Gillespie family

Martin, aged eight years, was the product of a family home filled with violence, anger, chaos and unpredictability. His parents also took drugs and abused alcohol.

Bedtime for Martin was not a peaceful, relaxing time. He often went to bed hungry, dirty and at the whim of the adults caring for him. Lying there he remained on the alert for sounds of violence that could erupt at any time, fearful for his own safety. These feelings, difficult enough to manage during the day, were overwhelming at night when he was alone and most vulnerable and his terror at its height. Martin brought the resulting 'night-time survival template' with him into his adoptive family, remaining vigilant and unable to feel comfortable when alone. Our aim is to help Martin and his parents, **Hazel** and **Colin** Gillespie, make sense of why going to bed and night-time is so distressing for Martin and to explore ways of helping Martin feel safe enough to sleep.

In addition Martin regularly has tantrums in which he tries to punch, kick and spit at Hazel. During these scenes he shouts at her, telling her he hates her, she never lets him do anything and that she is the worst mother in the world. Hazel recognises that Martin learned this abusive pattern when he was living with his birth family. Work is undertaken to help Hazel empathise (nurture) with how hard it was for Martin as a baby, and to recognise he may have learned to hurt others through witnessing violence and being assaulted himself. She can then provide structure for Martin by reminding him that hurting other people is not a healthy way of showing anger and by giving him numerous, supported opportunities to 'practise' other ways both of letting her know how he feels and of managing his feelings.

The Manghezi family

Until she was five years old **Valerie** lived with her birth mother and mother's succession of partners. Valerie struggled to keep her mother's attention and frequently turned to her 'uncles' for care and attention. Sadly not only were Mum's relationships turbulent and transient, at least two partners are believed to have sexually abused Valerie.

Valerie came into care following concerns from her class teacher about her emotional and physical welfare. Her capacity to learn at school was described as seriously impaired due to her tendency to be over-anxious, to find change difficult and her inability to make and sustain friendships. She was often very 'attention seeking' in class, unable to complete her work without verbal or physical support from staff.

After several short-term foster placements Valerie was placed with **Hilary** Manghezi, an experienced, single adopter, at nearly nine years old. Almost four years on Hilary was finding Valerie's anxious and rigid behaviours very stressful. Therapeutic interventions centred on helping Valerie, and her adoptive Mum, make sense of her current feelings and actions in terms of her past experiences. After lengthy discussions and direct observation the mentor devised a long-term programme of parenting interventions. Currently the focus is on reducing Valerie's need to cling to obsessive bedtime rituals through increasing her basic sense of security.

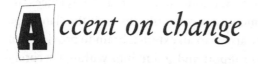ccent on change

Jemima Crackit and the new family script

Figure 5: Panicchio and Jemima Crackit

Most people know the story of Pinocchio, the wooden puppet who wanted to be a 'real' boy and achieved this with the help of Jiminy Cricket, his moral conscience. The concept has been expanded in this book to embody 'Panicchio', the traumatised child who reacts with panic, fear, anger or dissociation to the challenges of life. His moral conscience and 'external brain' is 'Jemima Crackit', the adoptive mother who works to 'rewrite' Panicchio's disorganised 'scripts' and help him develop not only a conscience but also a more mature 'feeling, thinking and reasoning brain'. In doing so he becomes a 'real', more securely attached child.

Although rewriting the family script represents a broader global enterprise than Pinocchio acquiring a moral code and internal conscience, the analogy is sound. Panicchio communicates primarily through the 'language of trauma' and continues to require access to an external brain to provide him with essential information, and to support and guide him within a securely structured framework, whilst he rehearses newer scripts, and explores more mature ways of thinking and being. There is no one better fitted to fulfil this leading role than the adoptive parent.

Sufficient research and preparation time is essential for caregivers to 'get into role'. If Jemima Crackit is to become skilled at interpreting her child's old scripts and help him create a new, shared family script, she must first be familiar and comfortable with her own childhood narrative. She can then draw on these experiences to embrace and interpret her child's story and develop a reciprocal dialogue with increasing confidence and fluency. By first casting the spotlight on the past and making it real, she becomes more able to breathe real life into her child's existence and help him feel truly part of their new family script.

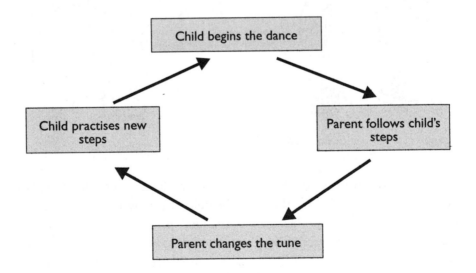

Figure 6: The dance of attunement, attachment and development

Whilst Panicchio needs ongoing access to Jemima Crackit's external brain to achieve greater reality, this is not a one-way process. Jemima Crackit must continually 'upload' information from her child, holding it and processing it for him. Simultaneously she continues to 'download' material from her own childhood and mature parental scripts, allowing Panicchio to elaborate his own 'mental software'. It is through simple, repeated moment-to-moment activities that Panicchio and Jemima engage in this dramatic 'dance of attunement, attachment and development' (see Figure 6).

Jemima Crackit may need to continually revise and choreograph Panicchio's movements, senses and emotions, as well as his thoughts and beliefs, in order to reduce his knee-jerk, trauma-based reactions and nurture a 'real little boy' with increasing self-awareness and self-control. To do so she must feel confident with her leading role in this intense drama and be able to 'ad lib' with ease, good timing and good humour.

Since Jemima's role is a strenuous and challenging one, it demands plenty of rehearsal time in comfortable surroundings. It involves a good deal of thinking oneself into the parts and the capacity to trust one's gut feelings that comes from getting a real sense of the role. Not only has Jemima to practise her own vital part in the dialogue, she also has to get under the skin of her co-actor Panicchio, providing sensitive and timely cues to draw him into the performance more fully.

The steps in this dance are numerous and complex: there are stresses and risks that need to be identified and spotlighted. Jemima must guard against becoming rooted to the spot through identifying too closely with Panicchio's woodenness, or through getting tied up in knots by his string-pulling and acting-out behaviours. She must be confident her backing group will keep her from inadvertently dancing to Panicchio's discordant tune. Outstanding performances are rarely the result of individual inspiration and energy and cannot be staged without substantial resource implications. A veritable panoply of stagehands is required to provide sufficient support, encouragement, direction, prompts and feedback to promote success. Opportunities for new performers to work alongside old stagehands and to introduce innovative practices are also essential if Jemima and Panicchio are to co-create a new family script and rehearse their real-life story together successfully.

These two characters provide useful images when trying to understand the 'language of trauma and attachment' – you'll find they crop up in different places as you read through the Alphabet of Issues.

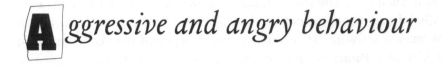ggressive and angry behaviour

The term 'domestic violence' conjures up images of adult males abusing female partners or of children being abused by parents who are unable to control their tempers. It *may* conjure images of female to male abuse. Rarely, if ever, does it conjure images of children abusing parents, particularly of young children abusing loving parents. Yet this is the lived experience of many adoptive parents caring for children who hurt. Often they feel isolated, helpless and confused, alongside intense feelings of self-blame, shame and hurt.

Social workers and other professionals who try to help may see parents as angry and rejecting as they act out their distress in ways that often mirror their experiences of abuse; they may see parents as depressed and not coping, as they practise the skills of dissociating from their pain. They rarely see parents' behaviour as symptoms of their child's distress: a reflection of how their child felt at his abuse and potent expressions of how he has communicated this to parents; how they have 'heard', yet not fully understood, what their child has tried to 'tell' them.

It does not need to be like this. Children who have learned violent ways to express anger can be helped to reduce their rage and violence, they can learn to love themselves and the people to whom they are closest. Parents can get out of the loop of aggressive or passive responses and learn to manage their own reactions as a powerful way of managing their children's. While violence is one of the most worrying and destructive behaviours of children who hurt, it responds, just as well as other behaviours, to the mixture of structure and nurture that forms the cornerstone of an attachment-based reparenting approach.

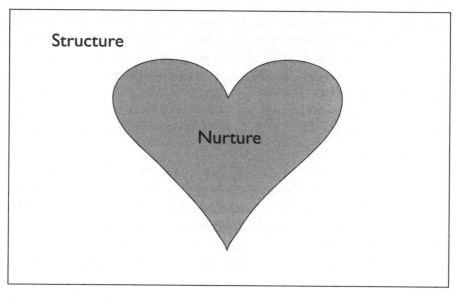

Figure 7: Nurture and structure

The concept of nurture helps parents recognise their child's behaviour as his language and to create the 'dictionary' that begins to make sense of his 'mother tongue' in terms of his history of maltreatment. This means making a dramatic shift from asking the question, 'What is this child doing to me?' to asking 'What is this child trying to say to me?' Gradually parents can add to this the question 'How can I help my child "do it" differently?'

Introducing structure helps parents recognise and name what is going on in their family. It is essential to begin to 'call a spade a spade' by acknowledging that hitting leading to bruises is assault, that hurting another person is physical abuse and calling other people derogatory names is verbal abuse – no matter the age of the abuser or his victim. Naming what is going on in their family can help parents gain confidence and understanding, thereby helping them create secure boundaries that can allow a terrified, out of control, abusive child to feel greater safety and containment. This in itself often reduces the need for a child to act out his rage and panic, as he increasingly senses his caregivers are taking safe charge.

The blending of structure and nurture stems from an understanding that, at heart, children who act violently are not in control of themselves or their feelings, despite their 'controlling' behaviour. This apparent contradiction deserves further exploration. While specific incidents of violence may give the child a feeling of mastery and control at that moment, it simultaneously perpetuates his deepest fears: that he cannot control himself and that the adults charged with parenting him are unable to contain him. It is overwhelmingly distressing to a child to feel both uncontained and helpless. Terror, panic and toxic shame-rage (see 'Terrible shame') are therefore at the heart of a child's use of violence: as a means of trying to control his seemingly chaotic environment. Thus violent children are fundamentally as vulnerable as children who become over-anxious, shame-filled or openly fearful under stress, and no less in need of empathy.

With nurture and structure at the heart of their work parents can name, without shaming, as they begin the process of helping their child change. Parents can help their child first of all by remembering that anger is a feeling like any other and is therefore 'OK'. Its expression in violence and aggression makes sense within the context of his early experiences: may even have been learned at the hands of his birth parents. Adopters need to communicate their empathy and understanding of this to their child whilst simultaneously making it clear that aggressive and hurtful behaviour is *not* acceptable. They can then begin helping him 'practise' new ways of managing his overwhelming panic, terror and rage.

Before beginning to look at specific ways to help children manage anger it is important to look more closely at the impact on children of living with the trauma of maltreatment. Human bodies are complex, organic 'machines' that are highly sensitive to the world around them. Just as neurobiological patterns are affected by early experiences, so too are the body's biochemical balances. The effects on the hormonal balance in a child's body of living with the constant dread of being abused, neglected or abandoned are profound. Faced with such dangers the body reacts by producing a complex cocktail of biochemicals, two of the most well known being cortisol and adrenalin. These stress hormones allow the body to respond to potentially threatening situations by alerting it to danger and preparing it to respond immediately (the flight, fight or freeze response). The more a child experiences trauma the more of these stress biochemicals his body produces and the more likely it becomes that these responses will become habitual: a 'Panicchio' body-state is likely to result.

While this is part of the body's natural process, it creates major problems for youngsters who have experienced repeated early trauma, when the neurochemical processes defining their experiences were developing most rapidly. For example a child may be so used to living with high levels of adrenalin and cortisol that he actively engages in dangerous behaviours, to maintain the 'norms' to which his body has adjusted. Hence Panicchio may neither show appropriate fear in potentially dangerous situations nor experience calm and relaxed situations as safe or comfortable. (See also 'Basic building blocks of the brain', 'Critical connections' and Jemima Crackit pieces.)

Trauma neurobiology can also explain why a child may seem to thrive on anger and confrontation. Faced with a massive over-production of 'rapid response' biochemicals, he has little option but to find ways to get rid of them. One effective way is to create angry and confrontational scenes that allow him to discharge these uncomfortable biochemicals and to feel, albeit temporarily, a sense of peace. This is probably one of the main reasons why a child may seem indifferent, or even happy, after there has been a blow-out. Parents, on the other hand, are often left with uncomfortably high levels of distress. If not recognised and managed, these can interfere with their normal capacity for reasoning and communicating, especially in challenging situations.

Armed with understanding, and some practice in managing their own stress responses, it becomes increasingly possible for parents to find effective ways to support their child (Jemima Crackit-mode). Talking to a child about adrenalin production and the part it plays in his panic and anger can help him gain some sense of control and mastery. It could help him to think, with parental encouragement, about safer ways of discharging adrenalin. A child who feels understood will, almost by definition, feel safer and more contained. This in itself can reduce the automatic stress responses that so much control Panicchio's life and increase his capacity for self-control.

Exercise is an effective and fun way of expending adrenalin, and enhancing well-being: so encouraging a child to take regular exercise as a prophylactic anger control tool can really help. If parents can recognise that their child is likely to become angry in specific situations they can gently but openly anticipate this for him and suggest an adrenalin-reducing exercise in advance. Thus, a run around the park on the way home could help ease the tensions that often arise at the end of the school day, as children struggle to cope with changing from one environment to another. It is vital that parents help their children in these 'co-regulating' experiences. If running around the park feels above and beyond the call of duty, parents could work with their child by timing his circuits, shouting encouragement or making suggestions about how to alter the circuit or exercises involved to make them more fun. In this way they are simultaneously providing some of the nurture and structure that can help their child to change.

Nurturing an angry child is difficult but can be achieved if parents imagine a tiny scared kid inside their big angry kid (seeing the panic beneath the controlling Panicchio front). Remember that a youngster's anger is a learned, survival response, albeit unconscious, and his most powerful way of letting parents know how he felt as a helpless baby. Sharing this knowledge with a child sensitively helps him make sense of emotions that often feel over-whelming. Empathising with the fact that he learned about anger when he was living with his birth family and being sad that he now has to work hard to find new ways of expressing anger gives a youngster two powerful, parallel messages: that his anger is a reflection of his early distressing experiences and that, with his parents' support, he can learn new ways of 'doing anger'. This can give children overwhelmed by their feelings hope that, with help, they can begin to take control of their anger, rather than their anger continuing to control them.

While it may be easier to empathise with a child whose anger clearly seems uncontrollable, children who appear able to control their anger, or seemingly take pleasure from hurting others, also deserve empathy for their struggles. It is important here for parents to remind themselves that, while their children might be able to control specific incidents of anger, they were not responsible for the early experiences that led to them needing to act out this way. Nor do they have good control over the neurobiology that underlies their responses and drives their need to be in control. Parents must walk a fine line between understanding and accepting their children's feelings and remaining clear that they will not condone or tolerate aggressive behaviour.

A colleague, when asked what he does for a living, often replies that he works with 'frightened animals'. Parents of angry and rejecting children should remember that their children are no less 'frightened animals' than youngsters who show their distress in less aggressive ways. Panic and fear are at the heart of all violence. The terror children feel is the terror of accepting love that might again turn to abuse and abandonment; the terror they feel about relinquishing control is the terror that doing so will result in helpless-ness and annihilation; the terror they have in loving is the terror that they are not good enough for the love of their parents, who will ultimately see this and turn away from them.

Nonetheless, it is vital that empathy for children's struggles does not stop parents from helping them find new ways of managing their anger. Loving nurture is not about finding 'excuses' for unacceptable behaviour: it is about helping children find the springboard from which they can begin to change. This must start with the implementation of a 'zero tolerance' policy on violence, coupled with a proactive listening approach to avoid escalation by the youngster seeking to be heard. Just as responding swiftly to a baby's whimpers and acting swiftly to pick him up and sooth him can prevent increasing distress, so it is with the poorly regulated, traumatised child. Parents should always strive to contain their angry or out of control youngster as soon as they see the tell-tale signs, in an effort to co-regulate his distress, giving him greater opportunities to calm down and thus prevent destructive, aggressive outbursts. However, full-blown outbursts of rage are not always predictable or avoidable, just as it is impossible and potentially unhelpful to prevent an infant experiencing some discomfort, at least briefly. Then, just as for the mother of an upset baby, it is essential that parents remain as calm as possible, allowing him to use their calming heartbeat and breathing to begin to calm his own. These, shared experiences of distress and re-regulation provide the template for the child's developing 'thermostatic control system', eventually avoiding both physical and emotional over-heating. For trauma-tised children whose bio-systems remain grossly disorganised, parents will need to be prepared to put in exaggerated external regulators (Jemima Crackit-like, using their own organised bio-systems) for some time, to com-pensate for the heightened sensitivity of their youngsters to stress.

Understandably this can prove more difficult to achieve with older children, where parents' efforts at physical containment are more likely to be resisted and could lead to someone being hurt, intentionally or accidentally. However, here too, it is important for parents to take hold of their feelings and use the calmness and control of their presence to reach out and 'touch' their child, albeit at a distance. With enough confidence in themselves, parents will still be able to provide the essential psychological containment for their youngster that will enable him to manage his terrifying feelings more safely. They should then welcome their child back with open arms as he returns to 'normal'. Gradually the child will tolerate greater physical closeness, which will further enhance the parents' important co-regulatory role.

Providing such structure might also mean reminding children they will need to pay for any damage they do during their angry outbursts. While this could be financial, it could also involve other means of reparation, such as clearing up any mess or undertaking extra jobs in the house. In this way parents are reflecting the societal realities that may face adolescents and adults who, unable to control their violence, find themselves facing charges, fines, criminal compensation and community service orders. Moreover it provides positive opportunities for youngsters to practise reciprocity: the 'give and take' that forms the lifeblood of healthy attachments.

Most adopted children display anger and toxic shame reactions, although not all do so using aggression directly. Throughout this volume there are further suggestions for managing shame-based, angry and 'out of control' children; verbal aggression is also addressed in some detail under 'Rudeness and swearing'. In addition effective ways of managing children who might be termed 'passive–aggressive' or who tell us of their panic and anger in more puzzling and less direct ways are discussed. Armed with belief, courage and confidence that they can make a difference, parents can gain the impetus they need for positive and sustained change within their troubled families.

It is important not to forget parents themselves, and to speak directly to them. Living with aggression has a profound impact on everyone involved and parents will probably have found ways to manage their feelings: including dissociating themselves from their negative feelings, by 'normalising' their child's behaviour through minimising it, or by increasingly distancing themselves from their child. These ways of responding to anger are entirely understandable and have probably served them well in the past to protect them from the pain, fear, shame and powerlessness of living with aggression. However, working towards making changes for their child must start with exploring the ways in which parents have personally been affected by their child's distress and how they can begin to heal themselves. They may need to find individual therapeutic help to get in touch with feelings from which they have learned to switch off, or to begin to take the risk of reaching out with greater understanding to their child. To do so is to demonstrate great courage and commitment both to themselves and their family.

Sadly, some parents retaliate to aggression from their child with aggression, often in the form of smacking. While this may be understandable it is neither an appropriate nor helpful way to manage an angry child (see 'What not to do!'). At the very least it gives him the message that the only way to manage anger is using aggression, which is likely to reinforce the child's anger 'hard wiring' and perpetuate his behaviour. If parents find themselves in this position it is vital that they seek help immediately. It is also essential that they take personal responsibility for their actions. They can begin by wholeheartedly apologising to their child for their actions and acknowledging that they were unacceptable.

This should be followed with the firm resolve that aggression (including hurtful words or angry glances) will no longer be a mechanism through which they try to manage their child. This may involve acknowledging to themselves the sense of powerlessness and shame that they have been experiencing: feelings that are likely to resonate with their child. Showing their child that they are prepared to admit their mistakes and try to change by seeking professional help, could be invaluable steps for themselves that could also help their child find the courage for change.

In summary, to live with aggression, either as victim or perpetrator, is terrifying and potentially dehumanising. Aggressive children, like adults, can learn different ways of managing distress but they cannot do this alone: they need to begin practising this with supportive caregivers as early as possible. It is much easier to help a toddler manage a tantrum than it is when your 'toddler' is 14, bigger than you and becoming increasingly out of control. Parents who are living with an aggressive child owe it to themselves, to their child and to all the people who are affected (or are likely to be affected) to take the first brave step right away, to move from being a victim to being a proactive agent of change. Stepping out of the shadows of secrecy, collusion and isolation will allow parents to see and be seen, to recognise their family's needs more clearly and to reach out for the compassion and support they all deserve.

Letter to the Ponting family

Dear Grace and Peter

We have talked about how children who have been abused and neglected have a right to feel intense anger, fear and sadness at what has happened to them: feelings they were unlikely to have been able to express safely at the time but which they carry with them into their new families. While the feelings may be universal, children's means of expressing them differ to a considerable degree. Each child in a family has had subjectively different experiences and each finds his own unique way of expressing what he feels inside. This situation may be compounded in families where a sibling group is placed together; if placed sequentially, the impact on family members may be particularly profound. The first child placed may feel his initial sense of security and attachment is threatened, whilst the later-placed child desperately needs to find her place within a pre-formed family unit, with its own rules and expectations. If children don't have their unique 'world views' recognised and validated they may resort to behaviour that goes on 'telling' their parents how they are feeling.

Justin and Juliet are demonstrating this within your family. Justin communicates his distress by angry and rejecting behaviour, in part because his angry feelings towards his sister have not been validated. Most likely this resonates deeply with the painful, shame-filled feelings of rejection and worthlessness he experienced in his birth family. Juliet communicates her feelings by using the 'language' she learned in her birth family, a combination of sexual acting out and anger. Although both children need to learn different ways of communicating their distress, you should begin by understanding their 'language' and validating their powerful feelings.

The single most important issue coming out of our discussions about Justin is the level of physical and verbal aggression he demonstrates. That must make it so hard for you to feel safe in your own home and to continue to feel good about yourselves as parents.

It is essential you understand the root causes of Justin's hurtful behaviour and try to remain loving towards him (nurture), whilst simultaneously providing adequate containment and avoiding responding with anger or punishment, as these last only confirm his perceptions and expectations of the world as unsafe and vengeful. It is impossible for children like Justin to take in all the good things parents have to offer, until they begin to feel safe and sense secure boundaries (structure). Only when Justin is able to experience safe limits and begins to feel less 'out of control', shame-filled and 'dangerous' (messages he'll go on picking up about himself as long as he continues to act out his anger and hurt) will he really be able to take in your loving care and make good use of it.

We've already discussed how early abuse and neglect leaves children with distorted 'looking glass' views of the world and of close relationships. If you are loving and accepting without having established very clear, 'firm but fair' boundaries, Justin is likely to continue trying to control his life (and yours) through aggression. Using the language of trauma he may interpret kindness as weakness and use his physical and verbal power to take control.

Sadly this power, although a very real threat to you and your family, is only illusory for Justin: deep down he still feels like the terrified, helpless infant he once was. Justin's attempts to feel safe by controlling his environment (more specifically, you), using threats, aggressive language and violent behaviour demonstrates that, at a very fundamental level, he has not built up 'road maps' inside his head of the world as bounded and safe, with parents who can be trusted and with whom it is safe to be dependent. Hence Justin is telling you very clearly, through his actions, just how desperately he needs to feel securely contained and helped to modulate his panic, shame and rage.

Furthermore, it is highly disempowering for you to feel bullied, threatened and intimidated. It does nothing for your self-respect and belief in yourselves as parents. Since these are essential prerequisites to helping Justin begin to change and heal, this is where you will need to start. By showing Justin you are worthy of respect and intend to take good care of yourselves, you will be giving him very positive messages about your capacity to take care of him responsibly and respectfully too. Conversely, putting up with aggressive behaviour does Justin no favours. Rather it may encourage him to continue this behaviour: essentially 'preparing' him to be abusive in his future relationships with partners and children.

It is vital you work together, as a team, towards establishing real safety within your home, for every family member. Fundamental to this is a 'policy of zero tolerance' towards aggressive or destructive behaviour. Only then will Justin feel secure enough to begin to let go of his old 'survival' patterns. To do this you will need to continue showing Justin you can see and understand that he is angry or upset, whilst maintaining your 'line in the sand' about what is acceptable behaviour in your home. You have already shown you are capable of defusing distressing situations. By continuing to spot trouble brewing, and even predicting for Justin when you see this is likely, you will help him to begin managing his arousal (distress) levels. He will need lots of practice, but eventually he won't need to let you know he is feeling 'bad' by 'acting bad'.

Justin will also need lots of time to practise recognising his feelings and making connections between what happened to him as a baby, what has just happened to 'set him off' and what he does now: not as excuses but as reasons, so that he can begin to take avoiding action himself. For example, this may be useful when Justin has to share you with Juliet, or he's expecting, or recovering from, contact with birth family members. Justin must have very mixed up feelings about 'mums': he knows deep down his birth mum hurt him and let him down, yet part of him still hopes she will take him back and love him, 'if he could only get it right'. There's also the question of Justin's projection of angry 'mother' feelings onto you, and of divided loyalties, towards you and towards Juliet. Justin may need therapeutic help to unravel and make sense of these conflicting feelings, in addition to your ongoing help in recognising and making sense of them.

It may be unhelpful to try to make Justin feel better by 'jollying him out of it', or minimising his distress, which is actually very real and understandable. Instead help Justin find ways of recognising how he feels and dealing with his feelings safely, whilst taking great care not to trigger his shame response: Justin needs practice in feeling acceptable, even when his behaviour clearly is not.

Try to find ways that work for you and Justin, so he can express himself in controlled, shared ways with which you are all comfortable. Some people clean when they are upset, some eat chocolate, others go out for long walks or go jogging. Whatever you choose, *doing it together* mimics the shared regulation patterns of infancy you all missed out on: especially if you can be playful and have some fun!

Justin desperately needs you, as his parents, to help him practise identifying his feelings before they get to the point where he does something he (or you!) might regret. Initially you, as the 'Jemima Crackit' adults, will have to do most of the feeling and thinking for Justin. By telling him gently what you see is happening (not asking him but letting him know that you know) you are helping Justin 'feel felt': that is to feel someone can make sense of his muddled, chaotic life even if he cannot (yet). It is also important you acknowledge positive outcomes to Justin when he manages to cope with tricky situations. Don't go 'over the top' with praise but do get the message across that you have noticed and are pleased for him.

Similarly, I think you both know Justin and his moods very well. Perhaps you could make a point of noticing out loud, as often as you can, how Justin (and you) are feeling and managing: again keeping it simple and low key. It is especially important to acknowledge positive aspects of Justin's behaviour in order to begin to change his negative perceptions of himself. For example you might say:

- 'I notice how much you enjoyed that game/ice cream/TV programme. Nice one.'
- 'It's good to see you looking so relaxed!'
- 'I do like it when you can wait your turn and give me time to get ready.'

Noticing when Justin had a difficult feeling he was able to manage well is also crucial. You might say:

- 'I could see you felt angry then. You made a good choice by walking away and going into the garden.'
- 'You managed my having to spend time with Juliet very well just then, even though I know that wasn't easy. Good job!'

Clearly it is also important to notice when Justin is struggling with feelings although here it may be better to *do* something to help rather than *say* something intended to be helpful that could trigger shame and rage.

It would also be good if Peter could try to be there for Grace when Justin 'has a go' at her. It is vital for Justin that he sees you as a real 'dynamic duo'. It would be particularly good if you could both change your dynamics a little – so that Grace takes the lead (or appears to, for Justin's consumption at least) in making family decisions. That could begin to challenge Justin's long-held view of women, especially mothers, that is reflected in his disrespectful and bullying behaviour.

It was good to hear Justin has made, and is maintaining, friendships and how well he responds to 'peer review'. It is particularly helpful that his friends disapprove of his hurting Juliet. Hopefully they would also disapprove of his hurting his mum or dad if they ever saw him behave in such a way: you may be able to capitalise on this at home when Justin's friends visit.

As we discussed, Justin needs to learn how to express his angry feelings in safe ways: hitting out uncontrollably, even if he does not intend to hurt someone or break something, can never be acceptable. Although your first line of defence should be to pre-empt aggressive outbursts, there will always be some times when you didn't see it coming, or aren't in a position to 'divert, defuse or discharge'. Given Justin's age and size, containing his anger by cuddling him may no longer be realistic: he is becoming too big and strong to make this a safe strategy. We'll explore some safe, non-abusive ways to contain Justin physically that would give you more choice in how to intervene as your second line of defence at our next meeting.

Remember that confidence and belief in yourself and your capacity to contain Justin emotionally will go a long way towards maintaining control when physical closeness could put you at risk. Children who hurt have highly tuned 'antennae' and can pick up other people's feelings very quickly. If they detect doubt or fear they are very likely to continue using their survival-based responses to protect themselves. However, if they sense confidence and self-assurance, they are likely to feel and act as if they are in safe hands. This, in turn, makes it easier for you to use your ability to regulate distress to co-regulate Justin's.

To help give Justin extra incentive to work on managing his feelings he may also need to feel some of the consequences of making poor choices and not managing well. If you're concerned about Justin damaging objects you could remind him of your house rule that he must repay you or replace anything he damages. (You might decide to store any really precious objects safely until you feel confident Justin can manage not to break them). However, do not physically try to intervene at this point, since this could result in an escalation of the situation and somebody getting hurt. Here again, you can use emotional or verbal containment to step in.

If Justin moves to hit anyone try shouting 'stop!' loudly. You will then need to repair broken connections between you within seconds, perhaps by saying, 'I guess that may have shocked you but I have to keep you, Juliet and everyone else in this family safe.' You could also try saying, 'I love you too much to let you hurt other people. I know how bad this will make you feel later.' Justin can then feel understood and 'held'.

If Justin is not able to respond to your interventions and hits someone there needs to be clear, reasonable consequences. Don't feel put on the spot. Take time to think through an appropriate consequence. A useful phrase in this situation is to say: 'I'm going to take some time to think about what needs to happen now. Meanwhile we all need to sit quietly and calm down.' Consequences might include doing small tasks for the victims designed to make them feel better, to 'repair' feelings, or actually mend damaged items.

To help Justin take some responsibility for his behaviour it might be a good idea to involve him in thinking about what rewards and consequences would help him manage his angry feelings in safer ways. This doesn't mean he has the right to veto what you decide are appropriate consequences! However, it's possible that, if you sit him down and tell him you've been thinking about how to help him manage his feelings safely and tell him your ideas, he may come up with suggestions of his own. Parents who do this are sometimes amazed by the suggestions children make: they're often far harsher than anything the parents would think appropriate!

Try to choose consequences that 'fit the crime'. For example, withholding Justin's bike for a short period might be an appropriate response to his going out without permission. Paying for broken objects or doing chores to pay for them might be appropriate when Justin breaks something. Apologising verbally, writing an apology note and having time close to you to think about alternative ways to manage feelings could also be effective ways of dealing with Justin's hurtful or destructive outbursts. Having to miss out on a favourite activity, or on going out with friends, 'because I can't be sure you will be safe' could be the most appropriate consequence of his sneaking out of the house without your agreement.

Whatever you decide, always try to show Justin you are sad he didn't make a good choice on this occasion, rather than getting mad at him (which is likely to keep him angry at you!). Remember to let him know you believe he will learn to manage his feeling better in the future and give him the message that you'll be there to encourage and support him.

For the time being I'd limit the use of consequences to dealing with Justin's aggressive 'acting out' and to his going out/staying out without permission, since these are basic safety issues and have such an impact on every family member. We can look at Justin's swearing and rudeness when you've all had time to practise and feel confident with these issues.

I know you've been struggling for some time with Juliet's angry outbursts that seem to have sexual overtones. Few parents would find it easy to manage a child whose response to being told 'no' is to lash out and try to poke your boobs or grab Peter between the legs. The therapeutic work together has already helped us understand that Juliet's behaviour is a response she learned while living in her birth family.

It is great that, with your help, Juliet's sexualised acting out does not happen so often. However, it's still important to deal with it appropriately when it does. I'd suggest you take hold of both of Juliet's hands, look into her eyes and say, 'Juliet, in this family we don't touch each other between the legs, or on the boobs. If you'd like me to cuddle you properly I will.'

If Juliet is able to respond appropriately to this then giving her a safe cuddle may be the answer. If not, it would be important for you as the responsible adult to take charge of the situation by moving away to a place where Juliet isn't able to hurt you. Simultaneously it would be important to let Juliet know you're doing this to keep you both safe and that it's not meant as punishment. Remember that, due to her experiences of being left alone in her cot for prolonged periods, Juliet is likely to see your moving away as potential abandonment: she therefore needs a clear message that you're there for her and can have a cuddle when you feel she's able to manage this safely.

Juliet's tendency to cuddle up to you and then suddenly becoming enraged, grabbing hold of your hair or putting her hands around your neck, reflects her contradictory early experiences. She's clearly letting you know, through the language of behaviour, that she both wants and fears your love and closeness. Safe cradling could be really effective with Juliet here. (See also 'Cradling for comfort and closeness'.) We could introduce this at our next session, in the context of 'safe cuddles'; meanwhile I'll attach some material for you to read and consider.

It could be very helpful for you to point out to Juliet, very gently, that it must be hard for her to sort out the muddles in her head. Tell her you wonder whether she's letting you know how confused she feels when she pulls you close then pushes you away. Acknowledging just how scary this must feel could help Juliet to start 'getting a grip' on her actions.

However, I'd also suggest that at times, just as for Justin, a short, sharp cry of 'stop!' could be enough to bring Juliet back and interrupt the behaviour. The most important part of this strategy is 'after the fact': that is how you see Juliet responding and how you in turn respond and 'repair' fragile connections. Whichever way you choose try to make sense of Juliet's contradictory behaviour for her with both empathy and firmness.

If Juliet responds by crying or looking scared it's vital you acknowledge immediately that she's had a fright. Remind her she's safe and that you're not going to hurt her, whilst acknowledging it probably feels that way. You may also want to help her connect these current feelings to her experiences as a very little girl. Tell Juliet you shouted because she was hurting you and that it's your job to keep you both safe. Go on to say you know that when she was very little and she was being hurt she wouldn't have been able to shout 'stop' and that you wish you could have been with her then to keep her safe. Follow that by suggesting you practise keeping safe and saying 'stop' together.

On the other hand, Juliet's initial response to your 'stop' command may be to 'go into shutdown': you will need to be quite vigilant here. In many cases such children will be 'retrievable' through a gentle approach using warm words and touch. This 'interactive repair' can then be a valuable part of your 'dance of attachment'. However, you'll want to avoid this happening if Juliet's dissociative reaction is repeated, intense and overwhelming.

It may be easier to start by making this essential practice part of 'fun time', so that feelings don't run too high. Young animals and children do most of their early learning through play: allowing bodies and minds to practise invaluable skills, including relationship stuff like this. A simple game such as 'traffic lights' or 'traffic police' can introduce the concept of doing, then stopping on request, that could familiarise Juliet with the ideas of 'controlling' and 'being in control' safely. Puppets and stories could also be important learning aids.

Meantime, simply moving away to put yourself out of reach could give Juliet the 'safe' message. Again, be sure to make it clear you're not rejecting Juliet and that you love her too much to let her hurt herself or you. Keep the separation short and sweet, then reconnect with Juliet when you feel certain it will be safe. (See also 'Dealing with danger' and 'Sexualised behaviour'.) You may find that working as a team you can provide each other with essential 'backup' that helps Juliet to feel more secure.

Don't try to bargain, or allow Juliet to do so. Some children try to 'get back in there' prematurely, by promising to be good when they aren't ready or able to do so. You take safe control when you let Juliet know you'll make the right decision: acting confidently even if you don't feel that way. Just remember how valuable 'Dumbo's feather' was in enabling him to walk the high wire: then he found that with practice he could do it for real! Of course this implies you may need to be creative, to allow Juliet to have safe 'set-up' opportunities to practise feeling close.

Perhaps you could try saying, 'I'm having a bad day; I need a hug' in an exaggeratedly needy voice, whilst looking around the room for a suitable 'hugger'. Sometimes you, as parents, could hug each other; other times Juliet might be the 'volunteer'. Be sure to follow your hugs with more exaggeration: saying and acting out how good you now feel. Remember, good messages don't need to be direct to be effective!

I do hope these ideas help. However, if you need to talk through or check anything out please contact me right away: you have my contact number and can always leave me a message if I'm not available.

Letter to Justin, written to provide additional support for his adopters.

Under duress his parents could remind Justin of its contents, stating that 'Christine said we should do this', thus removing opportunities for Justin to blame *them* for the consequences of *his* actions.

Dear Justin,

I spoke to Mum today. She tells me you'd sworn at her, been rude and threatened to hit her. She says you've also been hurting other people and haven't been doing what she says, especially not putting your toys away. I hear you've been having struggles in the car too.

Do you remember we talked in therapy about how your behaviour lets us know how you feel inside? We also talked about ways you can let Mum know how you're feeling – in helpful and unhelpful ways. I was sad to hear that you've mostly been letting Mum know how you're feeling in unhelpful ways. I've told Mum that we'll talk to you about being angry when I next see you.

Meantime, I think it's important you're able to play safely. I've therefore asked Mum to put away any toys she feels you aren't able to play with safely, or that you don't tidy away when asked. This means you wouldn't be able to play with them until Mum and I feel you can play safely again. I do hope you'll soon work out ways to play more safely with your toys.

Mum and I also talked about your struggles to stay strapped in and sit quietly in the car on your way to and from school. It's important for you to act safely in the car: to keep everyone around you safe.

Do you know that when you're feeling angry or anxious you have lots of unhealthy 'chemicals' in your body? Although you can get rid of these 'chemicals' by acting angry or tough, you can also get rid of them through exercise. Thinking about this helped me work out a plan to help you and I've persuaded Mum that you would both benefit from walking to school and back when she feels you aren't able to be calm in the car. Because Mum is so good at knowing when you're feeling angry or upset she'll be the one to decide when to walk to school and when to drive. I do hope you'll be calm enough to go in the car, especially when it rains.

It would be a good idea to start practising travelling safely in the car on other short journeys too. Why not think of things you could do on your way, such as listening to your cassette player? Mum will help by reminding you to take this. She'll also jog your memory about the 'belt rules' and give you a hand with the straps if she feels it's necessary.

I'll hear how you are getting on from Mum when I phone her next week.

Meanwhile, if you want to talk to me about this letter please phone me – Dad could help you find the number. I'm also sending Mum two posters to put up in the kitchen to remind you that hurting is not OK and to give you some ideas of what you can do when you feel angry.

Good luck!

Family rules for Justin and Juliet

VIOLENCE IS NEVER OK

VIOLENCE IS:

Hitting	Spitting
Punching	Shouting in someone's face
Kicking	Pushing things close to someone's face
Pinching	Hitting someone in the boobs
Biting	Hurting yourself

HURTING IS NEVER OK

IF I AM HURT:

I'll tell Mum or Dad or another safe grown-up, straight away.

IF I HURT:

I'll try to remember I hurt people I love when I'm feeling lost, sad or angry. A cuddle from Mum or Dad would be much better than hitting.

I'll ask for help to think about how to say sorry so I mean it.

I'll ask Mum and Dad to help me work out how to show I'm angry in a different way, so we can all get on better.

I'll trust that Mum or Dad will help me if I'm unable to ask.

Agreed by Mum, Dad, Christine and Caroline

Date: ....

Ways to manage angry feelings

When you feel angry you get lots of chemicals, like adrenalin, rushing around your body. This makes it difficult to calm down, think well or make good decisions.

Here are some fun ways you could get rid of the adrenalin and the angry feelings too (remember all these can be done with Mum or Dad and feelings shared can be feelings halved!):

- Squeeze a bean bag

- Run around outside, shouting loudly

- Jump up and down 20 times

- Do 15 sit-ups

- Ask Mum or Dad to hold a pillow for you while you punch it

- Tear up paper and think (or shout) about what makes you angry

- Blow up a balloon with an angry thought with every puff, then either punch it until you get rid of your anger, or burst it to explode your anger (or both).

- Draw or write about your feelings

- Share a book

- Ask for a hug

- Accept there are things you can't do!

Mum and Dad have lots of other good ideas to get rid of adrenalin. They can help you if you ask. If you have too much adrenalin in your body, you may not remember to ask Mum or Dad to help. Then Mum and Dad will do their best to remind you.

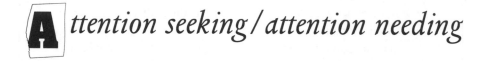ttention seeking / attention needing

Nobody much likes attention-seeking children or adults! There is a threat of being overwhelmed by endless demands for our attention that tends to make us withdraw sooner rather than later. So, sadly, the attention seeker's tactics frequently backfire on him: he gets less than he feels he needs and might otherwise attract and continues to feel unfulfilled and rejected. The caregivers do not feel good either: tending to end up feeling mean, irritated or angry. Thankfully, this situation can be improved upon if parents change their initial 'take' on the situation by decoding the language of trauma.

First and foremost parents need to understand attention-seeking behaviour in terms of 'attention needing'. A child (or adult) who has not had enough consistently positive attention early on still needs lots of attention 'to fill him up'. Babies are programmed to elicit life-giving responses from their caregivers. In addition to the survival basics of food, warmth and cleanliness, these include receiving plenty of comforting touch, movement, eye contact, interested and accepting facial expressions, vocal interactions and gestures.

An infant who receives sufficient 'good enough' care in the early months develops a positive view of the world and himself as a valuable part of it. He learns to communicate his needs openly and to anticipate that these will be met reliably. He gains a realistic, positive sense of self as 'good enough', bound up with a healthy sense of control over himself and his physical and social environment. He has no need to continue the attention-seeking behaviour of his infancy, since he feels fulfilled and confident that there will always be enough.

The hurt child, on the other hand, has never had the luxury of feeling he has enough, that his needs are acceptable and deserve to be fulfilled on a regular basis. He still feels empty and needy but he has learned either to deny his own needs, like the compliant child, or to use manipulative, attention-seeking behaviour to fill himself up. Asking for something, or standing just out of reach and doing something irritating to grab attention, just as parents are speaking on the telephone, are reminiscent of behaviour of toddlers. In adoptive families these attention-seeking patterns are frequently ongoing, and adopters may need strategies to avoid perpetuating patterns of deprivation and unhealthy interactions in their troubled youngsters, perhaps by acknowledging their child's communication attempts with a hand on the shoulder, a wave or a pre-prepared post-it note handed to the child with the message 'Questions here. Answers when I get off the phone'.

The 'child with no needs' can appear too quiet or 'invisible', with his needs not perceived or responded to sufficiently: consequently he continues to feel undeserving and worthless. On the other hand the demanding child can appear totally 'in your face'. So if we give him attention on his terms, it can seem as if we are rewarding him for his 'iffy' behaviours: a 'no-win' situation! Instead parents need to explore ways of giving their child what he *really needs*, rather than what he thinks he *wants*, thus creating a 'win-win' situation!

Simply not giving attention (ignoring the attention-seeking behaviour) tends to increase the unwanted behaviour, as the child will feel he has not been seen or heard. He is then forced to shout even louder for the care and attention he craves. At the same time parents unwittingly reinforce their child's inner belief that he cannot trust anyone to take good care of him and he is fundamentally unlovable.

Letter to the Warne family

Dear Elaine and Sam

I know how maddening it must be to cope with Mic and Sara's attention-seeking behaviour. It might help to view their behaviour as that of much younger children. Ask yourself: 'how would I respond to a toddler here?' and then respond gently but firmly. Your goal is to establish a solid, caring foundation (secure base) within your family from which Mic and Sara can explore the world around them safely, neither of which Mic and Sarah received consistently when they were babies or toddlers. This means you need to give the children appropriate attention to reduce their inappropriate ways of demanding attention.

Ironically, children who crave attention often find it hard to *pay* attention as their minds are focused on meeting their basic need for security. So, developmentally, it makes good sense to go back to toddler and babyhood to 'fill in the gaps' and 'fill up the child'. Of course you'll need to be realistic: you have a large family and your own needs to look after, as well as these two needy youngsters! Try to work out how much time you could realistically set aside every day to give your undivided attention to each child. Finding fifteen minutes in the morning and evening could make a big difference.

A particularly powerful (and time-effective) way to use the time would be to focus on personal care activities. Think back to when your children were babies: when did you spend most one-on-one time with them? All babies thrive on warm physical closeness, eye contact, gentle movement, singing and 'baby talk' from mums and dads. Washing, changing and dressing are times when these ingredients come together apparently incidentally but when much essential communication between parent and child takes place. By making sure you give support with the washing, teeth cleaning and dressing (including making good clothing choices for the day's weather conditions), you are simultaneously paying the children good, positive attention and encouraging greater awareness of their own bodily needs at a developmental level and stage that did not go well for them first time round. Bedtime stories, songs and rituals will extend your opportunities for 'baby' intimacy and possibly help both Mic and Sara settle more readily for the night.

At weekends and during school holidays, when there is more free time, you could try to fit in some simple fun activities, such as playing board games or throwing a ball about. Games such as 'piling on hands', picture snap, or bubble-blowing/catching could hold the children's wandering attention long enough for success and will bring you into 'legitimate' close contact. Rough and tumble games are very good, too, but you'll need to be watchful to avoid getting Mic over-excited, or provoking a sexualised response. You may need to keep a firm hand on the activity levels but I'm sure you'll be able to come up with lots of ideas along these lines from your own experiencing of parenting and your 'insider' knowledge of Sara and Mic.

Sometimes parents fear that by doing too much for their school-age children they are encouraging clinging and dependence instead of personal responsibility and self-care. On the contrary, by providing plenty of relaxed, everyday opportunities for youngsters to feel cared for and cared about they'll be so much more ready to do things appropriately for themselves. Both Mic and Sara have times when they try to be 'pseudo-competent' as well as their 'needy' times. However much you'd like them to be 'grown up', you can't expect them to build successfully on poor foundations: they both need time to go back and get it right with your support and the structure you provide.

You can help Mic and Sara understand when it is OK to practise being little (at home, within the family, with your approval) and when they need to act their age (outside, at school, with their friends and so on). I'm frequently amazed at how easy children find it to grasp this until I remember that most of them lived in two separate worlds within their birth families. The major difference here is that you will gradually be working towards joining up their worlds as they become more secure. I am confident that you will have no problem picking the moments or in getting this message across clearly to both children. If in doubt, use your gut feelings to guide you – and then have faith in your judgement!

Toddlers who experience consistent safe care and structure in their lives grow up to be confident and self-sufficient. Youngsters who have not had these essential early opportunities have to learn to manage themselves and the world as best they can. We can see this in the way that Mic strives to be the centre of attention, whilst Sara fades into the background and shuts off to avoid attracting negative attention. You can't afford to ignore Mic's challenging and boisterous communications, or Sara's disappearing acts, since in both cases, the children are crying out for the care and attention they were deprived of early on. They need and deserve to be heard. However, they will also need some practice at waiting briefly for your attention. So, sometimes, try saying 'I'd love to spend time with you. I'll just be a few minutes (finishing the washing), then I'll be there.'

High levels of activity and noise indicate high levels of arousal. Mic's neglect and abuse within his birth family means he lacks the capacity to manage his own arousal well. In fact, one of the unhealthy ways he seems to have adopted to deal with stress is to up the ante, especially around caregivers. All the self-care strategies we have discussed will contribute to Mic's growing self-awareness and self-control. However, he may also need *you* to sense when he is 'getting hyper', or when he has 'blown his fuse' so you can help him directly to manage his distress. Here you are connecting with him to provide Jemima Crackit external feedback, using your own finely tuned bio-systems.

Remember that preventing 'overload' and 'sharing the load' allows Mic to practise self-regulation and feel acknowledged and connected. This in itself should reduce his current need to be heard by shouting louder. Use your curiosity and intuition to work out how Mic is feeling and why; sharing this information with him will help Mic achieve sensory and emotional literacy. I'm sure you know Mic well enough to work out what's going on for him, letting him feel felt and understood and therefore safer and more contained. When it feels Mic is really winding you up, remind yourself that this loud noise is cover for a terrified, helpless little boy (Panicchio) who's too scared to speak out.

For example, when Mic starts becoming over-excited, with his high-pitched laugh and tendency to chatter incessantly, put your hand on his shoulder, look directly at him and say: 'Mic, I can see you're getting worked up. I wonder whether you've had a hard day at school? Let's go and get a drink and take it in the garden. We'll take the dog too and you can throw his ball for him. We'll all feel better after that!' Treating yourself with respect and empathy will not only show that you (and Mic) are 'worth it'; you'll also feel better and hence more able to be supportive.

It's also good for Mic to have some outdoor physical activities away from the house. This provides a good work-out, releases stress-busting biochemicals, and simultaneously gives you opportunities to unwind and focus attention on yourself. Looking after yourself is essential with high-maintenance kids like Mic and Sara, so take every opportunity you can get! I'll be in touch again soon.

Kirsty lives with her younger brother Danny and works hard to 'be good' and not draw attention to herself. Consequently, Kirsty tends not to be noticed in group situations and spends long periods in solitary play, or sitting still looking as if she is 'somewhere else'. Happily she is now living with adoptive parents who recognise that she needs as much attention as her brother, due to her early traumatic experiences. (This letter should be read in conjunction with the section on 'Dissociative states'.)

Letter to the Tait-Pritchard family

Hi there, Mel and Rae!

It was great to chat to you last night and to reflect on ways you could help Kirsty. I thought it would be useful to put down on paper some of the strategies we discussed, to flesh them out and aid our memories.

Kirsty's early abusive experiences in her birth family left her with quite different coping strategies from those of her younger brother Danny. Whereas Danny's survival strategies usually take the form of being very active, noisy and pushing limits, to make sure he's noticed and his needs are met, Kirsty has taken the opposite tack. She's responded by not only 'being good' but often by 'being invisible' at home, so as not to draw attention to herself.

With Danny and his brothers taking up most of the available space in their foster family, Kirsty increasingly withdrew, to ensure their caregivers weren't overloaded: in the hope that, if she was no trouble, the placement would last. The lasting effect has been that Kirsty has cut herself off from her self: because her feelings and needs were not adequately acknowledged in her birth family, she's so unused to voicing her needs, emotions and wishes that she's out of touch with her own feelings, especially the difficult ones.

It's vital to help Kirsty identify her inner feelings and change her view of herself and the world. She's unlikely to be able to do this for herself and, if asked directly about how she feels, she's likely to panic and withdraw further. One way to help Kirsty less directly is for you to find ways to 'notice' her, through the use of gentle touch. A hand on Kirsty's shoulder or arm when walking by or talking to her would help her feel noticed, valued and more connected to you.

Kirsty is a child who readily dissociates (a mechanism used by the mind-body to 'cut off' when situations become too stressful). Children, because of their immature development, are particularly prone to dissociation and may have great difficulty knowing their own minds (and bodies) and making choices. Crucially, they lack basic self-awareness and struggle with self-esteem. They're poorly equipped to identify and express their needs and feelings in any situation: particularly when they're stressed.

Kirsty therefore needs repeated opportunities and encouragement to recognise and communicate her feelings and needs. Initially this is likely to be very scary for her: even if Kirsty could identify her sensory and emotional feelings, to say what she feels and needs will feel like making herself too vulnerable. It will therefore seem safer to keep her feelings and needs under wraps.

We appreciate that it's difficult to help Kirsty articulate her feelings, as she often just answers 'yes' or 'no' to questions, or gives the responses she thinks adults want to hear, even if this is at variance with what *she* wants or feels. It could be more supportive to avoid asking direct questions and to be genuinely curious about what's going on for her, to help her stay with, and explore, her feelings.

Initially you should act as Kirsty's 'external feelings system' (Jemima Crackit): to notice out loud how you think she's feeling. For example, if she's having fun you might say, 'Oh Kirsty, it looks like you're having fun, I can see you're happy.' If you're aware something has upset her or made her cross, you could reflect to her: 'That must have made you sad, or maybe angry.' Show your own happiness, anger or sadness on Kirsty's behalf, to give her permission to feel. The more awareness and support Kirsty has around her feelings and the more opportunities to see and recognise how others feel, the better for her own self-awareness, and her self-esteem.

As Kirsty often takes a back seat in situations and activities, especially when Danny is around, it would also be beneficial if she were encouraged to develop her own voice and opinions. If Kirsty volunteers a view about something, this needs to be heard, remarked upon and praised: taking care to make your praise short and specific, so that she can accept it and avoid further dissociation. You could say: 'good job on speaking up' or 'that's a good one!' rather than the ubiquitous 'good girl' (that doesn't yet fit with her world-view).

Alternatively, and more typically to start with, Kirsty's opinion needs to be sought and actively listened to, even if you don't agree with her. If this is the case, be careful to avoid triggering a shame reaction by appearing critical: try saying: 'That's a really interesting point. Thank you', before moving on.

Another suggestion is to make use of Kirsty's little brown bear, Bruce. She seems especially fond of Bruce and sometimes uses him to manage difficult situations. Kirsty could be encouraged to use Bruce to signal that she's feeling frightened, or confused, and that she needs some help. This could be actively encouraged by regularly enquiring how Bruce is feeling, until Kirsty gets the message and is able to do this more overtly and confidently for herself. You can, of course, guess out loud how Bruce is feeling and playfully make suggestions as to how he could let you, and Kirsty, know.

You could extend this strategy by putting on little plays or puppet shows together, being sure to exaggerate the feelings for effect. I'm certain you'll also find plenty of story-books that involve children (or animals) and their feelings; why not have a joint go at writing your own, as Kirsty is such a bookworm? Children's TV programmes, and 'soaps', can also give you opportunities to bring feelings into conversations, both positive and negative! Try to watch these together and emphasise that *all* feelings are acceptable, 'good' and 'bad': it's what we do with them that counts.

Keep up the good work and don't forget to take some well-deserved breaks yourself: it's great that you have some really good friends who're ready to help you out for short periods with the children.

Basic building blocks of the brain

The human brain is generally understood to comprise three distinct horizontal layers that reflect its evolution, within two vertically divided hemispheres connected by a profuse bundle of fibres. Within these generalised areas there are numerous smaller brain systems; in the neo-cortex these are sub-divided into sub-regions or lobes.

It is essential to hold in mind, whilst considering brain structures 'in general' that each human being develops uniquely in response not only to genetic make up but also, in great part, to the impact of the environment, particularly during the periods of rapid brain cell growth, specialisation and interconnection that typify infancy.

Some useful 'rules' of brain development
The rule of 'use it or lose it'

> This dictates that brain cells used repeatedly will grow and mature, whilst less used neurons are lost through 'pruning'. The term 'experience-dependent' is perhaps more accurate as it more clearly suggests that early adversity stunts initial cell development.

The rule that 'cells that fire together wire together'

> This implies that it is *patterns* of electrical and biochemical impulses and hormonal messages from *groups* of connected brain cells that eventually become 'hard-wired' into established neural pathways. These are the brain's in-house 'information highways' that, with repeated use, provide predictive 'short-cuts', allow forward planning and promote 'the survival of the fittest'.

The rule of 'bottom-up' development

Although the brain begins its development during pregnancy, when basic brain cell formation occurs, much of the neural growth and specialisation of function takes place after the infant is born. Development is bottom up: with the core brain ready to undertake basic keeping alive and regulatory functions immediately. The middle cerebral layer comes on-stream in the days, weeks, months and years that follow; over time the top layer of the neo-cortical 'thinking brain' matures, reflecting the human evolutionary pathway. This rule can inform our developmental understanding of the thinking, relating and behaving patterns of children who hurt.

The rule that the 'thinking brain rules'

Once mature, the left neo-cortical brain acts as the 'factory or office boss', making mature assessments and taking executive decisions based on information supplied from every part of the 'corporate body'. However, its performance can only be as good as its lowliest shop-floor workers, its raw materials and its communications networks. As a rule of thumb, unless bottom-up brain development has gone well, top-down organisation and planning will be inefficient and often ineffective.

Basic model

Adhering initially to a simplified and stylised structural model of the brain allows readers to consider and make sense of much of the general development of human thought and behaviour. They can then move on (see 'Critical connections') to consider the structural and functional adaptations that can be brought about by early traumatic experiences and develop remedial therapeutic strategies.

Whilst internal connections *within* each area are vital, sophisticated communications systems *between* the basic structures are also essential. In the past these have sometimes been overlooked in what is referred to as 'cortical chauvinism': that is the tendency to focus on the more obvious, superstructures in our efforts at mapping the mind.

This could be compared to trying to understand the workings of a manufacturing plant through mapping its buildings whilst ignoring the infrastructure of public utilities, like gas and electricity, that underpin its smooth functioning. Although these neural communications networks may not generate works traffic themselves they are crucial to the economy of the plant and can amplify, damp down, withhold or even distort the information they carry. So it is with the brain.

Continuing the analogy, it is important to realise that few modern factories develop or thrive in isolation: they exist in a wider, global economy. How much more powerful is this factor in humans, being highly social animals whose early development depends crucially on close social intercommunication and interactions?

Essential extras

Below are listed some important information pathways involved in the reception and distribution of neural traffic, from both internal and external sources (some will be discussed further in the 'Critical connections' section):

- orbito frontal cortex (OFC)
- anterior cingulate gyrus (ACG)
- hypothalamus and hypothalamic-pituitary-adrenal (HPA) axis
- sympathetic nervous system (SNS)
- parasympathetic nervous system (PNS)
- neurotransmitters and neurohormones (biochemical messengers)
- neuropeptides ('molecules of emotion').

The OFC and ACG play a unique role, whose function could be compared to telephone exchanges, through which all calls are routed and connections made. However the OFC and ACG information exchanges are highly interactive, allowing time for interpretation, consideration and reflective processing of the basic data they receive from the 'lower systems'.

The HPA axis provides vital connections, for both 'in-house' and 'out-sourced' information about mind and body, throughout the horizontal layers of the brain. The SNS, PNS, neurotransmitters, neurohormones and neuropeptide messengers all provide 'fast-track' routes for information exchanges between body and mind.

Back to basics

The three basic, horizontal layers, often described as the 'triune brain', comprise the cerebellum and brain stem, or reptilian brain, the mid-brain and limbic system sub-cortical complex, or mammalian brain, and the neo-cortex, or human brain. Thus all animals with backbones possess brain stem and cerebellar structures; mammals possess mid-brain and limbic structures, whilst, in addition, human beings uniquely possess 'those little grey cells' of the neo-cortex, supported by the highly developed OFC and ACG.

Core functioning: brain stem and cerebellar structures

The brain stem is 'the basic brain' that keeps all animals, from reptiles through to human beings, alive by maintaining automatic life functions, such as regulation of heart and respiration rates and body temperature.

The cells that make up its structures are sensitive to information from the internal and external world that threaten survival, monitor attention and arousal and respond to restore the body's 'homeostatic balance'. In current medical circles, being described as 'brain stem dead' is understood to indicate that an individual can no longer perpetuate life unsupported.

Socio-emotional colour: the mid-brain, limbic system, OFC and HPA

These loosely defined areas are made up of a number of discrete sub-systems, with distinct, but often inter-linked, functions. It has been suggested that, in evolutionary terms, the 'emotional brain' allowed animals to become increasingly aware of their environment and to gain some degree of choice over their responses to it. These areas are defined by the 'feeling and doing' implied in the term emotion itself.

The evolution of the *amygdala*, within the limbic system, allowed mammals to 'weight' experiences in terms of emotional impact, which would be experienced predominantly as internal and external changes within the body. Although this began as an automatic, predictive response that increased survival chances, research suggests that mammals are able to learn, albeit subconsciously, from these experiences.

The amygdala is relatively mature by the time a baby is born. Closely linked to the brain stem and hypothalamus, it is bound up with the formation of intense feelings, such as fear, and the social expression of emotion. However, until sub-systems such as the OFC come on-line there is little capacity for mature control of emotional responses (see 'Critical connections').

The *hypothalamus* lies close to the amygdala and is intrinsically linked with the pituitary and adrenal bodies. Together they form the HPA axis, an internal information highway involved with emotional data and the stress and immune systems. Several neurohormones play a key role here, including noradrenalin, adrenalin and cortisol, all produced by the adrenal glands, located above each kidney.

The *hippocampus* is made up of a pair of tiny organs, one to each side of the brain, located close to the amygdala. One of its invaluable functions is to promote long-term memory storage and retrieval. In human beings this is what we normally refer to as 'memory': that is information from past experience that is usually accessible to verbal recall. These 'explicit' memories are prone to decay, distortion and insertion as the human mind contrives to make narrative sense of recalled fragments: memories can therefore change over time, in the light of additional experience or information.

Neo-cortex and ACG: the thinking person's personal guide

The newest cortical areas of the human brain allow reasoned thought, planning, negotiation and collaborative working. To achieve these uniquely human functions a major developmental shift is needed: from the social and emotional intelligence of the central layer, with its right-brain dominance, to the 'higher intelligence' of the neo-cortex, and greatly expanded left-brain functioning.

This is facilitated by the development of symbolic language, initially non-verbal through gesture, facial expression and tone of voice and then increasing in verbal sophistication, and the enhancement of both OFC and ACG (limbic) areas into 'broadband' telecommunications exchanges. The expanded use of language and the coming on-stream of these areas allow pause for thought, comparison and reflection that greatly increase the self-awareness, self-agency and social networking characterising human behaviour.

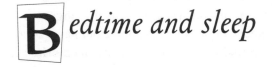Bedtime and sleep

Unlike most youngsters, traumatised children may not view evenings as times of calm, or welcome bed as somewhere to relax and reflect. Instead, many fear night-time and feel very uncomfortable with opportunities for peace, quiet and solitude.

Why would children have such negative views of what, for the majority, are pleasant and comfortable experiences? Like most of their difficulties, the answer lies in their distressing histories and what bedtime experiences meant for them. Bedtime for these children was not a restful time. As babies and toddlers they did not have settled nightly routines. They frequently went to bed hungry, dirty, smelly and vulnerable to the vagaries of their caregivers. They may have stayed up late into the evening before 'crashing out' on the sofa, surrounded by adults and with the TV at full volume.

Lying in bed youngsters may have been on 'red alert' for sounds of anger and violence erupting, perhaps listening out for the sounds of footsteps that may have meant hurt and abuse. All these feelings, difficult enough during the day, become insistent at night when avoidance or escape become harder and threaten to overwhelm them. This is the 'bedtime template' traumatised children bring with them to new families, often resulting in behaviour that is disturbing to all family members.

Moreover, many traumatised children spend their days trying to avoid remembering distressing experiences and guarding against intrusive feelings. Lying in bed at night, many of the mechanisms for forgetting they use during the day, such as aggression, talking non-stop, stuffing themselves with food, attention seeking or shutting down, become less possible. Children are expected to go to bed on their own and be quiet. Furthermore, when they fall asleep, they are frequently haunted by nightmares and wake feeling terrified. Consequently even the thought of bedtime becomes frightening.

Whilst some children fight to avoid sleep, others escape by falling into deep sleep states, seemingly retaining little awareness of physical sensations, such as full bladders, upset stomachs or overheating bodies. Puzzled parents may discover their children urine-soaked, covered in vomit, or dripping with perspiration, yet still soundly asleep. Research shows unusual patterns of dream (REM) sleep in such circumstances.

Adopters need help to recognise and understand these issues so they can help their children make sense of, and manage, their feelings of terror, as the first step in dealing with behaviours that make evenings and bedtime difficult. Acknowledgement and acceptance of the underlying reasons for youngsters' difficulties go a long way towards reducing their need to go on telling their parents loud and long of their inner distress.

Letter to the Gillespie family

Dear Hazel and Colin

I'm so pleased things have improved in terms of Martin's behaviour during the day – the reduction in his aggressive outbursts is great, well done! However, I'm concerned that you're still having disturbed nights. This isn't good for any of you: you'll be too exhausted to be at your best with Martin (and you certainly need to be!); Martin will be tired too and therefore less able to practise taking in the love and security you're offering. Tired children tend to be angry children, and angry children hurt themselves and others and find it difficult to think reasonably. In Martin's case it tends to bring his control issues to the surface: he then tries to take control any way he can! Hence it's vital we sort out Martin's night-time disturbances.

First, it makes sense to look at why Martin finds bedtimes and nights so stressful. Martin's behaviour is his way of telling you how he feels: given what we know, or can deduce, from the abuse and neglect in his early years, it's not surprising he finds darkness and bedtimes difficult. Thinking this through gives you a much better understanding of Martin's needs and how to help him cope better.

As a baby or toddler Martin wouldn't have had a settled night-time routine; there were times when he went to bed hungry, dirty and fearing he would be hurt. Even now Martin will not see bed as a safe place. Instead, looking through the lens of fear, he sees evenings as times of particular danger and bedrooms as places to avoid. He'll try almost anything *not* to feel the fear and isolation he associates so strongly with bedtimes.

This makes sense of Martin's battles to avoid going to bed, endless calls for attention once there, staying awake very late and repeated waking through the night, and provides invaluable clues on the way forward. Unless you help Martin feel comfortable and secure enough to relax and 'let go' he'll continue to use any means he can to try to stay in touch and in control. Since this is a deep-seated issue that may take many months to sort out, be prepared to take it slowly!

First, be mindful that you can't reassure Martin (that, for example, he's safe and you'll always be there for him) unless you've first stood alongside him, sincerely acknowledging his daily and nightly struggles. Only when Martin feels 'felt and heard' can he dare take his first, tentative steps on the road to trust and healing.

This must seem confusing as Martin is obviously attached to you and sometimes shows he believes you can keep him safe. However, his tendency to be very needy and clingy during the daytime suggests that, underneath the layer of closeness and trust you've worked hard to establish, he's still a terrified little boy who often feels panicky, alone and helpless. His troubled and troubling behaviour then kicks in, as he struggles to take control of the chaos and fear in his life.

Moreover, lying in bed at night Martin can't use the same tactics for avoiding and forgetting he uses during the day. In these quiet times he feels particularly alone and vulnerable to intrusive thoughts and feelings. Then, when he does finally fall asleep, he has scary dreams or night terrors. No wonder he fights hard to stay awake and keep you close at hand!

Your first step towards improving bedtimes is to acknowledge openly to Martin how hard you know he finds this and why he needs your attention so much. Help Martin think about how his nightly activities let you know he's struggling to feel safe, pointing out that bedtime as a baby must have been very scary. This will help him feel understood and make more sense of his behaviour. No child really wants to 'act up'. Martin is driven by feelings he doesn't recognise, let alone understand. He'll be more able to change his behaviour when he knows you've 'heard' what he has to tell you (without realising it himself) through his night-time performances.

Recognising that Martin is worrying about being swamped by the fears he's managed to avoid during the day will be more comforting and reassuring than trying to reason that his fears are no longer justified (though they clearly aren't!). Follow this with a matter-of-fact statement that now you've worked out what Martin's been trying to tell you, you can help him practise feeling safe enough to let go of some of his bedtime behaviours.

These messages need to be given long before the evening routine begins, at times when you and Martin are most relaxed and he's most open to 'hearing' you. (So it's probably not a good idea to talk to Martin about bedtime difficulties on the journey to school, when he'll be struggling with separating from you, or on the way home, as he often comes out of class feeling wound up.) Then keep it short and sweet, staying calm and relaxed so that Martin can hear your genuine concern for him. Another way in could be for you to have a conversation with a good friend, in Martin's presence: providing a less direct and intrusive situation to enable Martin to 'hear'.

Don't necessarily expect Martin to respond, or to agree with you: he may pretend he hasn't heard or vigorously deny what you say. This doesn't matter: your confidence and understanding of Martin's struggles will get your message over to him and set him thinking. Be prepared to repeat your message regularly until you see some change, and for several months beyond. Remind yourself you're altering deep-seated fears and survival strategies that have been established very early on, at neurobiological as well as psychological levels.

Having set the scene, your next step is to provide gentle reminders, just before starting your bedtime routine, of what seem to be the reasons for Martin's behaviour, alongside messages that you can help Martin manage his feelings. Again your approach should be confident, calm and matter-of-fact.

Try starting your bedtime routine earlier than at present and monitoring the television programmes you watch together. Many of the 'soaps' shown in the early evening involve loud family arguments and threatened, or actual violence. These may mirror Martin's earliest memories (he doesn't recall many of these consciously, but his body, his heart and behaviour remind him, and us, of their continuing power). Computer games that revel in violence are equally likely to retraumatise Martin, by triggering unconscious memories of his early experiences.

Being selective about programmes, switching off the television, or limiting use of the computer may not be popular but are what Martin needs to begin to change deep-seated patterns and beliefs. Getting into the habit of having soft background music would be a better option for changing the emotional ambience in your house: allowing him to begin to see your home as very different from the abusive ones of his past.

Your musical choices may be especially important since music, as with all non-verbal ways of getting in touch, impacts on children directly at the unconscious mind and body levels at which traumatic memories are stored. Music could provide a direct route to Martin's troubles and help alter neurological patterns in ways that are less susceptible to conscious avoidance and that words alone cannot accomplish.

Even when Martin has gone to bed he'll be extremely aware of sounds, movement, smells (alcohol, tobacco, perfumes) that could help him work out what's going on downstairs. Creating a peaceful, unthreatening atmosphere, perhaps using calming essential oils, is essential for Martin to feel safe when he's in bed and you're downstairs. However, beware of being too quiet, or creeping about since Martin will be particularly keyed into this: it often presented the greatest threat in the past.

Try acknowledging to Martin that he may be disturbed, and scared, when he hears your footsteps on the stairs on your way to bed. Let him know that you understand he finds it difficult to sleep through these, and other everyday noises, since listening out for sounds that meant danger helped him feel more in control and therefore safer as a baby. This is less likely to remain a problem if the evening environment hasn't been too quiet and you acknowledge Martin's struggle with needing to be aware of what's going on when he's in bed at night.

Before bath-time, offer Martin gentle reminders that you understand his difficulties, whilst interesting him in the opportunity of having a warm bath using his favourite bubbles. Remind him his rubber duck is looking forward to seeing him and wonder whether it'll be floating on the bubbles or hiding underneath. Simultaneously, ponder out loud whether Martin will be able to relax and have fun, or whether he'll need to let you know he's still feeling uncomfortable and unsafe by 'messing around'. Either way you're taking control of the situation by showing Martin he can rely upon you to cope.

If Martin becomes wound up, show him you appreciate he's letting you know he's struggling; if he's able to have a bath calmly, show you're pleased he's beginning to practise feeling safe. This basic process can be repeated at every point during the bedtime routine, gradually making it easier for Martin to feel accepted (and acceptable) and supporting him to make positive choices that will help him enjoy going to bed.

When Martin is tucked up in bed (and hopefully more open to bedtime stories) give him one short reminder that he may need to let you know that he has lots of difficult feelings (for example by running up and down stairs, or throwing his toys around) once you leave him. Martin needs to hear you can make sense of, and help him, with this. Muse to each other that Martin may need to do this, to stop thinking or remembering, wondering what needs to change and how you can best help him.

Try placing a family group photograph close to Martin's bed, as a visual reminder that you're always around. Another idea would be to make tapes of your voice (singing or just reminding him you're thinking of him), or of soft music, that you could switch on as you go downstairs.

Encourage Martin to look at your photograph and use the tapes you've made to 'stay in touch' and self-soothe during the night. Be prepared to help him with this initially, whilst giving him messages that he *can* do this for himself. This should help Martin feel understood, reducing his distress and giving him opportunities to practise 'self-soothing' in a limited way. This strategy could help whenever he wakes during the night and feels the fear that currently drives him to creep into your room.

Next, remind Martin you'll pop back upstairs in ten minutes' time, to check whether he needs another goodnight kiss. This will remind Martin that he's loved and can rely on you to stick around and keep him safe. Make sure you return after the agreed interval, as long as Martin keeps his side of the deal and stays quietly in bed. Repeat this, say two or three times each evening, gradually extending the return period by a few minutes. Counter any untimely shouting downstairs by sounding sad you won't be able to come up for your kiss, as Martin is making too much noise! (Repeat as often as necessary!)

Alongside this approach you may wish to think of some consequences if Martin starts messing about or trashing his room during the evening. Perhaps you could remind him of a planned trip at the weekend and be genuinely sad for him that you'll be too tired to take him out if your nights are disturbed. It's vital you state this as a *consequence* of Martin's actions, rather than as *punishment*, in order to reduce the likelihood that Martin's lack of self-worth encourages him to seek the punishment of missing the trip, or to blame you for the poor choices he's making.

There are a number of other strategies to help Martin with his bedtime difficulties. If he uses excuses or reasons for delaying bedtime, consider carrying on with your planned routine regardless of what he's doing. (One father whose child was a past master at inventing reasons to delay bedtime, decided to take control of this important area of family life by reminding his son once during the evening about the time he was expected to be in bed. He continued to remind his son only when he actively made excuses for why he was unable to comply within the agreed time. This took the form of saying 'Thank you for letting me know you may have difficulty getting to bed by eight o'clock. I'll be upstairs reading your bedtime story: I hope you'll be able to sort out your problem in time to be there as well.'

When, as inevitably happened, the son was not in bed on time, Dad read the story with great warmth to a teddy bear. He was very sad, when his son arrived as the story was ending, that he'd missed his story. Dad then tucked his son into bed, gave him his goodnight kiss, along with a fervent wish that both son and teddy would be there for the story on the following night. Next evening the child was indeed ready for bed in good time to hear his story, ending a problem that had blighted family life for many months and had been the source of much frustration.)

Perhaps you could consider this as a playful strategy with Martin. However it's important not to expect results too soon; you must also anticipate that his behaviour may improve, only to take a nosedive subsequently. This could be because something has triggered further feelings of fear or distress (such as a bad day at school). Conversely, Martin may be starting to feel safer with you: strangely this can feel too threatening or unfamiliar to a child used to taking control of his own safety.

Martin may struggle with these, and other, muddles for some time. As a basic rule, you might expect 'two steps forward, one step back' on this difficult journey towards change and healing. However, Martin will continue to make progress as long as you show him you're flexible, can cope and can make sense of his muddles for him. Whatever the nightly situation, it is important for you to continue with your bedtime routine and to have faith that it will have an impact in the longer term.

Martin's late-night wanderings, disturbing your sleep, demanding drinks or snacks, and constant requests to sleep in your room have the same fundamental cause as his 'going to bed' difficulties. Basically, they reflect his deepest fears about being left alone or being abused again and his desperate struggles to take control over 'everything', especially after dark.

You've been so good at taking on board Martin's past history, understanding his (literally) disturbing behaviours and helping him feel loved and secure. It's now time to share some of what we've worked out together with Martin: so he can make better sense of his feelings. Finding a common language to talk about his darkest fears and interpreting his behaviours will help address Martin's struggles and help him 'move on'.

Rather than continuing to follow Martin's lead trying to help him feel safe, and perhaps unwittingly 'buying into his fears', take the lead in establishing new ways of managing this together. The message you'll need to get across is that you absolutely understand why Martin feels afraid of the dark and being alone, and that you can help him work out ways to feel safer in your home. Don't expect Martin to believe this is possible: just ask him to consider what it would feel like if he did. Tell him you both need practice on this and use your new-found confidence to assure him you believe it can happen.

Avoid trying to comfort Martin by reasoning that his fears are unfounded: they do indeed have an all too real basis. Understanding and accepting this will be far more reassuring for Martin, especially if he hears your message that with your support he can begin to let go and move on, now he's settled with you.

I know you desperately want Martin to feel less anxious and have taken steps to set valuable boundaries for him. These include establishing one night each week when Martin sleeps in your room, to give him the experience of feeling more comfortable and relaxed. You've also tried varying the night, as a conscious choice on your part, to stay 'in charge'. Since Martin found this confusing it might be better to keep to the same night, or add in an extra night (or two), when it feels right. As long as you're in charge of 'when', Martin will continue to gain valuable practice in feeling more relaxed in bed: you may have more rest too!

Now you've become more adept at resisting Martin's entreaties or threats unless he gets his own way over sleeping arrangements, it's time to take the initiative further: acknowledging Martin's need to feel in control and to keep you on hand doesn't really make him feel safe yet probably sustains his distorted belief that it does. All the strategies you've used so far to show Martin he can trust you to be in safe charge will pay off here. You now need to continue to show him you've 'heard' his muddles about bedtime, can help him sort them out, and add some 'firm but fair' boundaries that confirm that it's OK to let go of his exhausting night-time behaviours.

The layout of Martin's bedroom, its contents, lighting, position of his bed, even the makeup of the bedding itself, can also affect Martin's sleep pattern. Continue with the trusty night-light and the gently closed door, since these seem to help. However, consider moving Martin's bed into the corner, against solid walls, so he can feel firm boundaries on two sides, and increasing the weight of his bedding. Gradually remove much of the clutter that collects in Martin's bedroom and work together towards keeping things tidy. These simple measures can increase physical security, provide deep-pressure calming (especially if well tucked in!), reduce over-stimulation and ease the pathway to sleep.

It could also help to intersperse nights when Martin has a timer, to help him practise managing difficult feelings alone for short periods, with nights when you sit in his room for a short time, reading, whilst Martin settles. You could also try belly-breathing, relaxation or visualisation exercises, either modelling these yourself or working them through together, to provide Martin with other ways of self-calming. Remember you increase the chances of Martin learning to settle down after waking if you leave once he's relaxed but *before* he falls asleep.

As you know, it's still important for you to be the one deciding on which evenings and the amount of time you spend there. As well as reassuring Martin his fears are being acknowledged, you're giving him vital opportunities to practise allowing you to be in control of important family decisions. This is an essential part of the 'structure' you're putting in place so Martin can start to feel more secure and nurtured all round.

When you've had a relatively good night, use all your extra energy to prance round the room madly, throw your arms round Martin, cook an especially big breakfast, try some rough and tumble play or plan an additional joint activity after school. Have fun dreaming up positive consequences of a dreamy night's sleep! Exaggerate your sense of being revitalised and then leave Martin to make the connections.

Conversely when the night has been disturbed, you can 'ham up' the exhaustion, maybe even staggering around in your curlers and nightie! Try to come up with some negative consequences of Martin's restless sleep that don't involve taking something away from him (potentially triggering feelings of abuse or neglect). You could be 'too tired to clear the table, fetch the washing and put the rubbish out' and suggest Martin could help you. This could be extended until after school, giving you more time to work with.

Alternatively, take time out for a shower to 'liven yourself because you don't want to stay tired and grumpy' and encourage Martin to give this a go too. You never know, it might just put him in a better mood!

While you're going through the tricky process of helping Martin feel safer and more cared for, make sure you take good care of yourself. This lets Martin know 'you're worth it', encourages greater respect from him and simultaneously shows him how to 'do' good self-care. Taking a nap when Martin is at school could also help you feel sufficiently rested to cope with additional broken nights, as you begin working on altering Martin's perceptions of, and reactions to, night-time.

I know you feel that overnight respite breaks would undermine the great work you're doing. However, you are more comfortable about short daytime breaks. So don't spend precious time rushing around catching up on the jobs you've been unable to do because of spending time with Martin and the other children: catch up on sleep instead! Your pattern of sleep deprivation goes back a long way, so there's lots of catching up to do and you really do need all your wits about you!

I know you'll give it a good go! Sleep well!

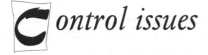# Control issues

Control is a major concern in many adoptive families. Parents sometimes feel that their child is in control of family life and the only thing to do is to impose bigger, more rigid controls, to redress the balance of power. Other parents, in attempting to be fully accepting of their youngster, may accept his power games and then concede the upper hand. In the first case there is over-emphasis on firm structure and risk of parents appearing punitive. In the second, the major focus is on nurture which can leave the child without necessary boundaries. To be successful, parents need to be firm but fair: to strike a delicate but essential balance between nurture and structure.

Sadly, early traumatic histories bequeath youngsters distorted perspectives of the world. Limited opportunities for integrating experiences and making good sense of them mean their perceptions and expectations of family life have 'all or nothing' qualities. Thus adopters or teachers giving such children stern looks to modify their behaviour, or raising their voices to establish authority, are easily misread by youngsters as overtly abusive.

Depending on their individual early experiences, children may react to attempts at adult control by becoming more confrontational (fight) or by running away physically (flight) or 'in their heads' (freeze). Whilst the freeze and flight responses are generally recognised as indicating terrifying panic, the terror underlying the fight response is easily overlooked; yet in all cases it is panic, pain and fear that drive children to try to control the world around them. Developmentally they turn the normal attachment sequence on its head: striving for independence without essential experiences of safe dependence under their belts. Furthermore they do so with poorly developed and weakly organised neural pathways, creating distorted feelings, thoughts and responses. Ironically they are attempting to achieve maturity whilst lacking fundamental self-control and self-awareness at the neurobiological level, the tasks of babyhood and toddlerhood.

Adoptive parents need constantly to remind themselves that traumatised children have had inconsistent, or consistently adverse, experiences of the use of power and control in families. Through the 'language of trauma' such children tell us in their current behaviour that control remains a huge issue for them. Youngsters who struggle to feel safe through aggressive behaviour are trying to create illusions for themselves that they are firmly in control. Their behaviour is organised towards that goal by making strongly persuasive statements to caregivers that 'this kid rules!' Since these views are highly distorted, it is up to caregivers to adjust their perceptions, expectations and responses to help children alter theirs.

In some cases the picture becomes more skewed. Some children appear so able to control their outbursts and controlling behaviour that they can stop 'midstream' when another adult walks through the door or their favourite TV programme is about to start. When the adult leaves, or their programme finishes, they immediately take up where they left off with 'all guns blazing'. Other youngsters, who become 'withdrawn' within the family, suddenly become animated and demonstrative should visitors appear, or the family set foot outside the home. Again, once the 'strangers' have departed or the outing is over, the child reclaims his previous 'distance'.

One could be forgiven for believing that in such cases children really are in control. However, in reality these youngsters have superimposed strongly controlling patterns of behaviour over a pervasive sense of chaos and terror. This is consistent with contemporary research showing that children with disorganised attachment patterns evolve 'organised' punitive-controlling, or compliant-controlling, patterns of behaviour by school age.

Below we briefly explore issues of control in relation to Matt (aged five years), whose outbursts of screaming often follow simple parental requests for compliance. For contrast we then discuss the almost obsessive bedtime behaviours of 12-year-old Valerie in terms of her attempts to control her persisting night-time fears.

Since 'control' is such a global concern, further discussion can also be found under 'Aggressive and angry behaviour'; 'Attention seeking/attention needing'; 'Dealing with danger'; 'Eating and food issues'; '"Good" child'; 'Managing separations'; 'Rudeness and swearing' and 'Bedtime and sleep' issues.

Letter to the McGrath family

Dear Josie and Freddy

I understand that Matt's screaming often feels manipulative, particularly when occurring in response to requests for compliance from you. As parents with a large family, that must seem particularly hard to deal with: I do hear how challenging this is for you at times. However, if we are to 'get out of the loop' and help Matt move forward emotionally and behaviourally we need to put different interpretations on his actions. This will become easier over time!

For now, you need to remind yourselves repeatedly that *at this particular moment* Matt cannot manage compliance which at other times wouldn't be problematic. Think of how disconnected Matt can be and how 'baby Matt' often 'runs the show', rather than the young, intelligent boy you know and love! Although I often call this 'thinking toddler', it should probably be 'thinking tiny baby' at times. When children have been seriously maltreated in infancy they aren't 'wired up' well neurologically. Instead they're 'hot-wired' to survive by any known (or unknown!) means: by four or five years old this often includes a good deal of controlling behaviour. It's vital to remind yourselves that controlling behaviour is a direct measure of the extent to which children have felt, and still feel, *out of control*, helpless and alone.

Moving onto the 'Looking Glass World' of Matt's mind (see Archer 1999b, pp.37–53), you can see that underneath this apparently well-organised 'total control' pattern is an out-of-control, terrified little boy with poor internal organisation. This means that Matt's 'road maps' of the world and of family life which he uses to navigate in the here and now are based on his chaotic and hurtful early experiences.

Hence Matt's expectations and interpretations of your 'good enough' family are made through distorted lenses. What you're offering and what he perceives to be happening in your family may be very different. He doesn't really trust you to control any part of his life. Understanding this makes perfect sense of why Matt often fights against your 'rules' and requests as if his life depends on it (which it once did!). Matt's future now depends on him learning to rely on good enough caregivers (you!). You'll therefore need to challenge the 'control loops' of his survival behaviours in creative and sensitive ways.

Remind yourselves repeatedly that you can't control much of what Matt does, especially what goes in and comes out of orifices, but you can control *how* you respond to him. Having good control of yourselves and your interactions with Matt is essential! Take care to make the choices *you* want to make *for* Matt, so you both 'win' and you don't end up feeling manipulated.

First, perhaps you could reduce the responsibility you give Matt for getting ready for school, and other self-care tasks. Why not think of your granddaughter, Lucy, and Matt as 'two-year-old-twins'? Although this might initially increase your workload it could considerably decrease Matt's 'controlling' responses. It would give Matt lots more of the baby-care experiences that weren't available to him in his early years, providing vital messages that he's now cared for and safe. This is fundamental to changing his perceptions from panic- and terror-based to security- and trust-based and allowing him to relinquish unhealthy control. It's also great for parents to have the chance to 'fill in the baby gaps' for their school-aged children!

Meanwhile, when Matt struggles with other simple requests and is building up to screaming point, you might say: 'I can see you need some help with this right now'. You could even admit you made a mistake in asking him in the first place ('silly me!') and suggest he'll need more practice on this another time. Giving Matt permission to scream could also be helpful if you are calm and confident ('I can handle that'). As often as not if children feel 'heard' and accepted enough, and see you taking safe control, they won't need to 'go ahead and do it'!

Frequently you'll find that what Matt *needs* and what he says he *wants* appear quite different: another potential source of conflict. At these times it's important to let Matt know out loud what choice *you* are making and why. Changing your mind (as circumstances may dictate) also comes into this category. Modelling 'making mistakes' and managing them well is very helpful for children like Matt who feel they were (are) 'one big mistake'. Your goal is to help Matt feel secure enough that he doesn't feel the burning need to take control of situations himself.

Finally, make sure you look after yourselves and recognise your limits. There may be times when you don't feel up to tackling situations: in those instances don't – and don't beat yourselves up about it! Perhaps you could try taking it in turns to handle the problem whilst the other gets some sleep, reads or goes for a walk. When it's 'over', do something just for *you* that helps you wind down and let go of all the pain and distress you've absorbed.

As you know, it can be helpful for Matt to see how upset you can be *for* him, when thinking about his past for example. However, it's vital you also model 'coping and containing' for him. You'll often need to stay tightly in control of yourself, your body language and your emotions and may need to make time later to work through your feelings. You could always call me at this point.

We can talk over these suggestions further when I see you. I'm sure you'll be able to take from them what you and Matt need: after all you're the experts on this one!

Letter to the Manghezi family

Hi there Hilary!

You seem to be having a tough time with Valerie just now. I know there are difficulties at school, at home and during the journey to and from school. Her eating problems must be such a worry to you, too. These are all issues we can work on in therapy during the next few months. However, as we agreed in our last telephone call, we'll concentrate on just one area with which Valerie has especial difficulty right now: going to bed and the obsessive routines she's developed to cope with her distress around this time. I know these include Valerie needing you to recite a number of prayers, always in the same sequence, and a rigid routine for being tucked up at night. Added to this there are the delays prior to going to bed and the constant shouting downstairs once she's there.

It seems three major elements underlie Valerie's bedtime routine:

- a pervasive sense of abandonment, panic and fear when Valerie feels alone

- the need to be in control that's a feature of many of Valerie's interactions

- obsessive routines that Valerie uses to provide some order in her life.

These controlling behaviour patterns were probably adaptive responses to her early life experiences, which we know were chaotic and abusive. Valerie would have experienced dependence as threatening: obsessive routines probably helped her feel some level of control in an otherwise chaotic environment. Her current behaviour patterns make so much sense in terms of her past, yet are no longer serving her well.

Initially you need to be accepting: helping Valerie understand where her behaviour responses originated. She needs to see they helped her to feel safe in threatening situations. Moreover she needs to understand that whilst these behaviours were absolutely appropriate then, they're no longer necessary or helpful now. To do this it might be helpful for you to set aside some time, though not at night, to talk to Valerie about her past and the ways she found to keep herself 'safe'. Talk to her about how her night-time behaviour would have helped her make sense of her world as a baby. Tell her she was really clever to figure out ways of keeping safe, then go on to say that, with you, she is no longer unsafe and you'll help her work out new ways of acting that reflect the new reality. Make sure you acknowledge that despite everything, Valerie does still feel scared and alone at times and that it's your job not only to *keep* her safe but also to help her *feel* safe.

Follow this by emphasising that although Valerie no longer needs to be in sole charge, or have obsessive routines to feel safe, you don't expect her to know or feel this is true for some time. What you'd like her to do is to test out the truth of what you're saying by practising different behaviours. Be clear you will help her manage the panicky feelings she'll have as she practises new behaviours and that she doesn't have to do this alone.

Due to the level of Valerie's fears it's important to choose one thing at a time to practise on: making small changes and trying each change for a week before introducing another. Try getting Valerie's agreement about the area to practise, since this will give her some feeling of control until she begins to believe you can safely be left in charge of family decisions. If Valerie cannot choose an issue, even with your prompting, *you* should choose the area to practise on, whilst acknowledging how difficult making good choices can be. Then let Valerie know what you decide and be empathetic about how hard she may need to work.

Be sure to remind Valerie that you'll be around to help her with her worries or fears, as she practises new ways of managing at night. It's important to discuss all of this with Valerie when she's most likely to be relaxed: perhaps finding opportunities at the weekend to chat about the new ways you're going to practise making her feel safe. Subsequently a gentle reminder just before bedtime should reinforce the changes you have discussed together.

Thinking first of Valerie's prayer routine, might it be possible to alter the words of the prayers you say slightly, where you say them, or the order in which you repeat them? It might be possible to say one prayer before tucking Valerie in for the night, or after straightening her duvet rather than before. If Valerie becomes anxious it'll be important to remind her that most people feel anxious about changes to their routine, her anxiety is understandable and that you can help her manage her feelings. For maximum impact, this needs to be stated briefly in a calm and confident manner.

It's also essential that you follow through on the changes you agree upon since, if you give in to Valerie's fears, this is likely to perpetuate her anxiety and fear. Remember that Valerie needs your confidence in her capacity to succeed and your gentle encouragement to deal with her efforts to let go of the routine with which she is familiar, but which is now a barrier to her progress.

After a month of practising changes in the prayer routine, remembering to introduce one new change each week, Valerie might be encouraged to think about changes to her duvet-straightening routine. If Valerie says you haven't straightened her duvet correctly, she could be encouraged to straighten it herself. Initially you might invite her to 'show me how you like it': you could then positively, and genuinely, encourage her to continue.

Another suggestion is to ask Valerie to practise lying for two minutes with her duvet less than perfectly straight. Acknowledge that she might not find this easy, but remind her that you're there to help her deal with her feelings. Be sure to congratulate her if she's able to manage for this short time. Subsequently, try to extend her tolerance in minute increments, noting and responding to any hesitancy or anxiety she displays. Do remember when working on this issue that your goal is not for Valerie to straighten her duvet or to sleep with it dishevelled but to help her feel safe enough to tolerate small changes to her routine.

I understand that the questions Valerie insists you answer are the same every night. Why not try typing the questions out, along with your answers and giving them to Valerie at bedtime. You might even consider recording your responses on audio-tapes which Valerie can play and replay at will. Tell Valerie that this way 'I can be with you, in your head and in your heart all the time'. Add that you will 'pop back' in ten minutes to kiss her goodnight again, as long as she remains quiet. Alternatively, you could suggest that Valerie asks the questions in a different order, or that you ask the questions and Valerie supplies the answers. Recognising that she'll find this scary, you can let her know you're ready to help with her feelings. Remind Valerie that you believe she doesn't need these questions to feel safe and you are there to help her practise letting them go. Wondering out loud, with genuine empathy, how long this might take could help Valerie 'feel felt' in her anxiety, whilst giving her hope that things can change.

Any further shouted questions should be acknowledged with the gentle but firm reminder that you've promised to come up as long as Valerie remains quiet. This quiet period should give her time to settle herself and yet be short enough not to trigger feelings of abandonment. Make sure you keep your word punctiliously! Alternatively you might suggest Valerie thinks about the answer she would like to hear, or that she thinks you'll give, and see if you agree when you return.

Valerie's constant request for you to come upstairs and answer questions does seem to be related to her need to keep you close. As you begin to change her obsessive behaviours, she may begin to feel safer in bed and less in need of your constant presence. In addition to the audio-tape and 'ten-minute return' proposed earlier, try giving Valerie a photograph of yourself, perhaps in a heart-shaped frame. Suggesting that she looks at this whenever she feels lonely or upset could provide her with an additional 'transitional object' to help her feel safe and remind her you're just down-stairs until she can really 'hold you in her heart and head'.

As an interim measure you may need to continue to 'check in' regularly. In order for you to feel in control of this it's important you set, and adhere to, the parameters. After you have tucked her in at night, remind Valerie that you will be coming back in ten minutes to give her a cuddle. Give her a timer or clock to mark out the time, which could otherwise feel 'endless' and be sure you return after the agreed time for the promised cuddle. Start by 'checking in' three times each evening and gradually reduce the number of times, whilst increasing the time between your 'visits'. If Valerie calls you before the agreed time, remind her how many minutes there are until your next 'visit'. This way you remain in charge of the interaction and therefore most able to help her.

Regarding the questions Valerie asks every night about whether she'll have a bad dream, I know you want to reassure her by saying she will only have good dreams. The problem here is that there will still be times when Valerie has nightmares, despite all your efforts to make night-time a more comfortable experience. Your reassurance is therefore unlikely to feel like reassurance to Valerie: it's more likely to feel like placating her. If she is not feeling 'heard', Valerie is more likely to need to 'say it louder' and try to take control using her obsessive behaviour.

Instead it would be more realistic to acknowledge that there will be nights when Valerie has scary dreams and nights when she'll have happier dreams. You should also let her know that you can help her with her night-mares. Here reassurance is provided in your acknowledgement of and willingness to help with her difficulties, alongside your efforts in helping Valerie feel secure enough to go to bed feeling more relaxed. In time this may well lead to her having a more peaceful sleep without being woken by dreams that reflect her current feelings of being unsafe and scared.

When Valerie does wake up following a nightmare she's likely to be overwhelmed by panic, terror and feelings of abandonment. At this point, respond to her as a much younger child, as this will accurately reflect her feeling state at that time. Use gentle touch, tone of voice and body language to communicate with 'baby' Valerie. Try singing familiar cradle-songs whilst holding her close, rocking her rhythmically and stroking her head. Leave discussing the content of the dreams until daytime, when Valerie's tolerance levels will be higher and she will be able to process them better. Even then you'll need to tune into her feelings and be ready to acknowledge how distressing the dream was, rather than trying to reassure by dismissing it as 'just a dream'. Valerie's bad dreams could be further addressed during her therapy sessions.

When you feel it's time to work on Valerie's fear of intruders, perhaps you could introduce some light relief whilst remaining sensitive to her obvious distress. You could begin by letting Valerie into a secret: that you were afraid of 'something under the bed' when you were little. This immediately allows Valerie to fee less alone with her fears, which at some level she probably judges to be silly and babyish. Ask Valerie if she'd like you to show her how your mum helped you feel less scared. Then grab a teddy and ask it to look under the bed for intruders: poke teddy under the bed then speak for it saying, 'there are no intruders under the bed but it could do with a vacuum!!' The simple humour should appeal to Valerie whilst slipping in a more realistic perspective – especially if you add, 'See! And I'm still here!'

Finally, when planning how you'd like to help Valerie with her night fears and obsessions, one thing you should be sure not to alter is ensuring that you give her a goodnight kiss and cuddle and read her a story. You could also put on some soft music, or use soothing aromatherapy oils, to help her settle. Not only does this reassure Valerie of your continued love and interest in her, but also provides her with the positive mother–daughter experiences she missed in her birth family.

Could I also just give a word of advice about your early evening routine? I know that Valerie enjoys watching *Eastenders* before getting ready for bed. However, this might not be in her best interests, since some of the scenes in this soap could replicate, to some degree, some of her early experiences and trigger powerful feelings of insecurity. Instead, I suggest restricting Valerie's evening viewing to programmes suitable for much younger children, or promote 'no television nights': replacing these with shared stories or listening to soft music.

Initially Valerie may well rebel at this so you'll need to be ready to respond (repeatedly) with words such as 'I love you too much to let you get upset just before bedtime'. Perhaps you could agree to record the programme and make time to view it together during the day, at weekends. You could then use the issues raised as a springboard to discussing pertinent issues at one step removed. Here you're providing containment through shared participation and jointly making sense of upsetting feelings and situations. By sitting close together as you watch you'll also be using your mature self-regulation to modulate Valerie's volatile system.

Good luck in the work you're doing to assist your daughter heal from the traumas of her early life. This is one of the most valuable gifts you can give her. However, do remember to look after yourself well, as you help Valerie towards greater health, and make sure you recognise and reward yourself for all the hard work you're doing.

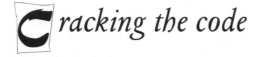racking the code

Jemima Crackit and Panicchio develop a shared language

The internal world of the hurt child is confused and confusing. His mental road maps are distorted, with fewer healthy neural pathways and some intensely powerful survival shortcuts transcribed into his neurobiology through the language of trauma. He tends to run on 'red alert': geared to respond to real or perceived threats that for others might appear insignificant. Once his panic buttons are pressed he relies on tried and tested coping strategies, based predominantly on hardwired fight, flight or freeze response systems.

As with any mother tongue, the traumatised child continues to anticipate, to perceive and to communicate with his world through the neural circuits established early in life. In this case he is well versed in the language of trauma and faces a 'double whammy' as his weak and distorted thinking and communicating patterns are further weakened and distorted by the survival strategies he unconsciously continues to select. During this process, vital energy supplies are channelled away from his already vulnerable thinking and language centres, creating a youngster who lives and survives in a highly stressed 'panic' state, with limited reasoning and cognitive skills. The stage is set for Panicchio, the archetypal traumatised child, to come into being.

Just as in the story of Pinocchio where the wooden marionette needed Jiminy Cricket as his constant companion to help him understand the moral code and develop his own conscience, Panicchio requires a parental Jemima Crackit to help him de-code his actions, thoughts and beliefs, in order to gain a more coherent understanding of himself and his world. Together they can create a 'family language' that gradually evolves into one that is more socially and universally understood and accepted (see Figure 8).

To 'crack the code' fully Jemima needs access to as much information as possible about Panicchio's early experiences, particularly his family and care history, and his past and current patterns of behaviour and of relating. But why go to the trouble and pain of delving into the past when Panicchio has the opportunity to start a new life in his new, 'good enough' family?

Panicchio's relational, behavioural and thought patterns were encoded into his neural pathways very early on: he often uses traumatic 'shorthand' to get by and finds it difficult to make sense of the 'language of love' his new family uses. There are frequent missed or mis-communications and misunderstandings. Exploring Panicchio's early history provides the essential, contextual lexicon for his caregivers, allowing him to feel heard and better understood by them. Moreover, a sizeable chunk of the 'experiential data' from which Panicchio currently derives meaning may be stored in relatively inaccessible 'files', either because the events occurred pre-verbally or because they were overwhelmingly traumatic and encoded non-verbally. Such files do not disappear, although the information may remain irretrievable or unintelligible to Panicchio himself for much of the time.

Although information remains concealed from Panicchio's conscious awareness in these 'dead-letter boxes' it frequently returns to haunt him in its spectral, encrypted form. As he stands little chance of making sense of this, its influence over Panicchio can be disproportionate: as these persistent 'ghosts from the nursery' continue to cast shadows over his thoughts, dreams, actions and relationships.

Figure 8: Learning the language of love

Adoptive parents like Jemima Crackit hold the key to breaking the traumatic code and its distorting, powerful influence. As the code itself is complex and deeply embedded in the child's life, powerful neural hardware and software are needed for Jemima to help Panicchio heal. To do so she must connect her more mature brain circuitry to her child's, so that she can 'upload' his data files and begin to decipher them. Simultaneously she must establish common communication networks, using primarily non-verbal language, through which she can 'download' vital software drawn from her own childhood and adult experiences into Panicchio's data banks.

For quite some time Jemima Crackit will need to continue to function as Panicchio's 'external decoding and data source'. Constant repetition, including both physical and mental rehearsal, is necessary to consolidate and elaborate these newly opened communication networks. Gradually Pannichio will become more able to 'read' himself, make sense of his experiences and gain increasing control over his feelings and actions. As he successfully 'installs' the new, mother–infant software he will become more truly self-aware, able to rely less on parental guidance and more on himself and consciously-made choices.

Clearly this can be a protracted and challenging process. Caregivers like Jemima Crackit may need help to ensure that they install effective 'virus scan kits' to prevent them from unwittingly 'uploading and reloading' their child's distorted software in negative feedback loops that strengthen his confused mental road maps, or from becoming affected by the 'virus' of secondary traumatisation. They must also avoid 'data overload' and 'personal systems burnout'.

These are very understandable, but preventable, risks for which caregivers must be adequately prepared. Ideally they should receive ongoing, skilled 'technical support' from knowledgeable, adoption-competent child and family practitioners. Working together they should establish regular 'service plans' that encourage effective 'self-maintenance', and determine essential back-up resources, including local community support networks. Regular opportunities for 'hardware check-ups' and 'information systems upgrades', in the form of specialised training and mentoring, are also vital to this ground-breaking and 'code-breaking' enterprise.

Cradling for closeness and comfort

All children need cuddles: to provide them with the closeness, comfort and containment that form the basis of sound attachment and development. Traumatised youngsters, having frequently missed out on their fair share of good cuddles in their early years, may join adoptive families with enormous 'cuddle deficits'. Family cradling gives adopters permission to fill in the cuddle gaps, with 'good enough' baby and toddler experiences, whatever the age of their youngsters. It can be a vital adjunct to the transformation of the 'language of trauma', through the body language of love.

Infants come into the world poorly equipped to regulate their own bodies: even 'automatic' functions like heart and respiration rates and body temperature need external regulation from caregivers, to establish comfortable 'set points' and 'install' the necessary neurobiological 'hard and software'. Maltreated children benefit from 'Jemima Crackit' adoptive parents who provide opportunities to practise these essential functions and extend their youngsters' sensory and emotional regulation and repertoire through physical and emotional closeness. However, youngsters may have spent years evolving survival strategies including mistrusting intimacy, except on their own terms. Their sensory and emotional control systems are frequently immature or distorted yet they may actively resist 'normal' close interactions.

Setting aside pre-planned times for 'concentrated cuddles' allows adoptive parents to interact with their hurt children in playful, accepting, responsive, curious, empathic, loving (PARCEL, see Figure 9) and healing ways. Taking a proactive stance, rather than reacting to puzzling or 'bad' behaviour, adopters can make sure they are themselves confident, calm and collected enough to help their child feel nurtured and safely contained. Frustration, anger, stress, helplessness and hurt feelings get in the way of the attuned PARCEL interactions at the heart of 'good enough' baby experiences.

- **P**layful: have some fun!
- **A**ccepting: warts and all!
- **R**esponsive: stay 'in tune'
- **C**urious: 'I wonder...?'
- **E**mpathic: 'I can see...'
- **L**oving: no matter what!!

Figure 9: PARCEL

Understanding, preparation and support for parents are therefore essential prerequisites for cradling for comfort and closeness.

Adoptive parents should be encouraged to build regular cradling opportunities into their family schedule, to enhance their relationships with their children and begin to counteract the long-term effects of their traumatic early lives. Here adopters replicate, in healthier ways, the arousal cycle through which infants move many times daily, nurturing their youngsters' capacity for self-regulation, self-awareness and self-esteem. Cradling thus forms part of the principle of going back and revisiting missed or compromised developmental stages, making resolution and healing possible.

Although initial cradlings may form part of formal therapeutic sessions, parents must feel comfortable with cradling at home, at times of their own choosing. Parent mentors can act as 'cradling coaches' during home visits, giving emotional support and encouragement to parents as they practise co-regulation with their youngsters. Pleasurable, predominantly non-verbal interactions allow parents and children to interactively 'download' and 'upload' vital experiences of nurture and structure.

Moreover, whilst being safely contained through family cradling, youngsters can better tolerate gentle discussion of painful and shame-filled issues without resorting to 'fight, flight or freeze' survival strategies. Access to detailed histories is vital so that adopters can make sense of their children's thinking and behaviour in terms of their past experiences. Sharing this information gently and sensitively with youngsters provides them with the key to understanding themselves, gaining greater self-control and enhancing self-worth.

Thus through their insistence on closeness and acknowledgement but non-acceptance of rejection, adoptive parents can get close enough to their children to provide new co-constructed messages of love, trust and well-being that can gradually overwrite the 'language of trauma'.

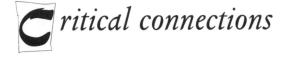

Critical connections

In young children the **orbitofrontal cortex (OFC)** is more developed on the right side of the brain and is closely associated with social and emotional 'traffic'. It undergoes a period of intense growth and development in youngsters between six and 18 months old. Its vital functions of managing arousal and providing emotional literacy, being able to 'read feelings' of self and others, are dependent on the quality of social interactions and emotional status of parental caregiving figures. It is closely connected to the amygdala, hypothalamus, HPA axis and sympathetic nervous system (SNS) and parasympathetic nervous system (PNS) sub-systems of the autonomic nervous system (see also 'Basic building blocks of the brain').

The OFC is held to be the location for social and emotional interactions, attachment formation, internal working models (road maps) of self and the world and regulation of motivational states. It is highly implicated in the capacity to 'put oneself in the shoes of others' and to be mindful of others' thoughts and feelings. It guides and informs thinking and actions, focuses attention, improves organisation and judgement, enhances impulse control and self-discipline, and enables cooperation and conflict resolution.

The OFC epitomises the 'use it or lose it' rule. Its growth and specialisation is dependent on copious early social interactions from 'good enough' caregivers, particularly during the first two years of life. According to Schore (1994), repeated exposure to 'the power of the smile' (see Figure 10) sets off a chain reaction of biochemical responses that helps cells in the OFC thrive and forge powerful connections.

Brain scans of Romanian orphans show very limited OFC mass, resulting from their severe physical, social, emotional and intellectual deprivation. Since the OFC is highly sensitive to the impact of excess stress hormones, such as cortisol, most maltreated children have undersized or poorly functioning OFCs. They are therefore vulnerable to the 'double jeopardy' of poor

Figure 10: The power of the smile

basic physiological and emotional regulation, compounded by the lack of additional capacity to think offered by healthy, well-organised OFC areas.

In individuals traumatised as children, the limbic **amygdala** can become the dominant 'memory system', bound up with powerful emotions of which they may not be consciously aware. This 'implicit' or procedural memory is durable and not readily amenable to alteration over time, without a good degree of cognitive maturity.

If the OFC is also compromised by detrimental early experiences its capacity to 'scan, review and buffer' the raw impulses of the amygdala will be reduced: leaving the individual prone to distressing over-reactions, via the SNS, and with limited opportunities to amend distressing memory traces that set a highly charged emotional tone.

Exposure to early chronic distress also reduces the functional size of the **hippocampus**, and therefore interferes with explicit (language-based) memory storage and retrieval. In large part this is believed to be due to ongoing, excessive production of the stress hormone cortisol in the adrenal area (the 'A' of the HPA axis) and the failure of feedback loops to the hypotha-lamic (or 'H') area that should control cortisol output and regulate glutamate secretion.

In small doses cortisol increases oxygen supply to the tissues of the brain and body, through enhancing blood supply, and thus promotes healing. However, over time, leaving the 'cortisol tap running' disturbs the neurochemical 'cascade' of stress reactions and, in young children, affects the establishment of 'set points' of physiological arousal. Like a dripping tap this can lead to permanently raised levels of arousal and a persistent 'drip' of stress hormones like cortisol, with their corrosive effects on other sensitive systems such as the hippocampus, OFC and anterior cingulate gyrus (ACG). In some children it is also evident in a tendency not to get sick, presumably linked to cortisol's health-promoting properties.

Eventually, if the 'leak' is not fixed, the cortisol 'tank' may become depleted. Rather than being over-reactive, individuals show numbed reactions, including dissociative behaviours, reflecting the dramatic 'resetting', but persisting imbalance, of arousal levels as systems 'run dry'. This long-term effect has been linked to immune system weaknesses and auto-immune diseases, such as arthritis, lupus and cancers.

The **anterior cingulate gyrus (ACG)** is described as the brain's 'gear shifter', enhancing flexibility, problem solving, cooperation, relaxation and the capacity to think positively. Held to be 'the seat of conscious attention', it is larger in the left hemisphere than in the right, facilitating its support and influencing other left-sided language areas, such as the area responsible for language production known as Broca's.

The ACG begins to mature when the child is two to three years old. Encircling the amygdala and hypothalamus, it enhances awareness of inner states of both self and others and diverts recurring thoughts that would otherwise have distressing effects. The ACG's involvement, with other areas, in speech production and verbal fluency promotes verbally-based thinking and reasoning, allowing interactive dialogue that enhances self-image and a sense of security. It also enables more sophisticated assessments and solutions to be reached.

Damage to, or poor development of, the ACG can reduce motivation to communicate thoughts and feelings and predispose individuals to 'get stuck' in oppositional and addictive behaviours; repetitive and inflexible thinking; anxiety; panic attacks; muscle tension and reduced body awareness. Its role of sustaining attention clearly implicates the ACG in disorders of attention, such as ADHD.

Sympathetic and parasympathetic nervous systems

These are branches of the autonomic nervous system embedded in the body, with strong connections to both the amygdala and hypothalamus. They are regulated by the OFC, so as to mediate emotional responses and motivational states.

The SNS is a high-energy-based, rapid-response system that promotes life. It ensures that tissues throughout the brain and body receive the impetus and fuel they need to 'leap into action': be it through joyous excitement or 'fight or flight'. In many respects it is a question of degree: 'enough' and the individual feels empowered and exhilarated, able to 'go up and come down' on cue. 'Too much, too often' and he remains on 'red alert', finding it difficult to 'get back in balance'. This can be seen in the distressing high-arousal behaviours that typify *acute* post traumatic stress disorder (PTSD).

The SNS is activated by neurohormones produced by the adrenal glands, at the base of the HPA axis, in response to messages from the amygdala. It raises heart and respiration rates, diverts blood supplies from the neo-cortical areas to the limbs and dilates the pupils of the eye. It is deactivated by the PNS.

As its name suggests, the PNS works in opposition to the SNS, damping down its activities: it is thus an energy-conserving system. In well-balanced individuals the 'give and take' of SNS and PNS allows free movement 'up and down' the arousal scale and a sense of 'returning to normal'. However, PNS dominance under extreme stress causes the 'freeze' response to be triggered. Whilst this 'playing dead' behaviour promotes survival in cold-blooded animals, it can have dramatically dangerous effects in warm-blooded animals, like humans, through enforced 'shutdown' of body and mind.

The PNS is responsible for the shame response, reflecting its de-energising 'conservation-withdrawal' characteristics. It is associated with breaks in attachment that require reconnection, promoted by the caregiver as a renewed, and renewable, energy source. Failure of this 'circuit repair' leaves the child 'out in the cold', both literally and metaphorically. The PNS freeze response is also associated with dissociative behaviour and the numbed responses linked with *chronic* PTSD.

Summary

It is the child's early environment that 'sets the emotional thermostat' governing all these systems. Maltreated children tend to lack equilibrium and are prone to extreme responses, even in relatively innocuous situations. Lack of 'good enough' parental interactions leave the child's poorly developed OFC unable to provide the necessary regulation for the amygdala and thus the SNS and PNS.

Both the OFC and ACG play major roles in allowing the neo-cortex to function at its best and to promote mature 'top-down' organisation and control. These structures are dependent on 'good enough' attachment experiences that promote healthy and timely 'bottom-up' development.

The 'bottom-up' maturity conferred by 'good enough', early caregiving also facilitates the movement from right-hemisphere-dominated, intuitive, holistic 'gut feeling' responses towards greater influence of left-brained logical, sequential thought. Equilibrium is found in the integration of all brain sub-systems over an extended period of time and maintained by enhancing communications between them. Increasingly it is being recognised that these functions are not confined to the brain and conventional nervous systems but also includes the 'body-mind messengers', the neuropeptide 'molecules of emotion', of the entire psycho-neuro-immunological (PNI) system.

It is a sad irony that those individuals who are most in need of good 'information exchange and monitoring systems' are least likely to have had the opportunities to set these in place. Their poor early attachment experiences stand them in poor stead in both psychological and neurobiological terms: their 'take on the world', and their responses to it, are distorted and frequently 'trauma-organised'.

Without significant levels of support these children tend to remain behaviourally disorganised, reactive and emotionally driven, since they lack the mature language of socio-emotional awareness and expression through which social and emotional intelligence can be harnessed and transformed into higher levels of consciousness.

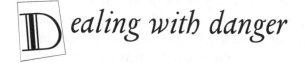ealing with danger

Some traumatised children have little concept of danger. They may wander off in public places, showing no apparent anxiety, even after quite lengthy separations. Others may balance precariously on furniture or walls, jump from great heights, leap into the deep end of swimming pools, lean out of top-floor windows or run into the road without stopping to look. In many cases they seem oblivious to parents' calls and entreaties. There is little 'checking back' to ensure caregivers are around and approve of their actions, or awareness of the concern their behaviour may engender. The maxim 'look before you leap' just does not seem to apply.

In developmental terms, 'checking in' and 'referring back' behaviours are put in place during toddlerhood, as emphasis moves from establishing a 'secure base' with parental attachment figures to engaging with and exploring the wider environment. As children become more mobile they inevitably take greater risks, needing increasing support and guidance from caregivers to negotiate these safely. Maintaining 'feedback links' with parents, through voice, touch, gesture and eye contact allows children to practise new skills without undue risk and strengthens the messages of security and trust that are being internalised. Maturing internal 'road maps' provide youngsters with sufficient inner guidance to negotiate the world securely and with increasing confidence.

When the process of establishing a 'secure base' does not go well, or the 'exploration' phase is compromised, youngsters' perceptions of themselves and the world go awry. Far from having a sense of trust and order, in the world and in themselves as part of it, alongside a growing understanding of the meaning of 'danger', maltreated youngsters struggle to construct realistic pictures of their environment. As with many biologically based systems where internal equilibrium is not well established, two extremes often emerge: going in fear of almost everyone and everything, or 'laughing in the face of danger', appearing oblivious to it. Traumatised children may swing between the two, depending on their behavioural state and situation.

The mechanisms underlying this reduced awareness or response to danger are not well understood but make good sense in terms of the 'language of trauma'. Every language is learned from repeated exposure to communications from caregivers. Gradually, children's dependence on parents' interaction and interpretations decrease as their own understanding, competence and fluency increases. In some youngsters there are identifiable gaps in their experience base that distorts acquisition of these vital skills, including understanding the 'language of danger'. This is supported by research with primates, that innate fears need to be 'turned on' by observing others' responses to potentially fear-invoking stimuli. Whilst some emotions, such as shame, may be intrinsically human, fear is believed to be common to all animals, evolving as a protective mechanism for the individual and species.

In many cases, children who hurt, yet know little danger, have been flooded with terrifying messages of which they have made little sense, rather than being starved of them. It is likely that birth parents' responses to their experiences would have been confused or distorted; their whole world would have seemed a hostile place, from which caregivers provided little respite. As with any other repeatedly overwhelming experience not contained by parents, or intensified by them, children's vulnerable systems must find ways to shut out these terrifying perceptions in order to survive.

Re-interpreting incoming messages of potential threat as relatively inert is a highly effective way of doing so in a world with few, if any, safe havens. The option of turning to caring adults for reassurance or security would not be high on these youngsters' internal agenda.

With age, traumatised children's behaviour may become increasingly difficult to handle. Not only will youngsters, and the wider community, expect greater freedom of movement and reduced supervision, their response patterns are also becoming firmly embedded. Since they have had insufficient early opportunities to learn to modulate feelings, emotions and arousal, they may exist in high energy and high activity states most of the time. They know little inner peace and understand little about their emotional responses. They may, conversely, come to depend on high intensity experiences, often involving great personal risk, to provide the 'buzz' they crave, or as a means of 'coming down' from such states in the only way they know. Here it may not be the perception of danger that is lacking, rather a predominantly unconscious over-riding of this, to achieve relative well-being.

Adoptive parents are bound to have preconceptions about their child's capabilities, based on their own childhood and caregiving experiences. Problems may arise where there are sizeable discrepancies between their own understandable perceptions and expectations and the child's equally understandable, but different, perceptions and expectations. It may be hard for new parents to recognise that their youngsters need to be handled as much younger children, if they are to be kept safe and practise acquiring a more appropriate 'vocabulary of danger'. They may expect top-down cognitive regulation to be in place (see pp.181–83), without realising that bottom-up, neurobiological development has been seriously impaired.

Hence adopters may need skilled help to make sense of their children's current behaviour in terms of their past. This diminishes perceptions that their children are manipulative, 'getting at them', 'beyond control' or possibly in need of mood-altering medication for impulsive and hyperactive behaviour. Irrespective of the age of their child and his particular pattern of responses, caregivers can regain their confidence and begin to hear and address their child's needs more effectively through retracing their steps developmentally.

Since children's difficulties stem from lack of positive experiences of a secure base during their early months and the consequent lack of capacity to self-regulate in healthy ways, the way forward becomes clear. 'Thinking baby and toddler' (see 'Think toddler think'), and providing sufficient opportunities for youngsters to make sense of, and alter, early 'feedback loops', is essential. In this way parents can encourage bottom-up brain development and help their children practise the close relationships and gradual exploration they need to make safer choices. Progress is likely to be incremental and depends not only on parents' responses but also on those of the wider community.

Parents who feel judged for babying their child, or for being overprotective or placing too many restrictions on 'danger-blind' or 'danger-focused' children may not have sufficient confidence to walk that fine line between taking appropriate responsibility themselves and giving appropriate responsibility to their youngsters. However, without the clear, containing, caring boundaries 'good enough' caregivers can provide, their children are likely to continue on their dangerous pathways through life: at potential risk to themselves and others.

Here the parent mentor writes some notes to supplement her discussions with Gill and James about managing six-year-old Sharon's 'dangerous' behaviours.

Letter to the Lee family

Dear Gill and James

It's probable that Sharon's lack of awareness of danger has the same root cause as her strange reactions to pain and her tendency to over-arousal: maltreating and neglectful parenting in the early months of her life, when she experienced poor care and lengthy periods of severe restriction. It's therefore essential you find ways of practising 'co-regulation' and of giving Sharon consistent, repeated messages that 'We'll keep you safe and help you to learn how to stay safe yourself'. This is likely to be a challenging and possibly long-term project but it underpins most of the other therapeutic parenting work you will need to do with Sharon.

Quite clearly, in the past, Carrie has taken on the role of looking after Sharon. That is not an appropriate job for a nine-year-old, although Carrie may need some help to let go of this responsibility. Occasional help from her would be fine but relying on her regularly could adversely affect her relationship with you (parent to child) and possibly also with Sharon.

Gently but firmly take control of keeping Sharon safe, telling Carrie: 'It's *my* job to keep you both safe. *Your* job is to practise being a little girl and having fun!' It could be very supportive to add: 'And it's my job to make sure you get it right!' Letting Carrie know what you plan to do, in advance, to avoid her 'leave my sister alone' response will be important. Although it will be hard for her to let go of her previous caring role ('this is part of who I am and if I don't do it who am I?'), it will probably be a great relief to her at the same time.

Making links between what you're going to do with what you know of the girls' early life will help Carrie make sense of the new world (your family) which she now inhabits. Some of that will trickle down to Sharon too: even though she was very young when she left her birth family her earliest experiences have informed her most fundamental beliefs about families and the world. Both girls' brains and nervous systems were organised to survive the chaotic world of their birth family and they will need repeated, very different, experiences in your family before these really begin to change.

From our conversations it seems that Sharon needs a great deal of help to stay safe on the road. In order for her to be able to experience feeling safe she'll need you to stay very close to her and to take her hand much, if not all, of the time. Sharon will probably not be keen on this since it could easily trigger unconscious memories from her past of being restrained but it is vital you get the message across that 'I need to keep you safe' or 'As your mummy it's my job to make sure you stay safe'. Saying 'I love you too much to let you get hurt' is another powerful way of getting your message over.

You could point out that you all need more practice at this because you haven't been together as a family for long. Sharing responsibility for problems make them more tolerable for children and avoids the 'shame trap' that causes much distress and difficult behaviour. 'Being in the same boat' can bring you closer together emotionally. Initially you should expect active resistance to your efforts, since Sharon's take on life is that she can't trust anyone else to look after her but herself: not a good basis for safety (or intimacy) in a five-year-old! Stick with it!

You could start practising 'keeping Sharon safe' with very short walks on car-free paths. Walking to the newsagent's would be a good start. Try to make it just the two of you initially. Calmly but firmly insist on holding Sharon's hand at all times. If she struggles (almost inevitable) you'll need to continue holding on firmly and say 'I need to keep you safe', followed by 'I can see this is very hard for you right now. It's a good job you've got such a good mum who knows how to take care of you'.

An understanding 'I know' can be an invaluable standby in the face of prolonged protests! If you meet continued resistance to holding hands then make it clear you intend to go straight home: being 'sad for, not mad at' Sharon. Try adding 'I can see we both need some more practise on this', in a matter-of-fact and calm tone, even if you feel you're beginning to lose your cool. Acting calmly helps you feel calmer! Remember, you can't judge or handle Sharon's behaviour like that of her peers: she's coming from a very different place.

You may initially feel uncomfortable about 'holding on' in the face of obvious distress, especially if you have an audience. However, keep reminding yourselves that Sharon desperately needs to feel safe and you're the right people (the only people) who can do this for her. Complaints that you're hurting Sharon should be taken seriously by checking your grip and your gut feelings. However, this is more likely to be 'you're hurting me' from her early days in her birth family. Try wondering out loud about what's really hurting Sharon and be sad for her painful memories: remaining confident you're doing the right thing and staying calm yourselves.

You may also find being playful helps with hand-holding compliance. For example you could send 'messages', by squeezing hands in simple patterns, or by gently stroking or tickling. Just be careful not to over-stimulate Sharon here, or you will lose the advantage. You could also try complaining of cold hands and wondering who will warm them up for you by holding them firmly – taking care to leave your gloves at home! Swinging linked arms to the accompaniment of lively songs could also do the trick sometimes. Remember, this is not about rewarding 'bad behaviour': it's about you being in safe control for Sharon's sake.

Sometimes 'mentally rehearsing' the scenario can help you come up with just the right things to say or do: it can be hard to think that way in the face of a tornado! Reminding yourselves of the potentially high physical costs of *not* keeping Sharon safe, as well as the heavy emotional costs if she doesn't feel secure, would be helpful. Repeating your chosen few 'keep you safe' words could help you to feel more confident and let potentially critical onlookers appreciate the task you are undertaking. Over and above this it's essential for Sharon to experience your calm and safe care repeatedly before she can begin to take it for granted.

Once Sharon has practised letting you keep her safe, she should start 'checking in' with you about potentially dangerous situations. This is the next step developmentally and will allow her greater autonomy whilst still ensuring her safety. You could introduce some games to play at home or in the garden that encourage this. The old favourite *Mother May I?* would provide Sharon with opportunities to check things out verbally, and give her some much needed 'asking' practice too.

However, most early checking back is non-verbal, involving touch, gesture or eye contact, so perhaps you could focus on those areas first. You could devise a reverse form of *Sly Fox*, in which players can only move forward and away from you when your eyes are wide open and you're looking in their direction. This could be emphasised by throwing your hands away from your eyes as you uncover them.

Simple games with bubbles could also provide opportunities to practise getting non-verbal permission. When you blow the bubbles ask Sharon to wait until you wink or nod before trying to catch them. You could also adapt the game of *Pirates* so that you have to test out the 'islands' before you wave Sharon over with your hand. A 'seebackroscope' might be a fascinating way to encourage looking back for previously agreed directions from you! Games at home are great fun *and* provide much needed mental rehearsal for children, in relatively safe surroundings, that can eventually be taken beyond the home.

Until you're sure Sharon is regularly 'checking in', you'd do well to keep her close to you, within 'eye shot' and reach. That way you can make sure she doesn't face, or take, unnecessary risks. The less practice Sharon has at risky behaviours the better and it's probably the only way you can be sure to keep her safe. You could try asking yourself 'would I allow a toddler to do this on her own?' then act accordingly.

There are lots of stories that cover risk-taking for small children. *My Naughty Little Sister* has some useful messages you can slip in undetected. Interestingly A.A. Milne tends to reverse the message in *A House at Pooh Corner*: with Tigger (the bouncy toddler) outwitting Rabbit in exploring and 'getting home safely'. This could give you the opportunity to talk about whether it's safe for young animals (or children) to be out on their own.

Milne's poem 'Disobedience' in *Now We Are Six?* also springs to mind. Here the little boy invokes the message 'don't go down to the end of the town without consulting me' to his mother: reflecting the separation anxiety Sharon still clearly lacks.

If Sharon continues having difficulties in letting you keep her safe, try using a teddy bear. You could call the bear 'baby Sharon' and show Sharon how you'd have looked after her as a baby. Wondering when Sharon will feel able to let you care for her this way would add emphasis and show her you're confident that she'll soon be able to let you keep her safe.

As a couple you could also talk to each other, in Sharon's earshot, about the ways you'd have liked to look after Sharon and keep her safe. You could express sadness about what she missed out on and hopes that she'll soon be able to feel safer and more cared for. It would be helpful to give specific examples of the safe caring behaviours you're hoping to introduce: for example, wondering when Sharon will come and ask you before she goes out to play. Global statements are less effective with children who haven't had their needs met; Sharon is unlikely to know what you mean by 'safe care' unless you spell out ways she can practise it.

Knowing how oppositional Sharon can be you could also use your conversations with each other to gently challenge her. Perhaps you could say that you feel Sharon isn't ready for hand-holding yet. She may set out to prove you wrong: you create a 'win–win' situation and can express pleasure whatever Sharon chooses to do. Be pleased she's beginning to learn about being cared for if she holds your hand; conversely show her you're glad she's letting you know she's struggling (literally!) and continues to need help if she doesn't hold your hand.

Even after all this effort there will be times when Sharon seems oblivious to danger or actively engages in risky activities. If you are prepared for these and understand that 'three steps forward, two steps back' is to be expected, you can avoid feeling disappointed or frustrated. You can help Sharon feel held and understood too, by gently reminding her that there's plenty of time to practise. 'Getting it right' and 'getting it wrong' is a valuable part of the learning process for all of you.

Perhaps the most essential elements for you to bear in mind are:

- working globally on Sharon's high arousal and encouraging shared activities that promote co-regulation with you

- remaining in safe charge of your own feelings and actions and Sharon's

- recognising Sharon's desperate need for structure and safe containment (which would normally come from 'good enough' parenting in infancy)

- being confident that you will not hurt Sharon: even if she's screaming that you are; as long as you're gentle but firm you run little risk of hurting her

- making sure Carrie understands what you are doing and why (so that she doesn't inadvertently sabotage your work or feel rejected)

- establishing an initial period within which Sharon has very limited opportunities to 'go it alone' or make poor choices; this will be hard on all of you but forms the foundation for her learning to stay safe

- encouraging Sharon to 'check in, check out or check back' on a regular basis, once this initial period is over and you begin to allow her more freedom to explore

- taking things slowly; so that you can remain in safe charge the whole time, whilst simultaneously providing regular practice in feeling safe for Sharon

- avoiding bargaining and offering rewards for 'good behaviour' – I feel sure Sharon would try to weasel her way round this, as for most things! (ignoring plea-bargaining is a sound general principle at all times!)

- building in some fun, such as singing loud songs as you walk, could be very useful (if you are having fun there's less time for complaints and confrontations!)

- expecting a good deal of initial challenge from Sharon and being 'sad for' rather than 'mad at' her difficulties

- anticipating things to slip back, especially at stressful times: bottom-up development dictates that when push comes to shove we revert to our earliest learned patterns; the capacity to think it through is then seriously limited, so top-down control would be difficult, even when you think the lessons have been learned.

Some of this may feel quite hard for you to take on board initially. As parents we often want to give our children as much freedom as possible and not to appear restrictive: particularly when that's been a very real part of their early lives. However, establishing 'who's in safe control' is absolutely fundamental to Sharon's healthy attachment and development: I'm confident you'll give it your best shot. I'd be very happy to talk this through further with you as you may have some initial queries and understandable doubts.

Meanwhile, keep up the good work and make sure you take good care of yourselves. It could be really helpful for both girls to see you looking after each other and showing realistic concern for each other's safety. In particular if either child becomes verbally or physically threatening at home, you could 'ham it up' and exaggerate concern for the 'target' parent whilst making it clear your intention to keep everyone safe: parents and children alike.

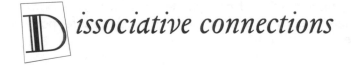

Dissociative connections

Many parents might feel uncomfortable with the term 'dissociation' in relation to their child but would immediately identify with one or more of the following descriptions:

'he goes off in a day dream'

'he goes into shut down'

'he blanks us off'

'he changes from one minute to the next'

'it sometimes feels like we have "two little Freddies"'

'when he explodes he's so strong it takes two of us to contain him'

'sometimes he doesn't even hear what I say'

'he doesn't notice when he's hurt himself'

'he rarely cries or shows his feelings'.

These almost everyday behaviours are often not recognised as part of a dissociative continuum that runs from 'highway hypnosis' at one end to controversial diagnoses such as dissociative identity disorder at the other. However, since expressions such as 'I'm not feeling myself today' and 'I was in two minds whether to . . .' are familiar to most of us, the phenomenon should hold more fascination than fear, more promise of 'normality' than threat of 'craziness'.

Introducing 'dissociative thinking' into our developmental reparenting approach increases parental understanding, leading to greater empathy and connection with traumatised children. This, in turn, allows youngsters to make stronger connections with their caregivers and with their external and internal worlds. It is helpful to consider dissociative children in terms of inter-rupted attachment and development and the consequent lack of opportunities to establish healthy neurobiological and psychological connections.

These dis-associations, disconnections, missed connections, disconjunct-ions and misalignments, are evident not only in the lack of 'joined-up thinking' demonstrated by maltreated children but also in many areas of functioning: sensory, motor, affective, cognitive and behavioural. Here we refer to the weak connections and misconnections between children's behav-iour, their emotions, sensory and motor coordination systems, conscious awareness, memory, perceptions, expectations, beliefs and responses, all of which may show noticeable variations throughout the day.

Infants respond to changes in the internal environment (like feelings of hunger or cold) and the external environment (such as noise, smell, movement and changes in caregiver) by becoming distressed. They cry and show through changes in facial and body expression just how upset they feel. In 'good enough' families, babies' cries will be heard, interpreted and responded to swiftly, predictably and appropriately. Caregivers initially must act as their infants' 'sensory thermostat' or 'arousal regulator', using their own mature self-regulatory systems and self-awareness, to support their immature infants, who arrive in the world ill-equipped for self-regulation. Over time, with repeated practice and consistency of care, young children's brains and nervous systems make the connections that allow them to cope increasingly well with distress and to acquire good levels of self-awareness. They evolve increasingly integrated views of themselves and their relationships.

Without 'good enough', early co-regulatory experiences, youngsters cannot make sense of all the sensations and emotions they experience. The lack of attuned 'interpreters' who can reflect back and give meaning to their expressions, gestures, gurgles, cries and movements, means they have no one to 'join up the dots' in their bodies or in their thinking. A child might not feel the cold, refusing to accept the need for a coat on frosty days, or knock into things because he doesn't seem to know where his body ends. His 'inner road maps' of relating to the outside world are also discontinuous or distorted: he is likely to misinterpret his social environment using the 'language of trauma' rather than the 'language of love'.

Young children also need sensitive 'state shifters' to help them move from one feeling state (such as anger) to another (such as joy), if they are not to 'get stuck' or feel overwhelmed and out of control. Over time and with practice, transitions from one state of mind and body to another become more automatic and fluid, as youngsters become fluent in their own 'mind–body language'.

Most people are now familiar with the concepts of fight, flight and freeze in response to distress. These are extreme neurobiological states that evolved to ensure survival; they can become 'burned in' or 'hard-wired' responses to repeated traumatic experiences. Current thinking in the field of developmental psycho-neurobiology defines the freeze state in terms of major dissociative shifts to very low arousal states, in circumstances where the high arousal states of fight or flight become ineffective or unviable. Some researchers believe that criteria for dissociation should include all extreme state dependent responses, high and low, that involve hard-wired neural pathways. It is likely that much of the troubling behaviour seen in traumatised children has strong dissociative components and is therefore not readily amenable to standard 'cognitive-behavioural' approaches.

However, since creating connections is an ongoing developmental process, children whose developmental connections have been interrupted or distorted through poor early attachment experiences can be supported in their adoptive families to 'join up' the cognitive-behavioural 'dots'. This is good news for families, far outweighing any fears that use of the term 'dissociative' could engender, once fully understood. Again adopters will need to 'crack the behavioural code' embedded in their child's trauma history in order to begin to 'hear' and understand their child's puzzling responses. Grasping, for example, that their child's inability to do what he's told may be due to a dissociative state 'downshift' (can't) rather than deliberate stubbornness (won't), allows parents to stay in control of potentially volatile situations.

Children's distress states may be brought about by external 'triggers', thoughts or recollections of incidents from the past. It can take just one aspect of a state dependent memory pattern to set off a train of feelings in children's bodies that have come to be integrally associated with that old familiar, but overwhelming, sense of terror or abandonment. Parents who understand this can find ways of co-regulating these unbearable feelings with their children, giving them vital, shared practice in modulating arousal and moving between feeling states.

Adopters must use their acquired 'Jemima Crackit' knowledge of their children to help them manage their feelings and make sense of their behaviour without blaming or shaming. A calm, quiet voice, with a firm but gentle touch, can help their child re-connect. Caregivers should also help their youngsters practise taking responsibility for *all* their actions at levels that are appropriate for their functioning age *at that time*, since ability is frequently a state dependent variable. In addition, they may need to be clear about what really happened for their children, stating this matter-of-factly, to fill in the memory gaps that dissociative state shifts frequently leave. Gradually, with parents' understanding, commitment and support, youngsters can begin to acknowledge 'all of themselves' and hold more integrated views of their relationships with the world.

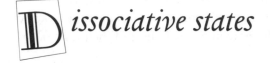issociative states

Dissociative children find it difficult to identify the physical sensations and emotional feelings that let them know their body's needs and that form the basis for good self-awareness. Their neurobiological systems are 'hot-wired' to respond to situations in their current environment bearing some resemblance to past trauma, or that are perceived for some reason as threatening. In addition there is frequently some sensory over- or under-sensitivity that is part of the birth family legacy of neglect or abuse.

Traumatised children have difficulty moving from one feeling state, or state of mind, to another and in developing an integrated sense of self. Thus they may temporarily 'get stuck' in certain behavioural patterns that, over time, can become more or less fixed. Frequently they will be unable to transfer information or skills acquired in one state of being to another, so that social and emotional learning is impaired. Unfortunately these difficulties can be misinterpreted as deliberate behaviours and the child labelled as 'stubborn', 'oppositional' or even 'slow'. Hence learning the 'language of trauma' is essential for decoding and managing dissociative behaviours.

Some children appear to be more or less permanently 'shut down': they may show little emotion, may move and respond slowly and keep their distance from people. This pattern has been particularly linked with pervasive neglect in the earliest days of the child's life. Others seem to cope fairly well socially and emotionally but will suddenly 'go away inside their heads', with little obvious reason. In both cases such children will desperately avoid eye contact and 'visibility'. Still others may 'go ape', displaying uncontrolled rage and 'the look', during which their eyes can appear terrifying and penetrating.

Reaching a child who 'shuts down' or 'goes away' may seem to demand quite different handling from those who 'go off on one' or 'crank up' when distressed. However, since they are all examples of altered, alienated states of being, they respond to similar approaches. Caregivers need to be able to make contact with the child and help him to find his way back to the here and now. Empathic tone of voice, non-intrusive eye contact, an accepting physical stance and confident gentle touch can re-open closed communication channels. On a repeated basis this gives the child opportunities to learn to modulate his volatile arousal and practise managing 'state transitions'.

Dissociative children may have very real problems with 'the truth'. Their internal world is 'all over the place', since their early experiences did not provide them with opportunities to become 'well joined up'. What they know may remain 'state dependent', that is they may have restricted access to 'all the facts' in certain feeling states. Thus there exists a genuine 'information gap' that cannot necessarily be over-ridden by 'putting your mind to it'.

In addition youngsters may have become highly practised at forgetting or denying overwhelming or unpleasant feelings and events. In the past this was necessary for survival; now it may be an ingrained but unconscious habit. In daily life we all tend unconsciously to take out or make up bits of 'our story' to make it feel more acceptable and complete. This becomes exaggerated in dissociative children whose memories are already fragmented. Hence their 'truth' at one moment may differ from the truth they can access or recognise at other times.

Adults often perceive this construction or denial in the face of overwhelming evidence as lying. However, in many cases these are not deliberate strategies but unconscious attempts to make sense of the confusing muddles surrounding these youngsters' lives. Sadly, some older children do eventually learn to use these tactics more consciously, if they realise that it puts them in control. Parents therefore need to be their child's 'eyes, ears, mouth, heart and mind' in order to help him process what is going on for him and to develop a truer awareness of himself and his behaviour.

This is the 'Jemima Crackit' approach (see pp.29–31 and 80–2) that helps 'Panicchio' avoid not only panic but also many other distressing states, make sounder connections between mind and body and to accept a shared reality. Rather than being faced with 'the Spanish Inquisition', that would inevitably cause Panicchio's nose to grow, as he digs himself deeper into his 'lies', the child needs to feel understood, so that his brain grows and he can come to understand himself more fully.

Whilst an accusatory or punitive approach is likely to perpetuate dissociative feelings, thinking and behaviour, through further isolating an alienated child, gently but firmly 'presenting the facts as they see them' brings the parent alongside the child. Together they can explore what went on, with the parent providing most of the 'evidence' and providing her 'best guess' as to what really took place. Exploring these sequences of cause and effect with good humour keeps the child in touch and allows him to hear and absorb his parent's perspective. This internalisation by the parent increases internal communication and networking and gradually diminishes the internal state separation that underpins dissociation.

Here we discuss some practical implications of living with dissociative children: addressing two areas where dissociative states feature prominently in Mic and Sara's behaviour. However, dissociation is a common characteristic of many traumatised children and several of the worked examples touch on this issue.

Letter to the Warne family

Dear Elaine and Sam

From what you've said, it seems that both children are skilled at dissociation and regularly enter puzzling dissociative states. This is understandable given what we know about the level of abuse they experienced in their birth family. On my last visit I noticed several times that Mic stopped listening and moved away/changed the subject/ignored me, if I raised difficult issues with him. I used playfulness – 'switching on his ears' – to let Mic know I could see he needed some help to stay listening. I was also careful to acknowledge how hard I thought it was for him to hear these things. That strategy in itself can be very effective in helping a child feel understood; increasing the chance he'll be able to 'stay in touch and listen'. Increasing parent–child connection is vital to the repair of damaged attachments and the reduction of dissociative patterns.

It's important to find ways of bringing Sara and Mic back when they are 'somewhere else'. 'Earth to Mic' might appeal to Mic's sense of humour. Putting your hand on his shoulder whilst you speak will enhance the effect. You may need a gentler approach with Sara, who seems to go much further away and for longer periods. Maybe you could wonder out loud where she is as you find some non-intrusive way of touching her and getting physically close. You could even say 'I can see you've gone somewhere a long way away. I don't want you to be alone. Can I come too?' Don't allow Sara to push you away or reject your concern here: if you stick around, staying calm and close, she will gradually start 'coming round' or 'letting you in'. This is vital if you're to reduce the feelings of helpless, hopeless abandonment underpinning much of her current behaviour.

In both cases you might like to talk to the children about these 'puzzling episodes' after the event. Choose times when they are not tired, rushed, excited or stressed so that they are really able to 'hear' you. You can let them know that it must be really hard for them to stay around when things feel bad, then explain that they learned this to manage the abuse and neglect they suffered. Telling them that they did the very best thing they could *at the time* will help reduce their sense of shame and enable them to 'move on'. You might wonder how much better they might feel, now they are more grown up, if they could 'stay in touch' more of the time. Helping them to see that 'zoning out' sometimes gets them into trouble may provide them with additional motivation to change.

Other examples of the children's tendency to dissociate seem to relate more directly to their reactive sensory systems: like Mic's keen awareness of, and reaction to, smells. This can indicate immature or interrupted nervous system development (just think how much babies rely on their sense of smell). Sara's non-eating and odd reactions to pain also fall into this category, indicating a lack of healthy awareness of her own body sensations. Why not explore some of the suggestions for working through the body and the senses that can be found in *First Steps in Parenting the Child Who Hurts* (Archer 1999a, pp.46–66)? In time we might look at more specific neurodevelopmental exercises that could support the children's systems and help them achieve greater levels of sensori-motor maturity.

When you're confronted with an apparently 'barefaced lie', begin by reminding yourselves that for children like Mic and Sara who regularly dissociate, lying is often not intentional. There are so many muddles in their heads, and they're often so cut off from their bodies and feelings, they don't really know what the truth is. It's your job to help them, before this becomes a firmly established behaviour pattern.

Start by reminding yourself that you don't need to get stuck in the trap of trying to prove the children aren't telling the truth or getting them to admit what really happened. You can be the 'Jemima Crackit' on their shoulder who can 'best guess' what went on and let them know that you know. Stay sensitive, understanding and even playful here: that will be much more effective than criticism or anger (although harder to sustain!). Using an 'Inspector Clousseau' approach as you wonder what might have actually happened could be fun. Working together to wonder whether the 'dog did it' is also an effective approach to get the children thinking!

Finally, I feel sure the children would benefit from regular cradling sessions with you both. Initially, the biggest challenge may be for you to create time for each child separately when your other children are otherwise occupied. Because both children have experienced such severe abuse of their bodies they'll need lots of extra practice of 'good touch': even if, like Sara, they initially resist physical contact. This is one area where you need to remain sensitive to each child's lead while being guided by your knowledge of developmental attachment needs. Cradling time would also help Mic 'reprogramme' his beliefs and behaviour systems in relation to his and other people's bodies. (See also 'Cradling for closeness and comfort'.)

Letter to Mic after he had talked to his adoptive mother about a dissociative experience

Dear Mic

I've been doing some thinking since we met and I thought it'd be helpful if I wrote something down for you, so that you can look back at it whenever you need to.

It must be scary to feel you sometimes do things and your head doesn't know what your body is doing. I know that sometimes children feel they must be crazy or mad if they feel like that: so the first thing I want to do is set you straight! You're anything but crazy!! Read on...!

I know from Mum, and from your files, that you had a very tough time when you were small and living with your birth mum. It seems as though she didn't know how, or wasn't able, to look after you as well as you needed and deserved. That's very sad and not *at all* your fault. I also know you're still very fond of your birth mum, which can make things feel very muddled inside. There may be a part of you that feels hurt and even angry that you weren't taken good care of and still another part that says 'but Mum loves me and I love Mum. She did her best for me'.

Interestingly, both those things are true: even though they sound contradictory! When we have very different thoughts and feelings inside and we can't 'make them fit together' we tend to keep them in separate boxes in our heads. That's one big reason why our heads and bodies don't always know the same things all the time.

Another big reason, as for many adopted children, is that when you were a baby and were left hungry, cold, in pain or on your own you would have been a very sad, lonely and scared little boy. Babies and little boys need their mums so much that if their mum isn't able to cuddle them, feed them, rock them and sing to them when they need those things (which is *most* of the time!) they could die of a broken heart.

But babies (like you!) are amazingly clever – instead they don't forget all the pain and heartache but put it in separate boxes in their heads. In particular the messages from their bodies are pushed away, so that they can bear the pain and stay alive. That's something very special and not every baby or small child can do that – but you did. It was the best and the most sensible thing you could possibly do *at the time.*

You were too small to look after yourself or run away and find someone to help you. So you 'shut off' most of the feelings in your body and your head and kept them very separate. Because it was such a helpful thing to do when you were little, it gets difficult to do it any other way when you're bigger and would like to do things differently. BUT it is possible to change – slowly and with lots of help from Mum and Dad.

So what can you do now?

First of all, keep telling yourself you deserved to be looked after properly – every baby does! You don't have to blame anyone – I'm sure Mum wanted to do her best but was just not able to give you what you needed. You also need to remember that you did the very best you could to be a baby and live through those tough times. It may take you a long time to really 'know' and believe this but you can practise telling yourself (with reminders from Mum and Dad) until every part of you in every box in your head can hear!

That brings me to my next point: talking to yourself is a great thing to do! People often say 'you must be mad' if they see people talking to themselves. Well, they are wrong! For children (and grown ups) who had to learn to keep their thoughts and feelings in separate boxes (some of them locked up very tightly), it's just the right thing to do. That way you get to 'join up' up the different parts of you and become a stronger more 'connected' person.

You'll begin to make more sense – to yourself and to other people too. It won't always be easy because some of those parts may know stuff that is very sad or hurts a lot to think about. The good news is that you don't have to do this on your own, or all at once. You can take your time and go at the pace you want to. Mum and Dad will always be ready to help.

You may even surprise yourself about how much you can remember (and understood, even as a very small child) and how it all begins to fall into place and make sense! (Remember, even though you probably didn't understand about your head and body not always knowing the same things, you were able to tell Mum – amazing!)

Maybe the best place for you to start is with your peeing at night – because you've already been able to tell Mum about your head and body not knowing the same things. It probably happens more at night because everything can seem scarier then. It's dark and you feel more on your own – and that can remind your body (without even thinking about it in your head) of the very scary times when you felt on your own when you were little. That makes it more likely that your head and your body will start to disconnect and try to keep things from each other – just as they did all those years ago.

Now things are much safer for you and you have Mum and Dad to help, you can begin to risk talking to yourself more! So, if you find in the morning that your bed is wet and your head doesn't really remember what went on, try asking your body! The trick is to be kind to yourself and not angry or critical. Just wonder (out loud or in your head) whether there's a part of you that remembers the peeing and could help fill you in. Perhaps the biggest reason this is still such a big deal for you is that there can be so much embarrassment and shame around peeing in the wrong place. Then it has to stay a 'secret'. By trying to talk to yourself more openly and with greater understanding and sympathy about what went on, and is going on, for you, you can begin to open up boxes in your head.

Some children find it helps to write these conversations down – sometimes using one hand to ask questions and their other hand to reply. Or you can just have quiet chats with yourself on your own (or with Mum or Dad). Just a few minutes can be enough – but you may want to spend longer, that's entirely up to you! I wonder whether it's already felt like there've been lots of noises in your head sometimes? That happens to some kids and it can feel very scary too! Now that you can be in control of the conversations, there should be fewer unwanted scary noises going on.

If you would like to know more about any of this, why don't you write, e-mail, phone or draw me a picture?

Remember, it takes lots of strength and courage to sort out the big muddles and join up the boxes in our heads – but it's worth it! AND I know you're strong enough and have enough courage to do it when you're ready – because you've taken care of yourself so well for years already. Keep reminding yourself that you don't have to do this on your own any more!

I'm looking forward to hearing from you and seeing you soon.

Poem written by Mic about his dissociative feelings

My Umbrella

It's like an umbrella
I can put up
To shut out the rain
And keep me dry.

The good thing is
That I don't get wet,
I know I won't get wet,
And so I keep it up.

The bad thing is
That when the heavens open,
And the rain pours down
I still get soaked through.

And the sad thing is,
When I keep it up,
It shuts out the sun
And keeps me in the dark.

Then how can I tell
When the rain has passed,
Clouds blown away,
And it's safe to come out and play?

So now I'm learning that
I can fold my brolly down
And carry it with me –
In its case, just in case.

And only when it's really wet
Do I need to put it up,
(Or turn it upside down
And float away.

– Just long enough
To escape the flood),
Then it helps me stay dry
To live another day.

Eating and food issues

Eating is fundamentally bound up with the sense of well-being. For babies, being nourished is an integral part of being nurtured: the sweet warmth of breast or formula milk reflecting the 'sweet warmth' of the 'good enough' parent. If either of these elements does not go well, the resulting problems can be long lasting and intransigent. Whilst feeding difficulties in the infant or parental difficulties with providing appropriate nourishment for the baby may be more obvious precursors of later issues with eating, the broader dynamic of poor general caregiving can be its 'hidden face'.

As food and eating are such 'big issues' very early in the child's development, it stands to reason that they can have inordinately large knock-on effects. Even in the womb, patterns may be formed that adversely influence the baby's well-being after birth. It is likely that maltreating parents will nourish themselves poorly during the pregnancy. In addition they may use toxic substances such as nicotine, alcohol or drugs, which could further compromise the developing infant's fragile nutritional status. Whilst poor physical growth is an obvious developmental sequel, there is evidence that poor nutrition in the womb leads to ongoing dietary absorption problems and potential food intolerances. (See also 'Nutrition'.) Current research also links relative malnutrition during pregnancy with metabolic changes and preferential food selection (for high carbohydrate, high fat foods) after birth, that promote well-being in survival conditions. This 'predictive adaptive response' appears relatively permanent, even when food supply conditions change, making the individual prone to obesity and ill-health.

Stress could also be a strong, indirect contributory factor to ongoing ill-health. Stress hormones such as cortisol are known to cross the placenta from the mother, with potentially adverse effects on the developing brain and nervous system. The baby that comes into the world already stressed is likely to be difficult to comfort and have more than his fair share of handling and feeding problems. Later cravings for 'carbs' may also form part of this picture, due to an ongoing stress response and consequent lack of appetite inhibition. In addition, the infant's gut may become overly sensitive, leading to colic and gastro-intestinal upsets, allergic sensitivities and a vicious cycle of unresolved distress associated with poor early feeding.

Omega 3 fatty acid dietary deficiencies in babies and young children have been linked with hyperactivity and Attention Deficit Hyperactivity Disorder, depression, sleep disturbances, poor coordination and impaired cognitive function. These essential fatty acids play a major role in the growth and specialisation of the cells of the foetal and infant brain, of which 60 per cent is fat. Breast milk is known to contain a higher percentage of these long-chain fatty acids than formula milks. Pre-term babies, those born to poorly nourished mothers and bottle-fed babies are therefore at greater risk.

Since poverty and social deprivation are associated directly with stress, the pattern becomes increasingly complex. Nutritional status will tend to be compromised, whilst stress may further deplete the vulnerable system of essential nutrients. It might be predicted that the majority of children placed in foster care or for adoption will have been exposed to several of these adverse factors.

After birth, how the baby is fed has a direct bearing on his physical and emotional health. Clearly breast-feeding provides the optimal nutritional start for human infants; it also sets the scene for healthy parent–infant interactions. Few fostered and adopted youngsters have had either this nutritional advantage or consistent opportunities for secure attachment interactions. Moreover, parents of bottle-fed babies perceived as 'difficult' or 'slow' feeders may be tempted to increase the size of the teat hole, to speed up intake. Whilst the intention is to improve nutrition, and therefore enhance growth and development, this significantly reduces the amount of 'sucking practice' available to infants.

Similarly babies who are repeatedly laid down in their cots and 'bottle-propped', or expected to self-feed from an early age, will not be in the best position for suckling, and will come to associate feeding with being alone and uncared for. Furthermore, like infants whose mothers do not respond to their cries of hunger, they are more likely to experience the isolation and powerlessness that is linked with later flattened emotions, and passive and dissociative behaviours. Since these are mediated by dramatically lowered cortisol levels, physical ill-health and immune system problems may also result.

Common sense suggests that poor suckling could lead to muscle tone problems in and around the mouth, including articulation difficulties, and could be implicated in the poor development of the 'social smile'. Dental problems may ensue, that have a further impact on subsequent eating patterns. Moreover, research also suggests associated weaknesses in other muscles served by the shared facial nerve, such as in the ears and eyes. According to HANDLE (see 'Parenting resoures', p.246), difficulties with auditory sequencing, balance and coordination and visual tracking due to poor suckling may be partially responsible for the speech difficulties, problems following instructions, dyslexia and dyspraxia found in many maltreated children.

Parents who have not received 'good enough' care themselves in infancy have poor self-awareness and will be especially vulnerable to further stress. Additionally, they are likely to find it more difficult to be emotionally or physiologically attuned to their baby's needs: they may provide feeds erratically, force the bottle into his mouth, handle him roughly, or expect him to feed himself far too early. They may also feed him foods for which his developing digestive system is not yet ready, or which is already sensitive due to ongoing distress.

Moreover the process of chewing and swallowing is not altogether innate: eating is yet another largely learned behaviour that can be adversely affected by early experience. The consistency and texture of solid foods offered to babies and young children can be crucial to later muscle tone and can lead to over- or under-sensitivity in the mouth area. Poor oral sensitivity may mean that lodged food goes undetected by the tongue, causing further damage to teeth, with knock-on effects to future eating habits. The child may also tend to 'mouth' things that are not food, such as cardigan sleeves, toys and play-dough in an attempt to satisfy his craving for oral sensation.

Adverse, early nutritional experiences may set the child up for many emotionally, as well as physically, based eating and digestive problems. If nourishment and nurture are regularly linked with discomfort, pain, rejection or abandonment the youngster's internal 'road maps' and neurological organisation will reflect this. He may come to use food as a substitute for love: consuming large amounts of sweet and fatty foods to compensate for his emotional emptiness. Further dental or body-image problems may follow.

Other children may engage in 'attention seeking' or 'attention needing' behaviours around food and mealtimes, in attempts to counteract the unpredictability of their early lives. Moreover lack of predictability and control over survival needs, such as feeding and physical closeness, have been identified as the most important elements associated with altered cortisol levels, which can be a predisposing factor in many later eating disorders.

Some children have such poor physiological self-awareness, due to poor patterns of nurture and ensuing poor stress regulation, that they do not recognise when they are hungry or thirsty or, conversely, when they have had enough. Consequently they may go for long periods without eating or drinking or binge eat until they feel nauseous or vomit. Here the lack of established 'set points' due to parental insensitivity or unpredictability lead to continued behavioural disorganisation in the child.

In addition some youngsters tend to hoard or hide food 'just in case', where supplies have been unpredictable or absent in the past. Others find it hard to ask for food or drink, since their early needs were ignored, or punished. They therefore tend to go without, contributing further stress to their already distressed systems, or become practised in taking food secretively or through manipulating others, often non-family members. Whether these patterns take active or passive forms may depend on the timing of adverse experiences and their nature.

Other children demonstrate ongoing difficulties with chewing. Some store food in their cheeks like hamsters, finding it difficult to break the pieces down sufficiently for swallowing; others appear to be 'playing with their food', taking long periods to eat even small quantities. Many have problems with certain textures of food and resort to eating narrow groups of foods, to limit their distress. This is often interpreted as 'pickiness', with youngsters perceived as 'controlling' or 'manipulative'. Certainly, feeding and mealtimes can become sources of added stress and major control issues if they are not understood and managed appropriately. However, once the origins and meaning of the behaviour are explored, the problem can be approached with increased empathy, patience and understanding.

Most of us are also familiar with the concept of 'gut feelings': that our 'bellies' behave quite differently according to changing emotional states. 'Fight or flight' hormones, including adrenalin and cortisol, tend to shut down our digestive functions, diverting essential blood supplies to muscles in the limbs and pupils of the eyes. Conversely the 'freeze' response, although involving cortisol, involves a 'letting go' that could account for the expression 'being shit scared'. This may be a contributory factor in traumatised children who exhibit bowel problems.

Moreover, the body may be as sensitive as the mind to our emotions. For example, research has shown that the gut contains as many receptors for serotonin ('the feel good factor') as the brain. Hence a 'maltreated' digestive system may carry as many traumatic memory patterns as the developing brain: little wonder that many maltreated children express their feelings through their stomachs, one way or another! Helping youngsters put these feelings into words allows them to 'inwardly digest' previously unpalatable or indigestible material. This contributes greatly to their overall physical and psychological balance.

In our first example we discuss the eating patterns of Sara (five years) and Mic (eight years).

Letter to the Warne family

Dear Elaine and Sam

You'll need to be quite flexible and cautious in your approach to Sara and Mic's eating habits. Being too rigid, or claiming particular foods are healthy, could turn the children against things they might otherwise enjoy. Similarly rewarding the eating of the first course with a 'nice pudding' can inadvertently give the message that the sweet food is better: this could powerfully reinforce their marked preference for sweet and fatty foods. Remind yourselves that, given their poor early histories, this is as much a physiological choice as a psychological one and may take a long time to resolve. Then try to offer fresh water, rather than juice, fizzy drinks or tea, to accompany meals and make this more tempting with curly straws. Better still, make these a regular, fun part of 'between meal' consumption for all the family!

Asking children to empty their plate, something you experienced in your own childhoods, may interfere with learning to set healthy limits. So, whilst you want the children to eat well, you need to keep in mind that you can't control what goes into their mouths (or comes out here, or at the other end). The example you set in your own eating habits and your approach to your body image can have quite an impact too. Parents being on a diet, or worrying 'whether my bum looks big in this' can unwittingly have a negative impact on children's choice of diet and their self-image. For youngsters like Sara who already 'feel bad' this could lead to persisting difficulties.

Another part of the underlying message you're aiming to get over to both children is how food is so closely bound up with the need for love.

When babies are breast- or bottle-fed and held tenderly in their parent's arms they come to associate nourishment directly with nurture. Sadly this didn't happen for either child in their birth family. It will help them if you can let them know how sad you are that things didn't go well for them and that you couldn't be there to give them what they needed. Go on to suggest that you *all* need more practice at the 'give and take' of food and love and that you'll find ways of working this out together. Here a problem shared *is* a problem halved: the children may even claim the solutions you've suggested as their own!

Given their poor early nutritional status, you may wish to consider supplementing the children's diets in the short term. You could start with Omega 3 fatty acids, which are important developmentally to babies' brains. These are readily available now, including some that are claimed to be especially palatable to youngsters. Perhaps you could talk to your GP or health visitor first: you may be able to get them on prescription.

As you know, Sara often went hungry for long periods or was fed very inappropriately. You could use 'think toddler think' to good effect now to address Sara's poor eating pattern: sitting with her whilst she eats, or even feeding her yourself. Feeding is so intimately bound up with nurturing attachments that eating problems can persist almost indefinitely if they're not sorted out: you'll need to be prepared for a protracted struggle here. First of all, make time to sit with Sara whilst she eats and give her as much help as you feel she needs. Let Sara know how pleased you are you have the chance to do this for her now; be sad that she missed out on so much for so long and relish the shared times you can have now. Make sure you're not rushed and that the other children are occupied, so you can give all the care and attention to Sara she desperately needs.

Often youngsters respond very positively to being spoon-fed their meals: as with toddlers you may find two spoons are more fun than one! This would give you opportunities to take turns popping food into Sara's mouth and will encourage her to be more self-sufficient when she's ready. Bottle-feeding is also an invaluable option, especially as part of 'family cradling' times.

At times when you'd like Sara to feed herself, as she's such a slow eater, it would help to give her relatively small portions and to cut up the food into bite-size pieces. It will be less daunting and more attractive like this and gives you more opportunities to praise Sara for eating well.

Remember to be very specific in your praise. Something like 'good job on clearing your plate', or 'great job eating that piece of carrot' if she hasn't eaten everything, with some positive eye contact and a hand on her shoulder, would be more likely to be 'heard' and absorbed than over-exuberant praise. General statements such as 'good girl' or 'well done' are so far from her view of herself that they are likely to upset Sara, or even trigger 'bad' behaviour subsequently. Similarly, star charts could be counter-productive given how easily Sara 'shuts down' when she feels too visible or too stressed.

Since Sara tends to be passive and compliant, 'keeping her head down', you need to be quite proactive in noticing when she needs help to know she's hungry or thirsty. You could do some 'asking practice' on less emotionally laden issues first to establish that it is OK to want something and to ask for it. Just occasionally you'll need to slip in a 'no', as painlessly as you can, so that Sara begins to manage this element too.

Try devising an 'asking game' and take turns making requests. You could make use of Sara's interest in dolls, puppets and pets to extend the practical experience. In addition, I suspect she'd enjoy checking whether the dog has enough water and food. As long as this remains a game and not a duty it could help Sara see that everybody (including Grommit) deserves to be well fed: mental rehearsal for feeding herself well!

You may have to persevere with extending Sara's diet quite slowly. At the moment she only seems to recognise 'sweet, fatty stuff' as food: the rest she avoids as if it were poison! This makes sense in terms of what we know of Mum's pregnancy and how Sara was treated as a baby. It will help Sara if you can 'translate' some of her thoughts and behaviour around food for her. At times when she struggles, let her know you can see it's hard for her to eat her roughage: and no wonder, given the rough time she had as a baby! Encourage her to realise that things *can* change and make it clear you intend to help her work it out gradually.

Consider introducing the 'try me' game: where you add one tiny portion of something 'new' to her plate alongside one of her favourites, perhaps with an encouraging cocktail-stick-flag attached. Choose times when you know Sara's not tired, upset or under pressure, to maximise the chances of her having a go. Be prepared to show her you're willing to have a bit too: you could pretend you really hate something first for added impact. Don't react if she can't manage the challenge. You might sometimes suggest that Grommit would be happy to oblige – but beware of this becoming Sara's 'way out'!

It would be good if you could find a few minutes each day for 'food playtime', when you and Sara can be messy and have fun with foodstuffs. There are plenty of examples in *First Steps in Parenting the Child Who Hurts* (Archer 1999a) to choose from but making bread (maybe from a packet mix) is one of my favourites. Few children, or adults, can resist the aroma of freshly baked bread, especially if they've made it themselves and can be in charge of sharing it with other family members. This can put food and eating in a new, more positive light!

Sara prefers to snack, meaning she's then unwilling to eat much at mealtimes. Given her history of neglect and her capacity to 'shut down', we must assume that having 'big' feelings, bodily or emotional, is too scary for Sara to tolerate. Again, you can translate this for Sara and help her make sense of 'now' in terms of 'then'.

Be prepared to become involved in finding and preparing food such as fruit for Sara when she asks for it, as she's been reluctant to let you know what she needs verbally. You might add a sensitive 'good job on asking' to encourage her to speak up for herself. Then try to encourage her to eat most of whatever food she has requested. You could join in the consumption too, by cutting the fruit into pieces and taking turns to munch, or create a rhyme to help the food go down. Eating a clementine to the tune of 'ten pieces of clementine sitting on a plate' can be good fun!

If proper mealtimes become drawn out it could be helpful to introduce a kitchen timer. Eating should not be a race and there should be no hint of stress or punishment here: you're merely putting in some structure to Sara's eating habits, setting valuable limits for her. If Sara is unable to finish her meal within the reasonable time you set, you could remove her plate without fuss and gently and sincerely hope she won't be too hungry before the next meal. You may feel you'd like to give some conditional praise for the amount she has managed, adding that she may need some more practice on this one. Alternatively, a 'slow eating contest' could bring some fun to potentially fraught eating situations: spaghetti is ideal as it can be sucked into the mouth strand by strand!

Make sure you emphasise to Sara that what she did to get through in her birth family was the right thing to do: it would have been too hard to feel all those painful feelings as a little girl. Gently help Sara think about some of the ways she tries to shut out the sad and scary things. Explain that when she looks down or moves away from you this lets you know how scared she is and yet how much she needs a hug from you. Your message is that you will go on being there for Sara and intend to find ways of helping her practise taking in food and love, especially when she's upset.

Beyond that you can congratulate Sara on sorting out the things that worked best for her when she was little. You can let Sara know her focus on sweet, fatty foods, particularly chocolate, is no accident. Baby milk tastes sweet and so has clear associations with being cared for; fats help us survive adversity. Moreover, an ingredient in chocolate acts on areas of the brain very close to the areas for love and comfort. Given the level of physical, emotional and sexual abuse in her birth family, it's not surprising Sara chooses chocolate for comfort!

You can point this out to Sara, wondering out loud how she'll learn to tell the difference between being hungry for food and hungry for love. Until she does, you'll help her practise taking more love in. It's essential that you don't let Sara reject your love, which she's become very accomplished at. If she tries to rub off your peck on the cheek, try being playful and suggest she's just rubbed it in deeper! Alternatively try placing a 'paper cuddle' on Sara's plate as a little message of love: at the very least you might elicit a shared smile!

You could also remind Sara that when she pushes you away she's saying even more loudly that she needs you but she's scared. The more you practise the easier it will get for both of you! Empathise with Sara by pointing out how hard it must be for her to sort out all the muddles in her head, more so because she was told that the sexualised abuse in her birth family was 'love'.

Whilst Sara is a poor eater, Mic constantly complains of being hungry, frequently asks for food between meals and tends to overeat. Fortunately you can use the same basic approach for both children. You are the caring adult, so you can make good choices about what kinds of food, and how much, they both consume: gently but firmly. These messages were so obviously lacking in their birth family and frequently result in chaotic, unhealthy eating patterns.

Try to have some nourishing food readily available at all times. This should be quite basic, so the children eat because they're hungry and not because of their poor early eating habits. (Keep most of the chocolate, cakes and biscuits out of sight and reach for the time being!) As the sensible adult you can at least take control over what sorts of food and drink you are happy to provide; healthy choices could be fruit, strips of raw vegetables, small pieces of bread and fruit juice. You will also need to be seen (not heard!) modelling healthy eating.

Mic needs to hear the message that he can help himself to as much of the foodstuffs you put out as he would like and that you'd like him to practise asking first. You may find he continues to binge but gradually, as he feels more secure there will always be 'enough', he'll be able to let go of his obsession with food. Meanwhile consider providing him with a 'food bag' stuffed with appropriate goodies that he could carry around with him, as tangible (and edible) reassurance.

If you find that Mic regularly continues to take too much you could leave little loving notes with the food supplies, letting him know you're thinking about him, or IOUs for hugs, to be collected when next you see each other. Tell him you're filling him up with love so he won't feel empty and help him identify that hungry feelings are his body's way of letting him know he needs a hug. You could wonder how long it will take Mic to work out the difference and that you'll be there to help for as long as it takes. Meanwhile a big hug before meals could help.

It could help Mic to manage better between meals if he had a clearer concept of time. Structure could help him feel more in control, and relieve his anxiety, as he can anticipate the next meal more accurately. A kitchen timer could be used to good effect so that Mic could see how much longer it will be before his next meal. This could pre-empt much of his repetitive questioning about 'is it time for dinner yet?' You would also draw up a colourful chart showing when meals happen and what food will be served. This could provide enough reassurance for Mic that he can tolerate the wait more easily. Further reminders about the 'help yourself' food store would also be useful.

Good luck and good eating!

In our second example we explore further how food can become a very emotive issue in families. Words of love are often stated in terms of food, such as 'honey' and 'sweetie' and parents naturally feel that providing their child with healthy and appetising food is one of the key tasks that demonstrate they are 'good enough' parents.

Here we explore the difficulties Anthea (aged 12) has around food and, in particular, how this affects family shopping trips.

Letter to the Katich family

Dear Jackie and Simon

Thank you for your letter describing Anthea's difficulties around food and shopping. I agree that these are related to Anthea's early experiences. When planning to help Anthea with these issues we need first to recall her experiences and consider how they relate to her behaviour now.

We know that Anthea was neglected and left alone for long periods; it's likely that, at these times, she would have felt hungry, sad, lonely and scared. This would have felt life-threatening. It's hard to imagine how frightening this must have been for Anthea as a tiny baby who couldn't meet her own basic needs, or find ways of getting them met appropriately. Anthea did well surviving in her birth family. This has made her quite tough, although she often gives the message that she's not. However, it also created huge issues for her around flexibility, control and dependence. She learned it wasn't safe to be dependent and that adults couldn't be trusted to keep her safe. These were appropriate beliefs given her circumstances then: they're no longer appropriate now she's part of your caring family.

Anthea's food issues relate particularly to this early period in her life, when she often felt hungry. Hunger pangs lead to babies experiencing distress. Infants who have learned that their parents will meet their needs can safely let them know they're hungry, by crying, squirming and screaming. These 'distress signals' are activated to let parents know what the baby is feeling and in the expectation they'll respond adequately.

Anthea, sadly, had very different experiences. Like all babies, she felt hunger as a tiny baby and expressed her needs in the only way she knew: by wriggling and crying or screaming to attract her parents' attention. However, Anthea was often ignored: left to cry alone for long periods while her mother wasn't there or didn't respond. Initially this would have led to Anthea increasing her 'distress signals' in the hope that appropriate help would be forthcoming. When this didn't happen Anthea learned other ways of managing her hungry sensations and distressing emotions: she found ways of 'switching off' (dissociating) from sensations and feelings that threatened to overwhelm her.

We can identify some of Anthea's ways of managing her 'baby' hunger in the way she currently relates to you around food. She is desperate to go shopping with you, to ensure that sufficient food is bought and to maintain control over choice and quality. This behaviour stems from a core belief that she cannot trust you, or anyone else, with the vital task of providing the means of survival. Her outrageous behaviour during shopping trips and her constant questioning about what's for supper can be seen as re-activation of her infantile distress signals, whilst her pickiness and food fads can be understood as ongoing, distorted attempts to manage and monitor essential food intake.

I absolutely agree that Anthea's food issues need to be taken seriously. You're right to be concerned that failure to tackle these issues now could lead to far greater problems in the future. As Anthea moves into adolescence your concerns around bulimia and anorexia could become only too real.

I feel you need to start by recognising that you cannot, nor would it be helpful to, force Anthea to eat, or to behave well on shopping trips. You should also remind yourselves of the underlying reasons for Anthea's difficulties: this will provide you with the understanding and empathy you need to make sense of Anthea's struggles with food.

Simultaneously Anthea needs to hear this from you and to be given opportunities to 'practise' that these beliefs, necessary for her survival as a baby, are no longer appropriate for life in the here and now. She also needs opportunities to start developing a different relationship to food and to you, in terms of nurturer and food provider. In essence she requires the mixture of nurture and structure that has been the cornerstone of all the strategies we've worked on together.

Hence, Anthea needs to learn that she:

- is no longer in a life-threatening situation
- can depend on you to keep her safe
- doesn't always need to be in control
- can rely on you to provide for her needs
- deserves to be looked after well.

Unless she has sufficient opportunities to learn these vital principles, she'll be unable to develop healthy, positive relationships with herself or others.

We've agreed that Anthea needs parents who can help her develop healthy dependence, to become healthily independent. Although it's essential she experiences you as dependable parents and providers, I wonder if your weekly shopping trips are too much for Anthea just now. They appear to trigger powerful, early feelings over which she has little control: her constant demands for things she knows she can't have indicate this so clearly. I would suggest that just one of you does the weekly shopping for now, while the other remains at home with Anthea and helps her manage the distressing feelings engendered by not being in control of shopping expeditions.

Anthea needs your help to understand that staying at home isn't a punishment and is intended to minimise the triggering of feelings she can't handle at present. Perhaps she could also practise managing her feelings better by going on short shopping trips to the local shop for just one or two previously agreed items.

Anthea will probably be unhappy whatever you buy on the weekly shop, because this issue relates to control, not to specific food items. This means you should approach this as a control, not a food, issue. Begin by asking yourself: 'How can I act in ways that put me in emotional control here?' At the same time you need to acknowledge Anthea's need for control, by interpreting her current feelings and responses for her in terms of her early experiences.

Tell Anthea you're sad she's not satisfied with the food you bought, then matter-of-factly say:

- 'Why not make a list of things you want as a guide for me next week?' (which she probably won't get round to doing). Go on to say:
- 'Telling me is not enough, my memory is so awful.' Avoid promising to get Anthea whatever she asks for, since her demands might not be appropriate or available.
- 'Won't it be fun to see if I make choices you like next week?' (playfully).
- 'Never mind, I'm sure you'll struggle by' (gently).
- 'How sad! Well, I'm sure Dad and I will enjoy what you can't eat!' (exuberantly).
- 'No worries! You can have lots of cuddles instead' (affectionately).
- 'What a shame! At least you were able to use my shopping time to go for a bike ride with Dad' (empathically).

Jackie, you must be prepared for Anthea to react to the situation with outbursts of temper, since she'll be feeling 'badly done to' and not in full control of her food supplies. If she does react, empathise with these feelings and give Anthea permission to take as long as she needs to feel upset and angry (but not to act in destructive or hurtful ways).

Here it's vital to avoid putting yourself in a 'risk situation' by trying to intervene. Instead, remain in the room with Anthea, talking gently to her, at a sufficient distance that she can't lash out and hit you, as she has done previously. This is not only dangerous for you, it will reduce Anthea's self-esteem even further, which could have further 'backlash' effects.

Simon, remember to use the time Jackie is out shopping to remind Anthea that she's very likely to get upset and angry when Mum comes home and to wonder gently if she'll have a temper outburst. Here you're putting yourself in a 'win–win' situation. If Anthea loses her temper and starts screaming, show you're pleased she's able to let you know she's still struggling with food issues. If she doesn't, be thrilled that she's beginning to manage her uncomfortable feelings, now you've worked them out together.

A 'wacky' alternative would be for you to have a tantrum about the food Jackie has bought. Here it's important not to mention that this is the way Anthea behaves: just let her figure this out for herself. You could go on to leave in a huff. As long as Jackie is well prepared to comment wryly on your 'awful behaviour', this has the added benefit of giving you some much needed time to yourself!

Both of you could be curious about how long it'll be until Anthea is able to deal with her feelings well enough to return to the previous shopping arrangements. Doing this together, in Anthea's hearing, could get your message across more powerfully.

Go on to wonder out loud whether this is about the food, or really about something else. Then make suggestions, such as 'I wonder whether it's hard for you to trust that we'll always have enough food for you?' to help Anthea understand the root cause of her difficulties. It would probably be better not to combine these conversations with any direct, food-related situation. Your trips to the park could give you good opportunities to raise the issue in less threatening ways.

Remember to congratulate Anthea gently on letting you know how difficult this issue is for her. Tell her she can practise coping with shopping trips by going to the local shop with you for milk, or fresh bread. Plan these visits for times when Anthea will be most relaxed. It's probably best not to combine this with returning from school, since we know Anthea struggles with transitions and because she's likely to be quite hungry then.

Remind Anthea that this trip is about practising managing feelings: that she needs to get to know that food is no longer a life-threatening issue, as it was for her as a baby. Tell her she can take as long as she needs to learn this thoroughly. You could even suggest that you know that this is such a difficult issue for her that you would understand if she had a tantrum. However, if you do this you must be prepared for the outcome: if she does, on this occasion, comply with your request!

One of the other parents I worked with had to deal with just this eventuality. Her daughter, also a very oppositional child, did as Mum suggested and had a major tantrum in the shop. Mum's response was wonderful: she suggested her daughter continued screaming while she got on with the shopping – on the basis that she could be sure her daughter was still safely there in the shop. While this was potentially very embarrassing for Mum, it did have a positive, longer-term impact on her child. She hasn't had any further tantrums on shopping trips: demonstrating the real value of putting parents in loving control in families.

However, it could be better to anticipate that Anthea may become demanding in the shop and act proactively by:

- offering Anthea some grapes before entering the shop 'to help you with your feelings'.

- hinting that you have a surprise (maybe a small game) at home 'just for fun!'

- telling Anthea you have some chocolate in your pocket to give her when you leave, 'to keep you going'. If she copes well, congratulate her on making a good choice and stump up!

- acknowledging calmly, should Anthea continue to be demanding, despite your thoughtful gesture, that she seems to be letting you know how difficult all this is. Then you choose: consider giving Anthea the snack when you leave anyway because she probably needs it; telling her you believe she needs and deserves it. Alternatively, be genuinely sad for Anthea that she's letting you know there's too much adrenalin in her system to manage more sugary stuff just now.

- proffering a 'special cuddle for chocoholics'.

- enlisting the help of the shopkeeper. To make this work effectively you need an understanding shopkeeper and to discuss your strategy with him in advance. For example, he could be encouraged to show he's unhappy about the commotion Anthea makes in the shop, rather than ignoring her or 'being polite for your sake'. The shopkeeper could go as far as quietly but firmly asking Anthea to leave the shop.

Then play it cool yourself, be sympathetic and avoid criticism or saying 'I told you so'.

- deciding, on the basis of Anthea's current anxiety levels, not to go to the shop. Be sad that Anthea isn't managing well today and remind her there'll be opportunities for another practice run later in the week. This gives Anthea the vital message that you believe she can succeed, rather than that she has 'failed'.

- leaving out a snack to share, for when you return from shopping. You'll probably both need it and you can 'recover' together.

We know that Anthea equates food with love: she needs to learn that 'food goes to your belly, love goes to your heart'. This could be a slow process and you'll need to give Anthea repeated reminders: either by talking to her about it directly or giving her 'messages' that emphasise this.

Your verbal messages should be short and direct, using curiosity, empathy or playfulness to lighten your statements:

- 'Where did you learn that food can heal a broken heart?'

- 'I would have difficulties around food if I hadn't had enough to eat as a baby. I wish I'd been around to fill you up with food and love.'

- Rush up to Anthea and, putting you ear to her belly, say: 'Is there enough in there? How about a super-hug?'

You can be creative in thinking of ways to give Anthea random, positive messages: in her lunch box, on her pillow, pinned on the door when she comes home. Your messages can be about almost anything, as long as they're short, loving and playful:

- 'Welcome home' (on the door).

- 'Hope you have a good lunch' (tucked in her lunch box).

- 'We love you' (absolutely any time!)

- 'Today I missed your smiling face' (especially if Anthea has been grumpy).

- 'You're my star!' (alongside a paper star in her school bag, to remind her that she is to *you*).

- 'Thinking of you' (popped under the door when Anthea has skulked off to her room).

These messages are aimed at helping Anthea connect with her deep-seated, but unconscious, fears of being unloved and rejected, so that she can begin to alter her internal 'road maps' and really take on board your commitment, reliability and security. I'm sure you'll have fun coming up with plenty of your own ideas!

You could use the 'No' strategies (see pp.173–4) we have already explored to help reduce conflict when Anthea makes unrealistic demands. These statements, too, are aimed at helping Anthea realise she's no longer in danger: you can be trusted to put in safe boundaries for her and she'll no longer go hungry or unloved. Simple statements, given with genuine concern, could include:

- 'You're welcome to have (an apple) in half an hour' (thereby avoiding the 'no' word).

- When you've finished packing your bag for school, then we can make a sandwich' (again avoiding negatives yet implying some cooperation on Anthea's part. Suggesting a shared 'comfort break' also pairs food with love more appropriately).

- 'It's hard for you to figure that when we say "no" we don't mean "no forever". We need more practice' (sharing the problem and implying it's resolvable, together).

- 'That's a big tantrum about such a small packet of crisps. Maybe it's really about some big feelings inside. Let's have a bear-hug!' (acknowledging playfully that you can make sense of Anthea's behaviour and support her).

I know Jackie finds it difficult to say 'no' to Anthea and we've talked about how this relates to the way you were treated as a child. I'm sure it will have helped you to make this connection. However, you don't need to feel good about saying 'no' here: try to remind yourself that by saying 'no' you are helping Anthea to become healthier. Act as though you're comfortable with this and, with practice, you'll come to feel it and believe it. Anthea also needs practice at coping with simple negatives, to find that neither she (nor you) dies or disappears if you say 'no', which will improve her sense of security and self-perceptions.

Now, turning to mealtimes, it must be very difficult when Anthea binge eats one day and refuses to eat at all the next. Since Anthea knows how much this distresses you, this adds to the difficulties and makes her behaviour more extreme. Again this is a control issue that only makes sense in terms of Anthea's past. Since you can't force Anthea to eat, you'll need to tackle this issue creatively. Anthea needs repeated, empathic reminders of the underlying reasons for her difficulties and opportunities to practise developing a different relationship to food.

Giving Anthea a cuddle before a meal, or leaving a positive message on her plate, will help Anthea begin to get in touch with the love you have for her. Through time, this should help her reduce her defences and allow her to eat just what she needs.

Suggest Anthea practises accepting that in your home there's always enough food to go round by leaving one item on her plate. This will help her 'listen to her body' more closely – and don't worry for now if Anthea 'manipulates' this by leaving her greens!

Consider putting together a selection of very small plates of food for Anthea. Cover them individually with cling-film so that you can return them to the fridge if necessary. This way Anthea can see 'there's plenty' yet opt for 'just a little' without overtly rejecting your loving care or wasting food. Just be accepting of her choices for now.

I hope you'll have some fun selecting strategies and using them randomly. Remember that it's better to do nothing when you're feeling angry, hurt or frustrated: give yourself a little time and nurturing and you'll soon reconnect with your obvious love and empathy for Anthea.

E*motional outbursts*

Bouts of screaming beyond infancy are closely related to tantrums in school-age children, often generating very intense feelings in caregivers and other family members. When dealing with children who can produce unbelievably piercing sounds for long periods, parents frequently describe feelings of frustration and irritation, bound up with a sense of helplessness and confusion (freeze) or the urge to escape the situation (flight). Sometimes they may feel tempted to shout or lash out 'to bring him to his senses' (fight). Given the intensity of the children's distressing behaviour, this is understandable and highlights the degree to which parents' reactions can reflect the underlying feelings (and fight, flight or freeze responses) of their children (see Figure 11). Recognising and understanding these parallels is the first step in providing healthier ways forward.

Screaming, like other distressing outbursts, can take place as often in public as in private. Here caregivers may have to deal with embarrassment and public censure as well as their own self-criticism. Sometimes children try to use this to their advantage, drawing observers 'on side' as they play 'the victim' to their parent's 'abuser' role. Parents need help to understand that this manipulative or controlling behaviour is a learned survival pattern, often mirroring actual early childhood experience. The caregivers' primary task is to 'get out of the loop' (see Figure 12) of being cast in that role and to provide their children with 'new scripts' for dealing with situations which they find distressing. Identifying antecedents, those environmental factors that may trigger outbursts, is useful in reducing repetition of troubling behaviours but, more importantly, caregivers need to decode the trauma-based behaviour patterns and relate more closely to their troubled children. Ignoring difficult behaviours plays little part in this agenda, since valuable pieces of codified information and opportunities to engage in meaningful conversations based on these data could be missed.

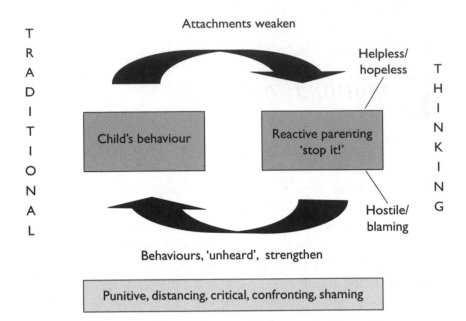

Figure 11: Staying in the loop

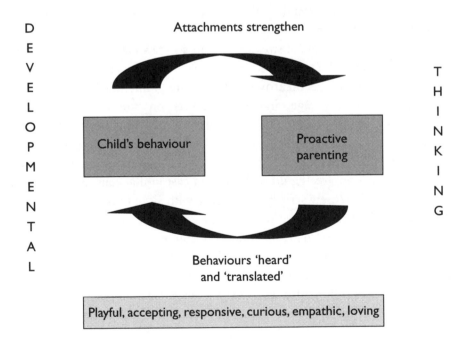

Figure 12: Getting out of the loop

Parents should focus on identifying and making sense of challenging behaviours and providing a framework within which they can formulate 'response packages', rather than on trying to prevent outbursts. This reflects the philosophy that children's behaviour is their 'first language', furnishing vital information for caregivers. Establishing a common meaning in children's 'mother tongue' opens the door to enhanced communications and relationships within which traumatised youngsters begin to learn the 'language of love'. The emphasis here is on parents and children gaining insights, so that they can achieve greater control over their interactions. It creates the essential attachment framework within which new patterns of relating may be practised and words found to express what otherwise would remain beyond words.

Understanding that children's behaviour has two major functions: to communicate and to try to work out difficulties, helps make sense of even the most bizarre actions. Once 'reasonable adults' begin to understand why 'unreasonable children' do what they do, they can avoid becoming embroiled in 'control battles' and help youngsters make sense of their muddles. The more they do this, and communicate their understanding of what is going on to children, the more they 'feel felt' and safely contained. They can then start making connections for themselves and eventually acquire a healthier sense of self.

Below we discuss the emotional outbursts of Matt (aged five).

Letter to the McGrath family

Dear Josie and Freddy

I've taken time to mull over Matt's difficult behaviours and I'm struck by how hard it is for us all to 'hear' Matt's screaming. Although we've discussed this several times in the past it still feels as though it's too hard to take in – almost as if the louder Matt screams the more we try to avoid listening!

What's particularly interesting is how you've told me several times how difficult the screaming is for all your family to bear, yet we've focused on other challenges, such as Matt's soiling and 'shutting down' behaviours. Perhaps this reflects what we've all unconsciously avoided doing: listening to the underlying, distressing messages he's been trying to communicate. It now seems important to address this issue directly, so that we can help Matt move on.

You've told me that Matt often screams for lengthy periods when asked to comply with simple requests, or when he needs help with personal hygiene, particularly after soiling. At other times there may be less obvious triggers for his screaming, which we may gradually begin to identify. Whatever the cause, the intensity and pitch of Matt's screaming are frequently distressing to all the family.

Before we consider ways of reducing this distress to manageable levels, it's essential to acknowledge the level of distress that Matt must be feeling to engender such strong feelings in you. This reflects the extent to which you're tuned in to Matt's physical and emotional states as well as how awful life feels at that point for Matt — like his repeated soiling and smearing. Sadly his attempts at communication (and resolution) go astray, since the screaming makes everyone feel so uncomfortable they try to shut it out.

It's important to find effective strategies that allow you to stay with Matt through his bouts of screaming and let him know that you can hear what he needs to tell you (non-verbally but very loudly). Initially this may involve you taking active steps to deal with the sound and distress levels for everyone. Only then, when your anxieties for each other are managed, will you be freed up and in 'the right place' to listen to Matt. Remember, too, that it will be predominantly your non-verbal communications Matt will pick up on, so stay aware of your body language, gesture and facial expressions as well as your tone of voice.

One effective way of coping with the piercing effects of Matt's screams would be to kit yourselves out with fluffy earmuffs, and personal CD players (with headphones) for the other children. When Matt begins to scream, and before the high pitch and intensity triggers too much distress in you, let him know that you know he has something really important to tell you and that you're listening. Next, say that it sometimes 'hurts your ears' when he screams, so you need your earmuffs so you can listen without it hurting too much. (If you feel it would be better to be less obvious, there are earplugs that mould into the ear and are relatively invisible.)

You may like to offer Matt some earmuffs too, as we know how sensitive he is to sound. You'll then be modelling good self-care and sensitive, attuned parenting. You can also make exaggerated play of your need to ensure the other children have their earphones or are preparing to go out: modelling good caregiving to other family members too.

Conversely, you could bring his siblings into the room with Matt, once you have prepared them for this possibility. It's often less upsetting for children to see what's going on than to listen from the outside and imagine the worst. For your older children this could give them increased understanding of what's going on for Matt and what you're doing to help. In that case you may need to bulk order the earmuffs! Moreover, given Matt's obvious fondness for Lucy, it could be valuable for him to see the effect his screams have on her, as long as she's not overwhelmed by the noise. Being sensitive parents (and grandparents) you'll know where to draw the line here.

Once you've made a performance of 'getting ready to listen', which helps you take control and helps Matt 'feel heard', hopefully you'll be able to stay close to Matt and bear his distress with him. I understand that Matt may be screaming for you to leave him alone *but* you need to 'let him know that you know' that he really needs you to be close.

Insistence on closeness and comfort (nurture) when children are being rejecting is initially hard and you may need to remind yourselves that you're doing the right thing. However it's essential, if Matt is to learn that you can 'hold all this stuff' for him. Moreover, giving Matt permission to express himself in this way, whilst you remain close, is likely to reduce the length of screaming time, since he'll become more aware that he's being heard. Simultaneously it can provide much needed co-regulation of arousal for Matt.

Choose one or two short, simple statements to repeat to Matt during his distress and practise these yourselves first. A gentle but firm 'I know, I'm here', or 'I'm listening' is much more comforting than direct reassurances, such as 'It's OK, you're all right', or invocations to 'calm down!' Having something to say over and over, can also help remind you that you're doing the right thing, as it's easy to lose confidence when faced with such distress.

As you know, Matt has told us that he believes he's a 'bad boy', so by gently but firmly challenging his attempts to push you away, before the anticipated rejection from you, you're actively letting him know that he is lovable. These twin messages – that Matt is 'good enough' and that you can listen to and handle anything he throws up – will need to be repeated time after time. Eventually Matt will 'get it' and he'll no longer need to use screaming, or other distressing behaviours such as 'blanking' you, to keep you at arm's length.

You could choose to wonder out loud when Matt will be able to talk about his hurts, instead of screaming them out: giving him hope for positive change. Let him know that he may need some help with this and that together you'll get through it. Meanwhile, you'll have to be prepared to show him repeatedly that you'll stick around and be there for him. Actions (including facial expression, gesture and tone of voice) really do speak louder than words!

You could also make valuable use of an egg timer. Here you're letting Matt know that you have time to listen but are setting clear limits (structure) for him. This could help Matt feel contained, limiting his distressing out-bursts and preventing him from distressing himself even more. Make a big deal about finding and setting the timer – choosing how long and so on – even if you really haven't a clue! This can help you feel more in control of the situation, which will benefit you both.

If the weather is fine, you could take Matt outside after the set time expires, since many children respond positively to the knowledge that 'the neighbours might hear', as well as to the 'cooling-off' effects of fresh air. Any comments at this point should remain empathic and non-critical. Try saying something like: 'I can see how hot and bothered you are. Let's go outside and cool down'. Here you're sharing responsibility for the problem, rather than blaming, which could push Matt further into a shame-filled 'shutdown'. Follow with a gentle reminder: 'I know how sad you'll be if Mrs X hears you sounding so upset'. Otherwise concentrate on keeping your non-verbal communications open and non-challenging, as these will be what Matt will mostly pick up on.

Alternatively you could ask Matt to go into a separate room for a short time (no more than five minutes, given his age), acknowledging that you both need 'a breather'. Try saying 'I can see you need some help here' or 'I need a few moments to calm down' as you gently but firmly move Matt towards your room of choice. You could use the timer to help Matt manage this short separation too. As soon as the time is up, go in and re-connect with Matt: perhaps a light touch on his shoulder would work best here. This would also help you establish whether Matt needs some more 'screaming time' or whether there's something else you feel you could do together to provide co-regulatory interactions that he could cope with.

Perhaps a furry, hot water bottle would be useful, to provide some tolerable physical comfort and security, if touch is still difficult. Being inanimate, this could be less threatening for a child like Matt who often has problems with touch and intimacy. It's sadly ironic that children's early distressing experiences can mean that they're least able to accept closeness when they need it most.

Having a well-defined 'screaming place' could be helpful: keep your tone light and playful and avoid anger and sarcasm at all costs, even if you, quite understandably, feel that way. A well-padded soundproofed room in the middle of nowhere is an unattainable ideal but maybe you could come up with a realistic alternative! Talking to your neighbours, so that they understand what is going on and don't imagine the worst, would also be invaluable.

Offering Matt a dummy to suck, or teething toy to bite on, normally very suitable for achieving a sense of balance and quiet calm, may have to wait until Matt has done 'enough' screaming, otherwise he may feel silenced, as he was so frequently as a baby. However, it's worth keeping these items in mind, as they could help him to end a screaming bout sooner, when you feel he's screamed enough but doesn't know how to stop, or when the timer goes off.

We cover other aspects of Matt's distressing behaviour under 'Control issues', 'F is for feelings', 'Self-regulation' and 'Sensory issues'. It's going to be a long road but you're getting there! Keep up the good work!

F is for feelings, not just 'fight, flight and freeze'

Helping children acknowledge and talk about feelings forms a vital part of parenting 'the child who hurts'. Feelings provide the impetus to the action, or reactive behaviour, implied in the term 'emotion'. One of the fundamental tasks of parenting is to provide infants with repeated opportunities to recognise, acknowledge and express their feelings safely. In effect, the parent's sensitivity to her child, and the downloading of her mature emotional software, helps the youngster 'feel felt' (Siegel 1999) and safely contained and encourages the formation of appropriate 'feeling' connections, physically, psychologically and physiologically. For maltreated children this is unlikely to have occurred, leaving youngsters in the thrall of powerful emotions they can neither recognise nor understand, let alone control.

In order to improve the relationship between themselves and their hurt child, adoptive parents may need to begin by improving the youngster's relationship with himself. Without improved sensory and emotional literacy the child's behavioural vocabulary remains limited and trauma-based. It is essential that adopters achieve fluency in the 'body language of emotions' and the 'outspoken and unspoken language of trauma' to improve essential family communications, as children with poor intra-personal skills (poor self-attunement and connections) frequently struggle with inter-personal skills (poor other-attunement and connections). The language of feelings must become more sophisticated if traumatised children are to move on from their reliance on 'fight, flight and freeze' survival responses, amend their core beliefs about themselves and others and achieve greater self-control.

Awareness of feelings, following neglect or abuse, can be shut down to the extent that the child fails to translate them into appropriate action (the expected emotional response) as with the youngster who does not cry or show fear. Conversely, feelings may be so blurred or distorted that the child misinterprets or amplifies his emotional state and acts 'over the top', or, for example, covers his pain with intense anger. In many cases there will be a lack of connection between feelings and the relevant memories or body sensations, reflecting Braun's (1988) BASK model of dissociation relating to Behaviour, Affect, Sensation and Knowledge. It is common for youngsters to speak about very painful events in their lives without showing emotion and, conversely, to experience 'big feelings' that are not consciously connected to past hurts. Bodies may hurt but not be 'felt' or the hurt is inappropriately connected to the present, as youngsters attempt to make some sense of their muddles. In some cases this can lead to unfounded accusations of abuse relating to present caregivers: such issues must be taken seriously and heard and understood with the '20/20 hindsight' provided by complete and accurately recorded case histories.

Letter to the Katich family

Dear Jackie and Simon

You're doing a really great job in supporting Anthea to help her understand her history and the impact it still has on her. As you know, therapy is just the kick-start in helping Anthea manage her life better. As we discovered, her early history of abuse and neglect led to Anthea developing such a 'thick skin' that she finds it difficult to connect meaningfully to the intense feelings that so often drive her behaviour. One lasting memory I have of the work we did was your distress (shared by the therapy team) when we really began to understand how terrified Anthea must have felt, lying in her cot, hearing the sounds of domestic violence downstairs, never knowing when her birth father might hurt her too. You were rightly shocked at how little this knowledge seemed to impact on Anthea. We all had tears in our eyes, yet Anthea looked at us with incomprehension and showed little emotion.

This demonstrates very clearly the profundity of the damage done to Anthea by her early experiences and the extent to which she's been able to 'switch off' from her feelings. What an amazingly sensible thing for such a young child to have accomplished! With nobody to help her deal with her feelings she did the only possible thing in the circumstances: stop acknowledging her feelings, both physically and psychologically. Yet it's so sad she had to do this and that, now she is safe with you, she continues to block her feelings.

Work over the next six months needs to focus on helping Anthea with these difficulties. We will of course use this as a focus of her therapy sessions but she also needs your help with this between sessions, in the context of everyday family life. Predictably, Anthea will resist your attempts to help her get in touch with her feelings, particularly feelings of fear and sadness that connect her so powerfully to the past. She's likely to respond to your efforts by becoming increasingly angry and defiant and wanting to lash out at you, or binge eat, as she has in the past. I therefore suggest that you reread the letters relating to both of these issues before you start helping Anthea recognise and feel comfortable with a full range of feelings. That way you'll be able to incorporate the strategies for these issues into the plan to help Anthea emotionally.

We talked yesterday about how difficult it is for Anthea when she falls out with friends. Since we know Anthea does this at regular intervals her intense response indicating feelings of abandonment and anger may seem totally out of proportion to what happened. I know you have been trying to help Anthea appreciate this when, for example, she comes out of school 'in a mood' because Sophie and she have had an argument. This may not always be the best response to the situation, since Anthea responds to your attempts to reassure her, through helping her gain a sense of proportion, by becoming even angrier.

This tells us something about what's going on for Anthea: that her feelings are not just about what has happened in the here and now but also about the other, huge losses she has experienced. Essentially the feelings engendered by falling out with Sophie act as a trigger into the feelings of abandonment Anthea would have experienced when her birth mother went out and left her alone in her cot, amplified by the moves from one foster carer to another. Anthea needs your help to begin to make these connections, so that she can make more sense of her reactions and begin to gain control over them.

You'll need to be very empathetic with Anthea as you approach this subject with her. Pick your moments: it's often easier to broach difficult issues when you are relaxed or enjoying another activity such as baking or walking; travelling in the car often provides valuable opportunities to talk. It might also be helpful to state your view in a curious or tentative way, to minimise the possibility that Anthea will respond to your suggestions with anger and denial.

Try to help Anthea connect 'small' hurts and losses in the present by referring to earlier, profound losses in her life. You could, for example, say one or more of the following:

- 'I wonder if the thought of losing Sophie's friendship reminds you of some of the other friends/people you have lost.'
- 'I bet you sometimes feel angry that all those people in your life left you.'
- 'I wonder if you think it was your fault that your birth mother hurt you.'
- 'It's so sad your birth mother didn't realise how special you were and wasn't able to look after you the way you deserved.'

It is vital that you do not expect Anthea to agree with you: in fact she may powerfully reject your suggestions. This doesn't matter. What matters is that you remain empathetic to her struggles and acknowledge that you're there to help her work out what's going on for her: this includes giving Anthea permission to challenge what you've said. Don't try to justify what you've said. 'I know that this is hard for you', stated with genuine feeling, is all you need to say.

You'll also need to talk to Anthea about what she *does* with her feelings. You could start by saying something like:

- 'No wonder you get angry or upset when you think of all the people in your life who left you.'
- 'Have you noticed that when you feel like this you seem to want to hurt someone, or eat lots of chocolate?'
- 'I've noticed that when you feel upset or angry you usually want to eat loads and be in control big time.'

Next talk to Anthea about why this may not be her best response choice, perhaps saying: 'I wonder where you learned that hurting people or eating chocolate would help you deal with your feelings. This must make you really confused. Maybe I could help you with these feelings.'

Follow this with suggestions of what she might do instead. Better still suggest some things you could do together, such as baking bread, playing 'snap' or even reading your horoscopes! When Anthea starts bingeing on sweets, try offering her a cuddle instead, saying: 'Chocolates don't heal holes in your heart; a cuddle might.' Take a look back at the suggestions for dealing with anger to give you some other ideas for managing Anthea's outbursts effectively.

If possible aim to talk about the way Anthea deals with feelings *before* the incident escalates. If you know she's likely to become angry, talk to her about this and suggest ways of managing, for example saying:

- 'I guess you're feeling upset (or angry, or sad) just now. I've noticed that when you feel like this you often lash out. I wonder if I could help you choose a better way to deal with those feelings?'

- 'When you have all those feelings, your brain isn't programmed to help you work out helpful ways to deal with them. Maybe we could work some out together?'

- 'You know when you hurt Dad or demand loads of chocolate that you miss out on treats. I'd like to help you come up with some other ways to manage your feelings, so you don't miss out on those treats.'

- 'You had such a hard time with your birth mother because she didn't know how to look after you properly. You really deserve some help to make good choices now, so you don't have to go on having a hard life.'

- 'Perhaps you could wave your hand to show me you need some help, instead of trying to deal with things on your own.'

The object of all of these strategies is to give Anthea the message that she needs your help to make good choices *and* that with your help she can't fail to 'get it right'. You know Anthea best, so I'm sure you'll come up with some great, creative ideas yourselves.

If Anthea persists in making unhelpful choices she may need to experience the consequences. For example, it might not be possible to take her in the car if you feel she's unable to act safely in it. This should be explained in terms of safety and helping Anthea make better choices, rather than as punishment. However, the consequence should have some negative outcome for Anthea, such as not going to youth club, rather than not going to school!

When Anthea makes good choices, congratulate her on this but don't overdo it, as Anthea doesn't feel good enough about herself to believe that she's great or wonderful and is likely to do something to 'prove' she isn't if your praise is too lavish. Try saying: 'I noticed you were getting angry and you decided to tidy up your room. Good choice.' rather than 'You were great/excellent/wonderful!'

You should bear in mind that the aim of all this work is to help Anthea feel comfortable with feelings, not specifically to reduce her angry outbursts or her binge eating. However, as Anthea gets help to understand her feelings she's less likely to feel so overwhelmed by them that she needs to switch off or over-react. As she begins to switch into her feelings her need to act them out should start to reduce.

It is important not to expect immediate results. Anthea has been using her dissociative response to feelings for so long that it'll take time for her to begin to trust that it's safe to have feelings. It's also important to recognise that any progress is likely to be up and down: one day you may feel you're making progress only to feel the next day you're back to square one. This is only to be expected. Anthea will have days when she is more able to manage feelings than others. Don't give up when you feel despairing. Instead contact me, so I can help you manage your feelings and, hopefully, give you the impetus to carry on.

Lastly the reparenting work you are doing is one of the most difficult life tasks you'll ever undertake. You need to feel that you can take a break from it at times. You also need to make sure you're emotionally fit by taking good care of yourselves. I'll phone to check whether you managed to arrange those aerobics lessons you've been promising to start.

Meanwhile, keep up the good work.

Feelings from the past

Angry and aggressive behaviour, food issues, soiling, smearing, destroying or taking things, 'shutting down' and 'blanking' people are just some of the ways abused and neglected children communicate their innermost distress to their adoptive parents. Although children may be unable to tell us in words about their hurtful pasts, their puzzling behaviour often speaks volumes. This can make family life uncomfortable, unpredictable and stressful and may lead to placement breakdown. In this second example we discuss five-year-old Matt's behaviour with his adoptive parents. (See also 'Control issues', 'Dissociative states', 'Self-regulation' and 'Sensory issues').

Letter to the McGrath family

Hi Josie and Freddy!

What a difficult job you're having dealing with Matt's emotional outbursts, his soiling and smearing and his 'go slows' must make family life so difficult just now. You're doing a great job hanging in there and in working hard to understand what motivates Matt's behaviour. We've looked at these, and other puzzling behaviours, in several different ways already. Here the aim is to increase your understanding of where Matt is 'coming from' in terms of his horrendous past experiences: to explore and understand Matt's history, so that you can help him make sense of 'now' in terms of 'then'.

Matt's early life with his birth mother was abusive, chaotic and unpredictable. He experienced abandonment and neglect on many occasions and undoubtedly felt a great deal of fear. He would have been unsure of what was happening around him and anxious that he'd be left alone and hungry. I feel certain there were times when, to Matt, this felt life-threatening. At the very least he would have developed core beliefs that the world was terrifying, that adults couldn't be trusted to keep him safe and that he didn't deserve to feel happy and secure.

Children who have experienced neglect, abuse or abandonment from their mothers develop insecure, disorganised attachments: they both need and come to fear their caregivers. As a baby, Matt 'needed' his birth mother for survival. However, she was also the source of his confusion, hurt, panic, neglect and abandonment, and thus simultaneously a source of terror. In such a 'hostile' environment Matt would not have learned to regulate his distress, since infants need the context of a consistent relationship with a caregiver who is herself a 'safe container' for difficult feelings in order to practise co-regulation.

Furthermore, Matt's birth mother contributed significantly to his distress, helplessness and despair. Matt's outbursts can be interpreted as a direct result of this: now when he feels upset he lacks the internal mechanisms to deal with his feelings and yet is often unable to use you as his 'external regulator'. Hence feelings quickly escalate to the point where he throws a tantrum; or, conversely, goes into 'slow motion' echoing Matt's early hopelessness. His contradictory (ambivalent) behaviour towards you directly reflects the 'irreconcilable conflicts' of the 'push–pull' relationship with his birth mother.

The nature of Matt's relationship with his auntie and her role in caring for him is also crucial to understanding his 'story'. Matt moved from one frightening situation (mum) to an equally frightening and abusive scenario (with auntie), where he received little consistency of care and was vulnerable to abuse from the numerous 'lodgers' and casual visitors to the house. This, coupled with the fact that his auntie left him alone for lengthy periods, hungry, dirty, smelly and in pain, confirmed for Matt the hurtful messages he received from his birth mother: that he had no right to feel safe or cared for. Consequently he sees himself, as he has told us, as 'a bad child' who doesn't deserve to be loved and nurtured.

Remember that the numerous incidents highlighted in Matt's files are likely to represent only a small proportion of the distressing events he actually experienced. In addition, Matt had a number of moves when in care, including a previous adoptive placement that disrupted. Furthermore, the move to your home (more 'strangers') is likely to have threatened any tentative feelings that adults were safe and could be trusted. He didn't receive much help in dealing with these muddled feelings, instead being presented with a positive picture of the move ('We've found you a new family. They're really nice. I know you'll like it there.') This failed to acknowledge Matt's understandably confused and frightened feelings about being introduced to yet another set of parents (who he probably expected would let him down).

Although Matt will have felt hurt, angry and frightened, it was often too dangerous for him to react with appropriate rage or grief at the time; instead he learned to rely on 'switching off' (dissociating), in trying to keep himself safe. This response would have been triggered as soon as Matt *felt* he was going to be hurt or abandoned and has contributed powerfully to the vicious cycle of misattuned interactions with caregivers he now experiences. Ironically this increases his panic, terror and rage deep down, leading to further dissociative behaviours or, more frequently now he is older, to outbursts of uncontrollable anger and frustration. We see both these patterns in Matt's 'switching off', tantrums, soiling, smearing when things don't go his way, or when he feels threatened. It's important to remember that all Matt's behaviours are clues that let you know how he feels inside and are not about 'getting at you' or even 'getting his own way'.

Do you remember when we did a guided visualisation during a therapy session? We asked you to close your eyes and talked you through how Matt must have felt, as a tiny baby, living with so much discomfort and distress. Imagining what it might have felt like helped you become more empathetic and understanding of why Matt does what he does and of the difficulties he's still experiencing in facing change. Remember, too, that whatever you felt represented only the tip of the iceberg of Matt's actual experience. Keeping this knowledge in mind is essential if you're to 'be there' for Matt when he can least show his real feelings.

It can be helpful to identify any triggers to Matt's distressing behaviours and then consider how these might relate to his earliest experiences. It may take only a very small trigger in 'the here and now' to catapult Matt into big feelings from the past. For example, asking Matt to do simple self-care tasks like putting his shoes away could easily trigger feelings of helplessness and abandonment, relating to his early experiences of being dependent and vulnerable and the pain of not getting his needs met consistently. He'll need a good deal of extra 'babying' from you (see the 'Think toddler think' section) to heal Matt's wounds of fear and mistrust. It's vital you create endless opportunities for him to experience adults as trustworthy and safe. Matt needs this not only to improve his relationship with you but also to develop a healthier template of life and of relationships in general.

Having said that, Matt also needs small, managed opportunities to practise dealing with the things he most fears, within a caring environment where he can learn that it's safe to do so. This means giving Matt loving messages that:

- you understand *why* he's having difficulties (say in putting his shoes on himself), even though you know he can do it
- you can be trusted to work out what he needs when he gets 'in a muddle'
- you know it's hard for him to really believe in his heart that you're a safe person to be with, even though he sometimes *says* he feels safe with you
- you believe he deserves to feel safe, cared for and special
- with your help, he can learn to do and see things differently now.

Putting these principles into practice

Before asking Matt to do something, such as wash his hands ready for dinner, tell him you're going to ask him to do something he may find hard: that you think he may even feel scared if he does what you ask. Tell him you often know when he's scared because he screams, 'poos' and smears or breaks things, then go on to wonder out loud (gently and curiously, avoiding criticism and sarcasm) how he's going to show you his feelings this time.

Now ask Matt to wash his hands (or whatever you want him to do), reminding him that you'll be there with him all the time. If he manages to do the task without screaming or going slow, give him a cuddle and show him you're pleased he's beginning to believe you are a safe mummy. If, on the other hand, he 'plays up', tell him you're glad he's able to show you how scared he's feeling and that you're ready to help him.

If you see Matt getting agitated try to give him a cuddle right away. Repeat to him that he's safe and you're pleased he's showing you how hard it is for him to believe this. If possible use eye contact or ongoing physical touch, such as taking his hand, to reinforce your message. However, don't get into battles over this if Matt can't handle it (partly due to his highly reactive sensory system – see 'Sensory issues' section).

Remind yourself, and Matt, that you are *not* his birth mother or his auntie: on the contrary, you're a safe mummy. Try to speak calmly, use as few words as possible and vary what you say to Matt. Actions and body language are 'heard' far more readily than any appeals to 'reason', especially when the child seems 'to have lost all reason'; it's vital you give your messages in a non-challenging, matter-of-fact way.

You could wonder out loud how long Matt's outburst will last and what it will take for Matt to feel safe and sure enough to put his shoes on himself: as long as you can remain unconcerned about the wait. However, it may be better to intervene early on Matt's behalf, saying: 'I can see you need some help right now. We can practise this together.' That way he has less chance of getting further 'out of control' and more chance of accepting your support and co-regulation.

I understand that control is a major issue for Matt (see also 'Control issues' section) and many of the disagreements at home seem to centre around his refusal to do as he's told or doing the opposite of what he's been asked. Although this feels like controlling behaviour it tells us just how little control Matt really feels he has over his life. His desperate need to feel in control stems from his early life experiences: when he was so vulnerable and helpless to make sense of the chaos and hurts at home.

The most important aspect of helping Matt is for you to make sure you control the emotional atmosphere in your home. This means working hard to meet Matt with empathy, not anger, and to find ways of accepting his behaviour regardless of what he does. Direct control of challenging behaviour is often difficult or counter-productive, whilst controlling the 'emotional environment' is feasible and provides the secure base Matt so desperately needs.

Making feelings part of life

Babies learn about feelings from their parents during their early months and years. This happens every time parents acknowledge their child's feelings and help him manage them (for example, baby cries, Mum interprets the cry as 'you feel hungry/lonely/need food/your nappy changing'; picks the baby up and 'sorts him out'; baby feels better). This sequence, repeated consistently, helps the baby learn what he's feeling and that he can get the help he needs.

Matt certainly didn't get these messages when he was little: his needs were ignored and the feelings he had were often denied or punished. For example, when his birth mum went out and left Matt alone, she implied that he *should* feel OK, when in fact he would have been very frightened. When he cried, to let her know he was upset, she didn't come to 'sort him out' as he needed. Sometimes she shouted at him for being upset, or even stubbed cigarettes out on his body.

This means that Matt is understandably very confused about feelings. This is probably a major reason for his angry or 'stubborn' outbursts: he may well be feeling sad or frightened but it comes out as anger, or 'shutting down'. Of course there are many valid reasons in Matt's life for him to be angry too! What it does means is that Matt needs an 'interpreter' (you!) to help him sort out what he feels and what to do about it.

It's important that talking about feelings becomes part of your everyday life: whether it's about how *you* feel, how other members of the family are feeling or wondering out loud how Matt might be feeling. Where possible try to make some simple connections between your, or other family members' feelings and what you remember about 'the early days'. Children love to hear about when you (or they) were little: it helps them to feel more part of the family: we all need some help to make sense of our stories (coherent narratives)!

Beyond this, Matt needs to hear, over and over, that you understand his angry, scared and sad feelings and to see that these feelings are not denied or minimised. Rather than trying to make Matt feel better, which he may interpret as you denying his feelings (repeating the messages of his birth family), he needs to hear that you can see he's angry, scared or sad and that it's OK to feel that way. Show him that you too feel sad when he's upset and that you can handle things for both of you: and begin to make sense of them too.

Sometimes dealing with dissociative behaviour, like Matt's 'go slows' or his ignoring you, can be harder than the 'in your face stuff'. Bearing in mind that Matt is often triggered into overwhelming feelings from the past, it would be helpful to acknowledge the difficult place you can see he's in. Although it may feel he's 'running away from you' or 'rejecting you' this isn't the case: Matt has very little control over his dissociative states and desperately needs your help to manage them.

Try to remain accepting, curious, calm and caring when Matt appears 'somewhere else', or 'in another time zone'. Let Matt know you can see he's upset and wonder whether his body is remembering something from when he was a sad (not bad!) baby. Remind him you are with him now ('I know. I'm here') and will stay with him 'wherever he goes' and 'whatever it takes'.

Keep your voice tone even and gentle and move closer to Matt, reaching out and placing your hand tenderly but firmly on his shoulder. Even better, if he'll allow you to hold him close, you can have a real 'heart to heart', using your rhythmic heartbeat to get his 'back in sync'. Don't expect immediate results: be prepared just to be there and to wait for Matt to 'come back'. The fact that you are willing to 'go there' with him will shorten the process and make it easier for him. Gradually he will learn to manage these 'episodes' for himself.

Only after being accepting and containing like this for some time should you try to help Matt think about different ways to deal with his feelings. This will give him sufficient time to practise 'getting' feelings before he tries 'doing' feelings.

I hope these suggestions are helpful and that Matt is able to use the excellent parenting you have to offer to begin to see the world as a safer place and himself as having some worth. I feel sure that when he begins to internalise these beliefs about himself, about the world, and your relationship with him, his need to 'act in' or 'act out' will diminish greatly.

Love Search

I sought to be loved,
But no one was there.
Day after day my heart ached;
I longed to share my passion.

One starless winter night,
My heart gave up.
It went empty and cold;
Life had no meaning.

Hatred washed over me,
Like a wave
Over a sunlit rock pool.
My thirst for love had gone.

My desire had evaporated.
I know my yearning will never be satisfied;
I will continue with my life,
A slave to hatred.

Francis (aged 12 years)

F 1 kids

Fast forward

Some children seem to run too fast and often look 'all over the place': the 'F1 kids'. Like powerful racing cars they have the potential to do well on the Formula 1 circuit but they may prove hazardous in busy, town traffic or narrow, country lanes. It seems as if their idling speed is too high, their 'engines' tend to 'over-rev', their 'brakes' sometimes slip and they experience occasional 'steering lock'.

Parents of F1 children have the choice of allowing them to race round the circuit, taking risks, including dangerous brake wear, over-heating, eventual 'melt-down' and crashes, or 'bringing them into the pits' and trying to 'tune up' their systems. This fine-tuning process may take a good deal of time, knowledge and commitment as it represents an extensive 'practice run' in providing the nurturing, loving interactions from 'good enough' parents to their infants that were often missing in the early lives of traumatised children.

A major piece of the 'tuning' process is to provide lots of 'practice laps' for the child, so that he has sufficient opportunities to try out and 'run in' his 'systems' as they are being 'retuned'. Just as the performance of the car depends a great deal on the design and wiring under the bonnet, so a child's performance relies to a large degree on the wiring of his neural circuits. Practice laps, under the close watchful eye of the construction team, allow subtle adjustments to be made until the racing car is running at its optimum. In the case of the 'racing child' the use of a 'Jemima Crackit' co-driver with 'dual controls' is a non-optional extra.

Parents, as the key therapeutic practitioners for their child, are uniquely placed to take on this vital co-regulating and co-constructing role. They can repeatedly tune into their child, with both sensitivity and understanding, observing his behaviour and interpreting what he is saying through his actions and words. They can then help him work out what he really needs and guide him round the course, downloading vital data from their own regulating and navigational systems as they go.

Perhaps the biggest pitfall is for parents to get so caught up with the adrenalin-driven child that they run ever faster to keep up with him, losing track of their normal, routine checks and 'race plans'. It is exceedingly hard to slow down and give direction to a 'speeding' child unless parents are in the right gear themselves! Regular 'pitstops' and self-care 'top ups' for caregivers must become part of the essential running order.

Becoming familiar with the developmental principles of modern attachment theory and understanding the impact of early childhood trauma on subsequent functioning and family relationships, allows parents to 'tune up' their children more effectively and efficiently. The acronym PARCEL defines the parental job description as: Playful, Accepting, Responsive, Curious, Empathic and Loving and provides the basic emotional blueprint for effective interactions between parents and children (see also p.84).

Additional strategies for 'F1 kids' take on board the 'practice gaps' in individual children's developmental pathways. Access to detailed early history is invaluable, allowing parents and mentors to identify the 'closed circuits' in youngsters' neural wiring that keep them racing round their fast but limited tracks. They can then devise 'interactive repair packages' that open youngsters to a broader repertoire of responses, directions and variations in speed. Individually designed and hard-wearing 'driving manuals' allow parents to 'fill up' their children with age-appropriate, interactive sequences in increasingly structured ways and to guide them more accurately and safely through the hazardous journey of life. Gradually parent 'pacemakers' can drop back, allowing their youngsters increasing opportunities to take the lead for themselves.

A consideration of optimal fuel input is an important adjunct. This takes account of maltreated children's frequently poor, or adverse, nutrition in the womb and through their early years, at times of maximum cell growth and specialisation. Supplementing children's diets, with omega 3 fatty acids that may enhance myelinisation of neural networks and vitamin and mineral formulations for children, can be an invaluable part of the parental 'fine-tuning' process (see 'Nutrition' pp.175–7) and, as always, reliable fresh water supplies are essential to the internal cooling system.

G ames to encourage attachment

Games form a crucial part of childhood. Like kittens chasing balls of wool it is through play that children learn the tasks that equip them for adulthood. Reciprocal play is an essential element in the process of helping youngsters understand who they are in relationship to the important adults in their lives: the simple game of peek-a-boo, for example, helps babies begin the process of differentiating between themselves and their caregivers and of working out that caregivers are still there when out of direct sight. Unfortunately traumatised children often have few opportunities for play: instead they spend their babyhood in 'survival mode', desperately striving to remain safe. For these children 'fun and games' played little part in their lives.

On entering new families traumatised children frequently need additional opportunities to play; they may also need more encouragement, support and practice generally in having fun. 'Parentified' children (pseudo-adult), for example, frequently need to be encouraged to relinquish their 'adult' personae and to be given 'permission' to be children. 'Think toddler think' ('T3') strategies and interactions that allow youngsters of all ages to play and learn at their *developmentally* appropriate age will help them heal from early trauma, through the process of practising attachment, experiencing dependency as safe, learning about themselves and developing self-esteem.

Working with the senses promotes closeness and gives youngsters copious opportunities to 'revisit' developmental stages which they missed or that did not go well for them. Below are some simple ideas for adoptive parents to consider for their hurt children, based on the 'six senses'.

- Counting fingers and toes promotes touch and provides children with opportunities to practise 'knowing their bodies' and establish 'self permanence'; checking body parts, such as nose, chin, ears, cheeks, 'to see whether they are warm/cold, hard/soft, wiggly/quiet' can also be used to good effect.

- Shared roly-poly games, dancing and musical bumps are fun ways of learning about how bodies work; rhythmic drumming, clapping, singing and marching also put children in touch with themselves (and you).

- Blowing bubbles allows legitimate closeness, promotes eye contact and turn-taking and encourages hand–eye coordination in fun ways.

- Making a mess together with clay, finger paints or packet cake mixes helps children who don't know how to play, introducing tastes and smells as well as vital touch experiences.

- Hide and seek, an extension of peekaboo, is a simple game that revisits early abandonment experiences, with the essential difference that children are now 'found' and 'claimed' by their adoptive parents, and strengthens the child's sense of self.

- Sand or water, plus old mugs, jugs and anything else that floats and is not precious can provide endless hours of fascinating play experiences – parents can join in, or take the opportunity to catch up with some gardening tasks within easy eye- and ear-shot.

- Reading stories together provides a wonderful end to the day. Choose stories that 'fit' children's emotional age and needs, rather than their chronological age: parents can always ask their youngsters to humour them if they protest that the chosen stories are 'too babyish'.

For further ideas on sensory-based games, see *First Steps in Parenting the Child Who Hurts* (Archer 1999a) or *Theraplay* (Jernberg and Booth 2001). Throughout this guide there are more suggestions for playful interactions with traumatised children. Parents can experiment with these or make up their own games, using their 'insider knowledge' of their youngsters. Adopters should remember to have fun as they 'work' in the knowledge that they are simultaneously providing vital components to encourage attachment and self development, helping their children heal from their earliest traumas and preparing them for adult life.

'Good' child
(or am I being 'good enough'?)

Most parents worry if their child misbehaves, is rude, oppositional, impulsive, over-active, hurtful to themselves or others or continually struggles in school. The majority long for a child who is pleasant, willing, helpful, compliant, sociable, successful at school and has many outside interests. To an extent this may reflect parents' own childhood experiences. Well-behaved children also reflect society's perceptions of caregivers' parenting abilities. There are occasions, however, when 'good' children can seem less psychologically and emotionally healthy than their 'bad' counterparts. (Here the terms 'good' and 'bad' are used as shorthand and not as judgemental categorisations.) All children swing from 'good' to 'bad', to some degree with changing times and circumstances. However, in some this pattern appears highly exaggerated: reflecting the polarised, insecure attachment patterns described in recent research (e.g. Solomon and George 1999). It is to these 'good' children, whose early lives have been traumatic, that we refer here.

In some cases, adoptive parents have uncomfortable feelings that 'something isn't quite right' with their 'good' child but find their concerns difficult to articulate or to have acknowledged by friends, relatives and supporting practitioners. At other times they are so relieved the anticipated 'trouble' has not occurred that they relish their child's 'goodness' and do all they can to encourage it. Who could blame them? Hence 'good' children often come to professional attention indirectly: adopters may have a group of siblings and approach support agencies with concerns about the overtly troubling behaviour of a 'difficult' brother or sister. Or they may cautiously 'whisper' their concerns, unable to put the finger on 'the problem', or feel unjustified in their anxieties about their 'lodger' child. Although these patterns of behaviour are not gender-specific, in general girls are more likely to 'act good' and boys to 'act bad'. Further research in the field of neurobiology may provide explanations for these differences, over and above the potential effects of early gender socialisation.

Working therapeutically with the whole family group is essential, as it allows information to be picked up, as much from what is not said as from what is said, that there may be 'trouble in paradise'. At times caregivers are only too pleased to turn their focus onto the 'quiet one' and are relieved to feel free to speak of their frustrations, irritations or even dislike of their child. With other families more subtlety and circumspection is needed, respecting parents' rosy perceptions of the youngster whilst gradually introducing the concepts of 'good enough' and 'too good to be true'. In all cases children's early histories and reported patterns of behaviour in previous placements must be explored in depth. This information provides vital insights into the origin and perpetuation of 'supergood' children that can help puzzled parents make sense of their ambiguous patterns of interaction. As with every family this supplies the 'lexicon' from which parents learn to 'translate' behaviours into thoughts and words for themselves and for their children.

Below we discuss Kirsty, a little girl who was eager to please, concerned about her appearance and anxious 'to do things right'. During therapy sessions she often showed her underlying anxiety by dancing around, singing or talking animatedly; she also spent much energy trying to 'keep her brother in line'. However, Kirsty found it difficult to engage in individual therapeutic work, seemed unable to access her emotions and showed little awareness of body feelings. Sometimes she appeared to retreat into her own world. She often tried to get too close physically to Mel and Rae and needed help to find her own 'space'. Nevertheless Kirsty's parents had few concerns about her initially and, naturally enough, focused on the demands on their time and energy that Danny posed.

Letter to the Tait-Pritchard family

Dear Mel and Rae

Now that the children have been with you for some months it sounds as though your initial surprise and pleasure at Kirsty's compliance is beginning to wilt. Your telephone call to the previous carer and recent contact with Josh, Alex and their adoptive family, when Kirsty became quite wild and uncontrollable, must have made you think you were looking at a completely different little girl! In some ways that could be true.

When Kirsty lived with her birth family she was often left alone with her three baby brothers for long periods. Food was bizarre and frequently in short supply; Kirsty was seen foraging for food from waste bins for herself and her brothers. Cleanliness in the home was non-existent and the children were poorly clothed, unkempt and prone to skin infections. Their birth mother could barely take care of herself and their birth father rarely helped out. Kirsty ran wild, used foul language and engaged in physically over-active and threatening play with her siblings. There were few opportunities for quiet times together, gentle intimacy, fun activities or 'childish' play.

In their first foster home all four children were together in a single parent household with two other needy children. Only after she came to your home did Kirsty begin to experience any sense of separateness, order or belonging. For a child who has had so little and experienced so many changes, the unfamiliarity of 'enough' can be terrifying; the fear of further loss is ever present. It seems that Kirsty is desperate to hold onto what she has and is striving to be 'good enough' to prevent the anticipated rejection. She is still too scared 'to be herself'.

Sadly during her early years, Kirsty received many negative messages about her own worth. As a result, she will believe: 'I must have been a "bad baby" to have been treated so badly.' She learned little about getting her own needs met and a good deal about taking care of other people's needs. Her birth mother expected her to take charge of household chores and she was the main carer for her three little brothers. There was little time or opportunity to be vulnerable or dependent or to become 'joined up'.

Early, internal 'working models' (road maps) of self and the world (based on early experiences) become firmly embedded in young children's minds, and bodies. These tend to be resistant to change, since they 'fitted' so well in former, distressing circumstances. Whilst many children cling to these old familiar ways of getting by, it seems that Kirsty has unconsciously moved into 'good child' mode in your family, trying desperately to forget how it was back then. Who could blame her?

Strange as it may seem, that makes good sense of her loud, boisterous and bullying behaviour with her brothers, which is in such stark contrast to her behaviour with Danny in your home. Being with Danny, Josh and Alex must have felt, to Kirsty, like going back home to her birth family, so she behaved in the way that worked for her there. That would have been quite shocking and distressing for you: this was not the Kirsty you have come to know and love. Nevertheless it provides us with a window into her abusive past and reminds us that Kirsty still has some way to go to become 'joined up'.

We'll continue to help Kirsty explore her past and connect her feelings to this in therapy sessions. We'll also start addressing Kirsty's worries about being 'good enough' in your family. Kirsty is certainly old enough to have some strong, conscious memories of birth family life and may be only too aware how she used to behave there. If 'she knows that you know' and can handle that, she may feel more secure.

You can start working on these issues at home by reminding yourselves that Kirsty is holding onto her earliest beliefs that she's 'a bad girl'. Whilst in the past she often 'acted bad', in your home she's unconsciously 'acting good' because she is terrified you'll find out that she's 'a bad girl' and send her away. This puts a huge strain on Kirsty: no wonder she sometimes shows her agitation in 'chattering' and suffers with terrifying nightmares. Moreover she has little idea of her own feelings and needs, not daring to try out 'being herself' just yet.

It's important that you find ways to 'let Kirsty know that you know', that you understand how scared she feels about 'being herself' and that you're sad she doesn't yet feel safe enough to tell you in words how she's feeling. When Kirsty is being 'too good' you could give some reassurance by being understanding and accepting, saying: 'Don't worry! You can go on showing me in your way how hard things are for you and I'll help you find the words.' You could add: 'I guess we all need more practice at trusting each other and becoming a real family. I wonder how long it'll take us?' Here you're taking shared ownership of the problem, avoiding Kirsty feeling shamed, and speaking positively about the possibilities for change, giving her realistic hope for the future.

It can be very difficult to change a child's oldest and deepest beliefs about herself. You could tell Kirsty you love her and that she's a good girl until you're blue in the face: she might even agree with you on the surface. However, deep down she 'knows' she's bad and that it's only a matter of time before you work that out too. What will have more effect, over time, will be your gentle acceptance of Kirsty 'warts and all' (if you can find any!). Beware of using everyday expressions such as 'good girl' as this will only confirm her belief that she needs to be 'good' to be acceptable. Specific praise is more likely to help her begin to 'feel good' about herself instead of just 'acting good'. Try using 'good job on the (whatever she has just done well)' or simply 'Nice one!'

It will be important to find ways of persuading Kirsty to let you look after her. Preparing food for her and sitting down with her whilst she eats is highly nurturing. Helping Kirsty with her bath and bedtime routine could provide you with many opportunities for closeness and playfulness. These times together could have direct, positive effects on Kirsty's sleep pattern as well as providing the developmental reparenting experiences Kirsty needs, to increase her self-awareness and eventually her self-esteem.

Meanwhile, it could be a good idea to cut down on Kirsty's activities outside the home, despite her obvious keenness to join local sports, music and social clubs and classes. In a few months' time these will be invaluable; but first Kirsty needs more time with you, practising the things little girls do with their mums and dads. This is an invaluable part of life she missed: developmentally she can't really engage 'out there' until she's had enough of 'in here' (you) to establish a sense of security and set boundaries for her.

When you're together as a family, try to let go of egalitarian concepts such as 'sharing' just for now. We have seen how Kirsty 'gives in' to Danny over toys and food. Although this behaviour is usually to be encouraged, there's a sense of submerged resentment in her 'altruism' that fits with what you said about catching Kirsty being unpleasant to Danny when she thinks they're alone. It's still too much to expect a very deprived little girl to share and feel that she 'has enough' at this stage.

The best 'quality time' with Kirsty would be time spent with one or more parent without Danny taking all the attention. This will give Kirsty essential opportunities to have a mum or dad all to herself: in the past she had to share what little attention was available with her brothers. Given time I feel sure Kirsty will feel more wholeheartedly good about sharing. There's a critical difference between 'doing the right thing because you feel right' and 'doing the right thing because you feel wrong'.

At some stage you could also talk to Kirsty about her rough, over-excited behaviour with Danny, Josh and Alex and be sad for her that that was the way it was in her birth family: making sure you avoid hints of criticism or anger of Kirsty in your tone or body language. Meanwhile it would be helpful to let her know you're 'glad that you were able to show us how hard that was for you'. You could then wish out loud that you could have been there to look after Kirsty when she was little: you would have made lots of time to play with her. Follow this with positive statements such as: 'We both missed out! Thank goodness we still have plenty of time to practise these things together now.'

Try also to find time for some 'rough and tumble' play and shared visits to the park, with its swings and climbing frame. Join in the fun yourselves, so Kirsty can see that it's 'OK' to laugh and mess about. You'll need to maintain clear boundaries here and to intervene sensitively if things start getting out of hand. Kirsty's capacity for managing her own arousal levels is still weak and she seems to discriminate poorly between excitement and fear. Neurobiologically the body sensations are very similar and equally highly charged.

When you give encouragement it might be better to say: 'do your best' rather than 'try your hardest'. For some reason children don't do so well when they 'try': perhaps it becomes a conscious thing and then anxiety gets in the way? From what you've said this could certainly be true for Kirsty.

In addition, Kirsty needs help to change 'feeling states' at times. At the moment she seems to *lurch* from one set of feelings and actions to another, rather than in any organised way. That is often a feature of children with quite distinct feeling and behavioural states. Remember that Kirsty's role models in her birth family were of a very 'flat' mother, who had unpredictable outbursts of uncontrolled rage, and a very intense but transient father. She will need lots of opportunities to practise feelings and managing transitions between them before she feels connected to all her 'parts' and can manage these comfortably and appropriately.

One aspect that may be particularly challenging is providing Kirsty with sufficient opportunities to 'act bad' in your home, with your 'approval'. I know this must sound crazy, as a well-behaved child is more acceptable, more popular and easier to live with than a poorly behaved one. But Kirsty doesn't 'feel good' although she is doing her utmost to 'act good'. After all she has to try to convince herself as well as you! Thinking about it, I feel sure you'd prefer to have a child who is 'up front' with her feelings than one who is 'sneaky'.

We can't make those 'bad' feelings go away by ignoring them. They may be 'pushed way down inside' but they'll still be there to creep out when you and Kirsty are least expecting it. Acknowledging and accepting the 'bad side' in all of us helps us take control of ourselves more fully. So that *you* feel in comfortable charge here, why not establish a 'funny half hour' routine, when 'anything goes'? This would have the benefit of setting limits on when, where and with whom Kirsty tries out being 'bad' and could provide her with a much-needed sense of containment.

Your responses to Kirsty's behaviour during this time are crucial. Initially she may need a good deal of 'egging on' from you to 'let herself go'. You could usefully model 'being naughty' for Kirsty yourselves, to give her permission. Choose small issues you are comfortable flouting and perhaps agree in advance which adult will be the 'bad child' and which the 'grown up'. Drawing funny faces on the steamy bathroom window, or leaving your dirty clothes all over the floor, could be good, low-key starters. Playing outrageous practical jokes on each other, with Kirsty as co-conspirator, could also be great fun.

Using unplanned genuine mistakes is also invaluable, allowing you to model coping with being wrong and putting things right without falling apart. Try bringing the dog into the equation too: I'm sure there are times when he's 'naughty'. Kirsty will see from how you handle these situations that it's possible to 'be bad' and still be 'good enough' to be loved.

There may be some continuing issues for Kirsty about Danny's behaviour too: she may feel 'they come as a package' and if Danny 'messes up' they will both have to go. Stories, puppets and 'plays' are natural media for exploring 'being bad' safely. The 'naughty little sister' books could be really helpful here, as could the Little Princess '*I want...*' series by Tony Ross. Introduce these into your usual quota of shared stories, rather than as anything special.

My all-time-favourite story about 'bad kids' (and young children's tendency to dissociate) is *Where the Wild Things Are* by Maurice Sendak. The central character is a small boy who has been sent to his bedroom. There he 'goes off on fabulous, wild adventures' before finally choosing to come home. The boy's appearance changes dramatically as he moves between 'small boy' and 'wild thing' mode; back in his room his dinner awaits him 'and it is still hot'. As this is a short book with copious illustrations you could read it to Danny too (in Kirsty's hearing!).

Finally, it could be helpful for us to talk to school staff about Kirsty's behaviour and your change of approach. If we alert staff to the issues they can keep you informed of any changes they see in class and react with understanding and equal enthusiasm when Kirsty 'acts bad'. They'll need to know how to avoid coming over as too punitive or too lenient and how to bring Kirsty back when she 'wanders off in her mind'. Make sure you also let them know you're trying to ease the pressure on Kirsty to 'perform' well and hope the class teacher is wise enough to adopt the same tactic.

All in all, this is going to be a tough one but I'm sure you'll support each other and 'seize the nettle' with courage and commitment. Don't forget to call me any time if you have any questions or concerns.

Impact on adoptive parents of living with violent and threatening behaviour

Violent and threatening behaviour from a child is not only difficult to live with, it is difficult to think about, let alone speak about, especially in the early times. One courageous adoptive mother has written the letter below to her son, in which she thinks through the evolution of her son's aggressive behaviour and begins, painfully, to help him face up to his actions. She follows this with a discussion of her feelings, or lack of them, over time and the impact of the secondary traumatisation she experienced at the hands of her son. She hopes that this letter will 'speak' to other adopters faced with similar experiences and give professionals some idea of the impact of living with violence from a child.

My dear son,

This is probably the hardest letter I've ever written. As you stand in court waiting the outcome of an assault charge I hope you know I love you and want the best for you. I am at court supporting you and hoping the outcome is one you can use to help you better manage the uncontrollable anger you sometimes demonstrate.

    I remember first hearing about you when you were five years old and in foster care. I remember hearing about how you had been physically abused by your birth father, witnessed fights between your parents; how you were not fed regularly; were often left in a dirty nappy for hours and how your cries frequently went unheard. When the social workers told me about the tantrums you sometimes threw in your foster family I felt an overwhelming empathy for you and a desire to make a difference in your life. I wanted to shower you with love and to keep you safe. I wanted to show that I would never hurt you the way your first parents did. I was certainly not going to let a few tantrums deter me from being your mother. In fact I felt a little angry hearing about your tantrums: surely all five-year-olds had tantrums sometimes, and after the life you had lived it was not surprising you had a few more than the average child. Perhaps the foster mother didn't know how to manage you; perhaps she didn't give you enough attention. She certainly didn't have as much love to give you as I had.

When I met you for the first time you immediately called me 'Mum' and rushed up for a cuddle. You showed me your bedroom and shyly asked me what your room looked like at 'home'. We got off to such a good start – you and I. And when you finally did come home, you were charming. Everybody loved your friendliness; your ability to chat to just about anybody and the way you always seemed to know what was going on.

The tantrums started after you had been with me for about a month. They happened when I asked you to do something you didn't want to do, like putting your shoes on. They only happened when we were alone together: you continued to be charming to everyone else and even treated me affectionately when we were with other people. The affection did at times feel false and left me feeling that this was to impress other people rather than a genuine wish for closeness. I wondered what I was doing wrong. I reasoned that it was early days and it was hardly surprising you got angry after all you had been through. I tried reasoning with you, cajoling you, bribing you to 'be good', and supported you through tantrums that might last for two hours and could be started by such simple things as giving you the 'wrong' breakfast cereal.

I then found, to my horror, that I started getting angry with you. I hated myself for shouting at you: that little smile of triumph you gave me when I shouted at you made me afraid. What was going on? Did you actually *want* me to become angry? You seemed to take such pleasure when I shouted at you, or if I cried. Meanwhile I told the social worker I was having a little trouble with you and continued making excuses to the teacher when we were late for school.

The years went on. The tantrums lessened for a time only to be replaced by episodes when you would wreck your room and damage property in the house. You seemed to know the things that were special to me and targeted these in your uncontrollable rages. Or were they uncontrollable? When you sought out something of mine to break, avoiding more obvious targets to vent your anger; when you would wait until your father left for work before flying into a rage; when you could stop if you thought someone else might be in earshot – I wondered whether you *could* control your outbursts, yet couldn't quite believe it.

The first few times you hit me were when you were having a tantrum. I reasoned with myself that hurting me had been an accident and happened because you didn't know what you were doing with your fists and feet. Later, when you responded to my requests by pushing me or hitting me I blamed myself. Perhaps my expectations were too high; perhaps I'd asked you to get ready for school in the wrong tone of voice; perhaps it was because I'd raised my voice in frustration. When you were at school I examined each and every situation trying to work out what had gone wrong and how I might do things differently. I began to 'walk on tiptoes', weighing up how to ask you a question in a way that would not incite your rage.

I told the school you were getting out of control but hid the bruises on my arms. They too had experienced some aspects of your anger: you had been in fights with other children and at times refused to do as the staff asked. The teachers suggested I should speak to you about your behaviour; they implied that I had not taught you appropriate ways to control your anger.

I remember one time in particular when we'd had an especially difficult morning: I lost my temper and shouted at you in the school playground. Your headmistress was there along with your classroom teacher. They gave each other one of those 'knowing' looks that said: 'Now we can see why this child gets so angry.' They blamed me; you blamed me; most of all *I* blamed myself.

I have read about 'tough love'. I have lived 'tough love', because despite everything I do love you. But now today I face the 'toughest love of all'; because today you are in court for a charge of assault. When years of trying to reason, cajole, bribe and watch my every move has made little difference to your violent outbursts: I sit in court knowing it was my call to the police and my agreement that you should be charged with assault that has led to you standing in front of the judge, facing the consequences of the last time you hit me.

My darling son, I want to tell the judge to stop; I want to say I have changed my mind; I want to say that the bruises weren't as bad as they looked; I want to protect you; I want to believe that if I did this you would change and there'd be no more anger. But in my heart of hearts I know the 'toughest love of all' means that I must not do this. I need to help you to stop this cycle of violence, I need to stop you from practising to be an abuser and I need to stop being a victim. And sadly I know that today in court is the only way this cycle can be broken.

I will always love you, I will always be there for you, and from now on I will be a victim no more.

I have faith that with my help and my love for you, you can change. I will be there to help you know this as well.

Love

Mum XX

Learning to hear – and to 'really listen': a personal account

Perhaps you, the reader, are asking yourself how it felt being abused by the son I tried so hard to parent. Perhaps you are asking how I coped. The two questions are so much inter-linked it is difficult to answer one without the other. Initially I felt puzzled, overwhelmed but also hopeful that with time and patience he would settle and no longer need to act out his anger by violent means. Or, more honestly, I thought that as he settled he would no longer feel as angry and the behaviour would gradually reduce. I imagined it might take several months before I began to see a difference.

When my son had been with me for six months and his behaviour was, if anything, getting worse the hope faded and despair began to set in. I suppose this was when real feelings of fear began to emerge. There were days when I did not want to get out of bed in the morning; I dreaded picking my son up from school; my heart beat faster every time the phone rang in case it was the school calling to ask me to collect him because he had hit another child or had a tantrum in the class and had broken something. I now recognise these feelings were ones my son had felt as a baby when he was being abused by his birth parents. He was so good at letting me 'hear' his pain: if only I had known how to 'really listen'. He had learned the language of abuse and trauma and found potent ways to communicate that to me in the only way he knew how.

This was followed by other 'lessons' in the ways I learned to cope with the trauma to which I was exposed. The denial of what was happening; the minimising of assaults by referring to them as hitting, or blaming myself for having provoked my son in some way: these are all things I also learned from my son not only in respect of his behaviour but also in his, at times, idealised picture of his birth parents in his dismissal of what they had done and in his feelings of lack of self-worth. He would blame himself for what had happened to him as a baby while at the same time blaming me for what was happening now. This was the time when the pain I felt was at its worst. I felt overwhelmed with fear and despair. I felt isolated and alone, just as my son must have felt when he was lying in his cot overwhelmed with feelings of pain and hunger.

How had my son managed to deal with this level of distress when there was no way out, when the people he depended on for his very survival were also the people who were responsible for his pain? He learned what so many babies learn who are faced with such circumstances – he learned to protect himself by 'switching off' from his physical and emotional feelings by dissociating himself from them. Essentially he learned not to feel. He passed that learning on to me. Overwhelmed by pain I learned a mantra that began to help dull the pain and fear that had become ever-present factors of my daily life. I would repeat over and over again: 'It's OK; It's not that bad; Stop feeling, stop feeling, stop feeling.' It began to work, my way of dulling the pain. I even got to the point where I did not need to use my mantra. When I began to feel fear and pain my body automatically found its way to stop the feelings, to switch off and feel nothing.

This was probably the only thing that helped me to survive those years when the abuse was at its worst. It offered 'protection'. But it also isolated me, more than anything else did, from other people. I began to see them through the prism of the trauma that was my life: I suppose in the same way that my son viewed me through the 'looking glass' of abuse, neglect and abandonment.

Now, after years of support and personal counselling I can begin truly to see, hear and speak the unspeakable on behalf of my son. This will provide the structure that, along with continued understanding and nurture, will help him to embrace the 'language of love' and reduce his need to act on the 'language of trauma' he learned from his birth parents and which has continued to dominate so much of his life with me.

Looking after ourselves

As parents we often think of ourselves in terms of looking after other people, in particular our children. If we have adopted children, they may need a great deal of taking care of, demanding of us a good deal of commitment and some very special skills. The more we do this, the better we become at prioritising and taking care of others. The downside, however, is that we can overlook our own needs. When the battery of a torch runs down the bulb goes out: no one can see clearly, or provide useful guidance for others. It is therefore a vital part of our job as caregivers to keep our batteries topped up if 'the lights aren't to go out' in the fragile world of our vulnerable children.

The family laws of self-care

- To every action there is an equal and opposite reaction. The amount of time and effort we spend on ourselves should increase in direct proportion to the amount of time and effort we expend on others.

- While it seems sensible to cut down on 'our time' to have enough energy to deal with our children's challenges, this is a short-term and short-sighted solution. Taking the long view, we must be prepared to 'act out of character' and 'be good to ourselves' so that we can do our best for those who depend upon us.

- It is essential that we cultivate the elements of nurture and structure that are at the heart of healthy relationships: we neglect our own nurture and structural supports at our children's peril.

- Pressure from society to act selflessly, rather than selfishly, should be resisted: with continuing education this pressure should diminish. Meanwhile ask yourself: 'If being selfless equates with having little sense of self how can that help my child, whose sense of self has been so severely compromised already?' Conversely, being selfish allows us to model all those 'self-attributes' that are sadly missing from his world.

- No one has the monopoly on fun! We each have unique feelings and perceptions of the world. Our approaches to enjoyment should be equally varied, although shared activities can increase fun levels dramatically.

- We do not exist in a vacuum. Nature abhors vacuums and so should we! We need to maintain our social and relational networks in good working order so that we can take from them as well as give to them. This is a fundamental tenet of relationships: they need to be bi-directional.

- Nature herself has much to offer. Tapping into the forces of earth, air, fire and water that provide life can be revitalising too!

- Breathing, eating and sleeping need special attention. Exhausted parents and exhausting children are not a happy combination!

- Practice makes perfect; rarely practised skills become rusty. Since learning is a life-long process our need to practise self-care should continue throughout our lifetimes. This may involve minor changes, or more 'radical rethinks', as our lives evolve.

Managing separations

Recent research demonstrates that babies hear, taste, move and feel months before birth and that they respond to mothers' physical and emotional circumstances. Unborn babies have only their immediate environment to prepare them for coming into the world: their dependence on mothers is absolute. Early separation from the birth mother therefore means loss of the only world they knew: trauma from which they need understanding and support to heal.

Similarly, separation trauma is suffered by babies remaining with birth mothers unable to meet their needs adequately: such as depressed mothers, who although physically present, may be emotionally unavailable to their babies, exposing them to feelings of loss over extended periods. Other infants experience abuse and neglect that leaves them terrified, distressed, confused and alone. These early, traumatic experiences have profound effects on their neurobiological development and strongly influence their beliefs about the world. Their sense of self, security and trust are seriously compromised; often they continue to struggle with issues around separation and loss, long after finding 'security' in adoptive families.

Good attachment experiences during infancy enable youngsters to tolerate separation. This process is evident during early 'toddler socialisation', when infants begin to explore the environment beyond their 'attachment figures'. Sensitive parents strike a balance between providing the security of closeness and the encouragement to 'go it alone' that allows youngsters to practise small separations, tolerate change and occupy themselves for short periods. Here youngsters can be seen 'checking back' to ensure that their parents are still there and approve of what they are doing. By school age, such youngsters can usually manage the daily separations and new experiences that increasingly make up their lives.

However, children who experienced traumatic separations and interruptions to their attachment and development often continue to find coping with these everyday challenges overwhelming. Sadly, despite the best efforts of their adoptive parents to create safe, nurturing environments, their attachment security has been seriously compromised and they are often unable to experience themselves as safe and secure. Some youngsters cope by minimising their need for others and striving for premature self-sufficiency; others continue to use infantile attachment strategies to try to keep caregivers close and control their terrifying world.

Luke struggles with situations that echo his early experiences, such as amusing himself for brief periods, or visits to his extended adoptive family that trigger feelings of abandonment. His adopters are having difficulty understanding and helping Luke with extreme clingy and controlling behaviour that challenges family life and threatens the stability of the placement.

Letter to the Kasprowicz family

Dear Maria and Anthony

As you know, Luke has a distressing history of abandonment and neglect. We know his birth mother left him with strangers while she worked as a prostitute to fund her drug habit: Luke therefore moved around a great deal before he was six months old. Birth mother's drug use also meant she often wasn't 'present' for him, even when she was at home. In addition he had several moves in foster care, before he came home to you. Since all this occurred in Luke's first two years, the period of greatest neurological development when the templates ('road maps') that shaped his view of the world were forming, this has had a profound impact on him at every level.

It's hard to imagine just how Luke felt as a tiny baby. He must have suffered hunger, fear, pain and great uncertainty about what was happening to him. Life would have been chaotic and unpredictable, with adults sometimes paying him attention and at others becoming angry or ignoring him. Research shows that adults find managing change difficult: house moves, job changes, new relationships, loss of loved ones, are all identified as stressful situations that can continue to affect them long after the event. If adults with their wide range of life experiences and maturity are distressed by just one of these major events, think how much greater their impact would be on tiny babies who have never experienced security and predictability. Luke's life could be likened to having all of those experiences, daily, on a random basis. Being mindful of this makes it easier to understand why Luke has such extreme reactions to any kind of change now.

Now, let's turn to the tantrums Luke has whenever he moves from one environment to another. I know he's only three years old and that friends and relatives have told you toddler tantrums are normal at that age.

However, I agree with you that the nature and extent of Luke's rages are greater than would be expected from securely attached children of his age. They indicate difficulties going way beyond the problems most parents face during 'toddler socialisation'.

I appreciate how undermining it is, as new parents, to be told you're exaggerating Luke's problems and that you're being naïve. I hope our discussions and the emphasis we place on parents being the 'experts' on their child have helped you feel validated. Your knowledge of Luke and your gut feelings that his difficulties stem from his early traumatic experiences are way ahead of your friends and relatives. Perhaps we could help get this across to your 'essential support network' by arranging to meet with them, and you, to share what we know. This would be a good way of beginning to help Luke: he needs a consistent approach to his difficulties, which could become more feasible if we could persuade friends and family to follow your lead.

It's essential to understand Luke's behaviour as the language he uses to let you know how scared he feels when something in the 'here and now' triggers feelings from the past. Bearing in mind that the 'dictionary' you need to understand Luke's language is drawn from his early experiences, it would be best if we re-read the information on file together. We can then use this to imagine what Luke must have felt: being moved from pillar to post and being cared for by so many unfamiliar people. Terror and panic must have been his predominant emotions: at times his experiences must have felt life-threatening.

Initially Luke may have shown his understandable rage by crying, screaming and wriggling his body wildly, in the way only tiny babies can. When this proved ineffective or even threatening he would have 'switched off' (dissociated) from his terrifying feelings, to keep himself safe and survive. Once Luke learned to 'switch off', this process would be automatically triggered as soon as Luke *felt* alone or threatened with abandonment. This is evident in Luke's behaviour now: when you try to take him out, or when he moves from room to room, unless you are with him.

Separation currently triggers fears for Luke that he may again face a life-threatening situation: being helpless and alone. This makes sense for several reasons:

- Luke is too young to recall verbally his early experiences, yet his body, mind and heart remember only too well. The feelings that come up now *feel* as if they're about what's happening now, although they're primarily about the past. Hence our emphasis on getting in touch with Luke's early history.

- Luke learned to dissociate as soon as he felt threatened: whenever he perceived the *threat* of abandonment rather than the actuality. The fear generated in the present when he, or others, leave *feels* like the same intense fear as in the past.

- Luke would have felt totally helpless (which he was) when his birth mother left him or ignored his 'baby needs'. This was influential in forming the belief that separation, or lack of close attention, meant 'danger'. He probably now feels that unless he 'takes control' he (or you) may disappear, threatening his entire existence.

- When Luke faces any 'leaving' situation his need to feel in control is overwhelming. His raging tantrums are best understood as attempts to control his environment and overwhelming fear. They also strongly resemble the 'infantile rage' behaviour of tiny babies.

Luke's behaviour is his only means of communicating his distress and letting you know how scared he feels. He's unlikely to recognise this: but it's essential that you do. I know, at the moment, Luke's fear is expressed as angry outbursts that can make it harder to 'hear' his behaviour as the language of fear, or to feel empathy for him. It must be so frustrating for you when Luke refuses to put his coat on and resorts to screaming and hitting out when you're trying to take him to the park, or to visit friends.

Of course you're also likely to feel angry at times. It could help to pin a note on your door reminding yourselves that Luke struggles with fears he cannot understand and that he's communicating this through angry behaviour. It would also be helpful to remind yourself that, while the anger is directed at you, it stems from the past and is not a reflection of your relationship with Luke. In fact it tells us that you are getting close to Luke and picking up on his feelings.

- 'This looks like anger – but really Luke is 'dead scared'. He needs me to help him remember this and to feel less terrified.'

- 'Luke must trust me a lot to show me how terrified he is feeling. He really is coming to know that I can help him.'

Letting Luke know 'the plan for the day' early in the morning could reduce his fears that 'things happen without warning'. Although he's too young to read, he could still benefit from having a diary of his day placed in a prominent spot, such as on the kitchen door. Pictures to represent what you'll both be doing that day could provide the visual reminder he needs that life with you is predictable and safe. Spend a few minutes at the start of the day reading the diary together and reflecting on what you'll be doing. This would be time well spent to reduce the times you spend dealing with Luke's anger and panic throughout the day, alongside the times Luke spends feeling upset and alone.

Given Luke's age, prepare him by saying 'we'll soon be getting ready to go out' about five minutes before starting to get him ready for any activity. However, you could experiment with this until you find the time that best lets him know what you're planning and gives him most opportunity to deal with his troubling feelings. If you tell him too far in advance, the event won't connect with what you're telling him; too near and he won't have time to process his feelings.

In addition to warning Luke about a forthcoming event (however small), give him a short verbal reminder that you know he's likely to feel frightened. Let him know, perhaps putting your hand on his shoulder, that you'll know that he's frightened if he becomes angry and starts screaming. Confirm to Luke that his fears are absolutely understandable: he wasn't in a safe place before he came to live with you. He now needs practice with you to work out that you can keep him safe and his world won't fall apart.

When you're ready to leave, invite Luke to practise knowing it's safe to go to the park. If Luke manages to get ready without a fuss, congratulate him enthusiastically on beginning to learn he's safe with you. Conversely, if he has a tantrum, thank him quietly for letting you know how scared he's feeling, saying, 'I know. No worries! I can handle that'.

Try singing quietly while you find Luke's clothes and shoes, to help create a calm atmosphere and minimise the triggering impact of tension. Why not try making up a song about Luke being safe? Use a simple tune, like *Ten Green Bottles* and improvise ('We're getting ready to go out to the park [x 2] / And when we're ready to go out to the park / Luke's going out and Mum is going too!'). Don't worry if you think you can't sing: your tone of voice is more important than the tenor.

If you see Luke getting agitated, pick him up and cuddle him. Repeat to him quietly that he's safe and you're glad he's telling you how hard it is for him to believe this. If possible use eye contact to reinforce this message; holding his hands might help. However, don't get into battles if he struggles with this: just be there for him.

I loved your idea of giving Luke 'paper cuddles' as a way of showing him affection when, most needing it, he's least receptive to it. For young children 'paper cuddles' can be simple 'o's, using the age-old convention, picture images that evoke 'safe hugs', or even life-size cut-outs of cuddling hands. Older children may respond to 'pay the bearer on demand' cuddle cheques, to be cashed in later.

Having a stock of paper cuddles could help for occasions when Luke pushes you away and your attempts at closeness make him more anxious. Moreover, your stock of 'love in the bank' would be invaluable when you're struggling to feel positive about Luke.

Friends and family could also use this idea when they're leaving your house, or when you leave after a visit to them. Paper cuddles, alongside messages that 'we'll see you again very soon' are potent reminders for Luke that parting from people doesn't have to mean abandonment or pain. In fact, most of the strategies I've suggested for going out would also work for letting go.

In addition you, your family and friends could also consider:

- talking animatedly to each other about when you'll meet up again

- promising to phone as soon as they (or you) get home

- (if Luke becomes agitated) telling him playfully they're pleased they'll be so missed

- giving each other big hugs, to show Luke what fun it could be.

As leaving situations for Luke may also have associations with hunger (not being fed when his mother left him) it could be a good idea to give him a drink, biscuit or piece of fruit as you say goodbye. This is not bribery: it's recognising Luke's difficulties and helping him to deal with them.

Then try varying when you give him these: sometimes before you leave, sometimes as you leave and sometimes after you've left the house together could help him concentrate on the snack he may be expecting rather than the empty feelings of hunger and abandonment that 'leaving' engenders. Gradually reduce the use of snacks when you feel Luke is beginning to manage better and is more sure of himself and you.

One of the principal reasons for Luke's difficulties around leaving is that he cannot conceptualise that he (or you) will return or still exist. This relates directly to his early experiences (for babies even minutes alone can feel like forever) and needs to be acknowledged, both verbally and practically. Showing Luke you're leaving out a change of clothes for his return or giving Luke something of yours (not an item of value he might damage) to look after in your absence could reinforce your verbal messages about returning home, as will consulting his daily diary before leaving the house.

If all else fails and Luke still refuses to put on his coat, pick him up and congratulate him on being 'clever enough to know you need a cuddle'.

Cradling Luke in your lap when he seems agitated could further help him to feel safely contained and more connected.

Don't wait until Luke is in 'full flight' before you intervene. Immediately (or before) you see Luke becoming agitated is the very best time to help him manage feelings: before they become overwhelming and he gets out of control.

Other strategies you could try to help Luke feel more comfortable with the idea of leaving would be:

- Practise brief 'leaving situations' with Luke's teddy bear: this could easily be incorporated into many of the games you play with him.

- On leaving for work in the morning Anthony could help Luke with his feelings by demonstrating how to leave safely and well: the messages, that he's leaving, what time he'll return and how much he'll miss Luke (and you) while he's out, are 'mental rehearsals' for Luke that should help him make better internal 'leaving' connections.

- Visual reminders are invaluable ways of reminding Luke that Anthony will return home. Start keeping a chart together, showing the times Anthony leaves and comes back each day, to help reduce Luke's fears; you could use colourful stickers and family photos to get your message across.

I hope this letter provides you with some ideas about how best to help Luke. Of course, as the experts on Luke, you need to decide which of these strategies are most likely to be effective, or consider creating your own. Let me know how you get on.

Finally, try to have some fun when you eventually make it to the park!

Good luck in the work you're doing. Luke is a lucky boy to have such caring parents.

N*o*

When parents say 'no'

The word 'no' is a trigger for many maltreated children: they seem to interpret 'no' as meaning 'never', rather than just 'no for now'. It often feels like a 'life or death' issue and frequently raises difficulties around control for them: leading to escalation of control battles.

A valuable rule for parents in dealing with the word 'no' is to limit its use wherever possible. This minimises the number of triggers to deep-seated feelings with which children struggle, thereby reducing unhelpful disconnections and confrontations.

When you need to say 'no', try reminding your child in advance that they are likely to struggle with hearing this *and* that you can handle this.

It is helpful to tell children what they can, rather than cannot, do

- 'You can (watch TV) after you've (dried the dishes).'
- 'I'm happy for you to (go out) when (we've finished tea).'
- 'All children dressed and ready by 6.00 p.m. can go to the cinema!'

If your child loses his temper after being told he cannot do a certain thing immediately, show genuine sadness for the choice he has made

- 'It's sad you've (lost out on playing with your football) today. I hope you can figure out a way of asking that allows you to have it next time.'
- 'What a shame you chose to shout rather than to work out how to get what you wanted politely: we need more practice.'

- 'I know this is difficult for you. Thanks for letting me know. How can I help you manage better when I have to say "no"?'
- 'I know you're going to be cross but the answer's still "no".'
- 'Let's run round the garden and burn off those feelings right now.'

Putting yourself and your child in 'win–win' situations is invaluable

If he's angry you can thank him gently for letting you know you were right, that you can see he's continuing to struggle with 'no'. If he avoids getting upset, you can show you're pleased that he's beginning to feel more comfortable with being told 'no'.

Empathising with your child's feelings is helpful

- 'I bet when I say "no" it feels as if I don't love you. It must be difficult thinking your mum doesn't love you any more. We need more practice at this!'
- 'I know it's hard to wait for something you really want. When it stops raining we *will* go out. Meantime I hope you find something to do that won't mean you'll have to wait until another day.'
- 'Grrr! I hate waiting too. Let's sit and read stories together to cheer ourselves up!'

Introducing games around 'no' can help your child practise feeling comfortable with the word 'no'

Make up statements and ask your child to say 'no' to them (let your child know what you're doing by saying you're helping him practise feeling OK with the word 'no'). The more fun you can put into your games the better: this could include making some outrageous statements about how difficult your child will have with saying 'no' (to things he doesn't want to do anyway) or, conversely, to things he really likes.

- 'This could be difficult. I'm not sure you can say "no" to this. Would you please clear the dishwasher/clear the table?'
- 'I'd like you to say "no" to a sweet/some crisps.'

Try turning these games on their head by encouraging your child to practise saying 'yes' instead!

utrition

Overseas adopters are routinely advised to screen their children for gastro-intestinal parasites and disturbed gut flora. Simultaneously, they are recommended to check for nutritional deficiencies and consider supplementing their children's diet for some time after bringing them home. This acknowledges the adverse conditions in which their children may have been raised and the detrimental effects of failing to recognise and treat the problems effectively.

In contrast, most adopters of children within Britain receive little advice about nutrition and its impact on healthy development. Is our society recognising the poverty and deprivation of children from developing countries whilst remaining blinded to the devastating conditions in which a sizeable minority of 'home-grown' children exist? Perhaps the closer one feels to the problem the less one is able to view it objectively?

The *laissez faire* approach to diet for children being placed for adoption also stands in stark contrast to levels of publicised concern for the nutritional health of unborn and newborn babies and the obesity of children today. Hardly a day goes by without media references to the beneficial, or adverse, effects of even the most mundane foodstuffs. Clearly, a wide range of child health experts and government agencies believe the quality and quantity of what expectant mothers eat and drink, and of the nourishment young babies receive, is important to their future well-being. There are also recognised links between these issues and proneness to obesity and ill-health throughout life.

This growing body of evidence often leads to concerned parents being ultra-cautious over their own diet and that of their unborn children. Many pregnant mothers are mindful of the need to avoid alcohol and excessive caffeine-laden drinks and to consume several glasses of fresh water daily; nutritional supplements are routinely prescribed by GPs and at ante-natal clinics. However, for the adopted population, economic, social and personal factors in their birth families often mean that their early overall care, including nutrition, is compromised. Traumatic distress can add to this cocktail of relative nutritional disadvantage.

Recent research showed the benefits of dietary supplementation for young offenders. Whilst the prison diet was described as 'balanced', there was a dramatic reduction in violent behaviour amongst those inmates who received vitamin, mineral and essential fatty acid supplements. This improvement dropped off when nutritional supplementation stopped. It was reported that the young men being studied often chose unhealthy food options, particularly fatty and sugary snacks and drinks. Consumers' Association investigations show a similar pattern of poor food choices amongst schoolchildren consistent with recent studies implicating environmentally-mediated genetic changes.

Food and water form the major building blocks of life: 'we are what we eat', and drink. Since most of the essential 'building work' of mind and body takes place in the womb and during the early years, what youngsters consume during that period is particularly important. Significantly, their food choices and eating habits are also being 'programmed' at that time. It is therefore essential that society becomes more active in promoting awareness of the nutritional needs of children being placed in new families. Just as love may not be enough, without vital specialised inputs, to overcome early social adversity, so the option of a balanced diet and an adequate intake of water may be insufficient to remedy past nutritional deficiencies. Establishing nutritional status and identifying special dietary needs could prove as vital as assessing attachment status and acknowledging social and emotional special needs in this vulnerable group.

Additional nutritional difficulties may be caused by long-standing alterations in gut bacteria, which are 'fed' by just the sort of 'junk food diet' and relative dehydration discussed above. We are only beginning to identify the causal factors and long-term effects of such changes: *candida albicans* (fungal infection) is, perhaps, one of the most widely known, though remaining subject to some controversy. However, adopters deserve, at the very least, to be made aware that this body of knowledge exists, in order to make informed choices about the dietary management of their children.

In-depth discussion of individual dietary approaches and supplementation is beyond our remit here. The intention is simply to highlight the issues and raise questions in readers' minds. There are many competent, informed nutritional consultants and many books and articles available; avid 'surfers' may uncover an array of relevant information on the internet, although care is needed to establish the reliability of sources. Specialist support groups (like PNPIC, see 'Parenting resources', p.246) and those providing help for specific conditions, such as Attention Deficit Hyperactivity Disorder, dyslexia and irritable bowel syndrome, also provide valuable resources.

Putting it all behind us

Those 'need to know' questions
(Why, How, Who, What?)

Why?

Commonly held beliefs persist that exploring traumatised children's pasts should be avoided, to spare unnecessary additional hurts and indeed, there is risk of retraumatisation, where information is shared insensitively, or in over-large chunks, with insufficient preparation and understanding of children's needs or capacity to cope. Adoptive caregivers would do almost anything to protect their vulnerable children from further suffering, so why place so much emphasis on 'the need to know'?

First, we cannot protect children from what has already happened, nor 'make it better' by encouraging them to 'put it all behind' them. Whilst adults, at one step removed, may feel more comfortable not knowing or 'not hearing', for traumatised children this is not a realistic option. They were there: they felt the pain, terror, grief, the shame of maltreatment and, try as they may to step away, this knowledge follows like a barely visible but threatening shadow.

It is argued that children have little memory of their early lives since they lack the brain 'hardware' associated with verbal recall. Certainly, the hippocampus does not mature until the third year of life, so that earlier experiences cannot be organised and stored in 'narrative memory files', readily accessible through conscious choice. Its structure and function is also vulnerable to excess stress. However, more 'primitive', automatic, memory systems are functional and, in the absence of mature systems that add reason to recall, these dominate children's perceptions and behaviour.

Since the hippocampus provides essential links to areas of the left brain that put feelings into words, traumatised children are less able to create explicit verbal narratives that allow them to process, and put into perspective, past or present distressing experiences. Thus they are unable to self-regulate well or 'put it all behind them'. Early experiences are *'unrememberable'*, reflecting hippocampal immaturity, the absence of autobiographic recall and access to verbally based cognitive strategies, and simultaneously *'unforgettable'*, reflecting the dominance of 'hard-wired' automatic responses that form traumatic and non-verbal memories. This is understood to be the neurobiological basis for the distressing symptoms associated with post-traumatic stress disorders and syndromes (PTSD and PTSS).

Sensory neural pathways begin to be laid down in the womb: researchers are increasingly aware of the effects of sound, movement, touch, smell and taste on unborn babies. These stimulate the creation of networks of response pathways, making up the implicit (non-verbal) memory circuits that help infants become aware of, interpret and predict their environment. The amygdala of the mammalian limbic system also plays a large part in early infantile memories: adding emotional resonance and relevance to stored experiences and providing children with increasingly effective 'early warning, learning and survival kits'.

Why then do children need to know if they 'know' already? Simply put: every individual has 'layers of knowing' that correspond with the layers of the 'triune brain'. The 'reptilian' brain is concerned primarily with sensing and regulating basic body functions that keep us alive; it is an unconscious process. Knowledge, or learned experience, here is 'automatic'. The 'mammalian' brain is said to have evolved to provide animals with greater choice through increased emotional consciousness and opportunities for learning from experience. There is still little or no symbolic ('verbal') processing of information. Finally the neo-cortex of the 'human' brain provides a sophisticated layer of neural 'hardware' that permits intelligent, reasoned thought and action.

It is at the level of the neo-cortex that mature 'executive function' is evident in the appraisal, organisation and execution of tasks and the resolution of problems. Information between the two hemispheres of the brain is increasingly shared as neural pathways become highly integrated, providing a mature, holistic overview of the self and the environment. This 'cognitive leap' is intrinsically bound up with the development of language: as experience becomes translated into meaningful word symbols. Implicit knowledge can become explicit and truly 'known'. Trauma actively interrupts this developmental process, skewing neural pathways and interfering with mature reflective thought.

The 'knowing' of traumatised children is therefore predominantly at the levels of 'reptilian' and 'mammalian' functioning: that is at unconscious or sensory-emotional response levels. They see, hear, smell, touch, move about and feel the world in terms of their immature neurobiology and hence without 'the full facts'. Their capacity to feel safe in, and make coherent sense of, their world is dictated by their incomplete 'bottom-up' brain and nervous system development: their knowledge systems are 'stuck' at sub-optimal functioning levels. Hence helping children recognise and make sense of their unconscious processes allows them to 'know' and integrate their 'hidden knowledge', in order to develop more mature 'top-down' controls and truly begin to put the past behind them (see Figure 13).

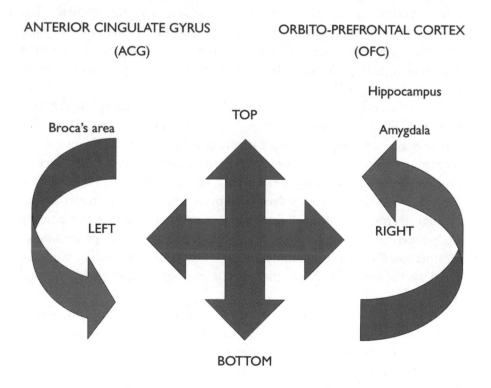

Figure 13: Brain development

How?

Much of our parenting programme is designed to 'bring on line' immature neurobiological systems, through providing repeated opportunities to 'revisit and redo' early parent–infant interactions that did not go well. In doing so adoptive parents consciously adopt a reflective stance that allows their child to see and feel themselves more fully (using the 'Jemima Crackit' model). Through 'right brain to right brain communications' they connect with their youngsters, allowing them to tap into parents' more mature information systems and to 'download' vital data. Simultaneously parents 'upload' information from their children that can be acknowledged, translated and fed back, to enhance 'top-down' thinking.

In children with painful histories there are often discrepancies between bottom-up experience and top-down knowledge that reflect interrupted attachment and development. Thus traumatised youngsters face 'double trouble': they have more than their fair share of sensory and emotionally based experience yet possess less than their fair share of reflective, cognitive and executive functioning capacities. Revisiting early history forms the essential cornerstone for improving children's bottom-heavy 'bio-feedback' processes. Children, literally, build up their knowledge base from their earliest experiences. Here, as they are helped to mature, learn more about the world and increasingly reflect on its meaning, they can interpret these experiences differently. This represents the transformation of a bottom-up developmental process into top-down self-awareness and self-control.

For parents, mentors and therapists, children's history provides the raw data from which they can crack the code of their puzzling thoughts and behaviour. They can then draw up 'lexicons' from which they can read, interpret and give meaning to these and begin to provide 'translations' for children. Without access to historical knowledge parents may be unable understand their child's puzzling behaviours or to sustain sufficient reflective insights for their youngsters to 'stick with them' through the process of healing disrupted attachments and setting development back on track.

For children, access to information about their earliest times can put essential images and words to life-scripts dominated by overwhelming and confusing feelings and sensations. It brings order and meaning to their chaos and muddles; replaces superficial control patterns with new, bearable realities and a newer language of understanding. It breaks down self-imposed barriers to knowing that evolved for survival but which now stand in the way of moving on and 'putting it all behind them'. It can be a painful, slow process of self-discovery that eventually leads to reflection, recovery and maturing self-control.

Who?

It is the adoptive parents of traumatised children who really need to know their youngsters' histories. Adopted youngsters are often terrified that their parents will 'find out the truth' about them and then reject them or treat them badly, just like previous caregivers. 'They wouldn't want me if they knew' thinking needs to be tackled head on with openness, acceptance and understanding. Adopters need time to get in touch with, and process, the pain and horror of their children's pasts with support and without their children present. They will then be in 'the right place' to share the 'knowing' with their youngsters: secrets, lies and fear can be transformed, bringing adoptive families closer and more able to 'speak the same language'.

Since adoptive parents are with their children day after day, they are best placed to do this on an intuitive, moment-to-moment basis, responding to current circumstances and making connections with past experiences. It is their continuous empathy, understanding and feedback that will help their youngsters make sense of their lives, build realistic personal narratives and gain greater top-down controls.

To do this confidently, adopters need the support and specialised knowledge of therapists, parent mentors and others skilled in 'real life story work', who can access files and give meaning to 'cold facts', 'suspicions' and 'maybes'. Their help in sharing this accumulated information first with parents and then together with their children, forms another essential facet of their work as practitioners: rendering the unspeakable 'language of trauma' audible and tangible.

What?

To help all practitioners, particularly adopters, undertake these tasks it is vital that they gain as much information as possible, preferably prior to placement. This should include:

- full details of the child's early life experiences, with special reference to the traumas he suffered in his first two to three years of life; ante and peri-natal history is also essential
- explanations of the physical, social, emotional and intellectual effects of these traumatic events

- clear accounts of when, how and why their child came into care
- number and duration of all placements, including moves and changes of caregivers, and partners, within the birth family
- reasons for each move within the care system
- behaviour problems on coming into care and those subsequently identified in foster placements
- current and proposed contact arrangements with birth family members and the likely impact on the child and adoptive family
- effective reparenting strategies to help adopters address current behaviours and repair the hurts of the past.

Caregivers need this information to help them communicate effectively with the child, avoid traumatic triggers and provide a safe and nurturing environment. For example, children who have been left alone for long periods may feel as if they are being abandoned again (and may in fact die) if adopters leave them for even short times, or are late to pick them up from school or friends' homes. They may respond with fear and anger or 'get in first' with rejection, withdrawal or self-harm. Parents alerted to their children's early experiences can help them make sense of their responses and practise knowing that they will not be abandoned or neglected, through repeated experiences of reliable and safe returns. Similarly where adoptive parents understand that their children communicate their distress by taking things, they can minimise their youngsters' opportunities to 'steal', by not leaving money around and making sure they feel 'filled up' with love.

Adopted children need to know that their adopters know 'everything' and will still be there for them. Where youngsters know that their caregivers know their struggles and are actively working towards helping them, they can feel emotionally 'held'. Parents will be less likely to blame and shame their children as they take more empathic approaches to help them deal with troubling issues. Youngsters can also be helped to blame themselves less and, unhindered by toxic shame, they can more readily accept their parents' support.

Hence sharing background information with adopters, from the outset, puts placements on a more open and honest footing and provides the basis for good working partnerships between caregivers, children and professionals, in order to meet the needs of these troubled young people more fully.

(The structure and function of the brain are also addressed in 'Basic building blocks of the brain' and 'Critical connections'.)

Puzzling pain responses

Babies' nervous systems are 'experience dependent': their body–mind systems develop according to their earliest experiences, mediated primarily through significant attachment relationships. Whilst common sense might tell us this would be true of social and emotional relationships, to accept this in terms of understanding pain reactions can feel like straining credulity. Surely pain is pain and little can be done to change that?

Now consider how parents instinctively cuddle, rock, sing to and jiggle their babies to soothe their pain; when faced with the bumps and aches of their increasingly mobile youngsters they automatically 'rub it better'. Animals and humans alike scratch at areas of intense itching, even if this leads to skin damage and pain itself. Without being aware of it, they are all tapping into a fascinating phenomenon of pain management known as 'gating'. At its simplest, the nervous system cannot respond to two simultaneous, differing stimuli: creating an alternative source of discomfort refocuses attention and reduces awareness of the original pain.

Emotional and cognitive strategies can also key into this internal pain management network, and block, or accentuate, the conscious sensation of pain. Infants react more or less to pain depending on their behavioural state: responding more when they are tired, hungry or highly alert than when sleeping, actively busy, or happily engaged with caregivers. There is also evidence that subjective 'pain thresholds' are lower in individuals who have experienced chronic sexual abuse. This suggests that pain responses are adversely altered by repeatedly raised stress levels, probably coupled with constant vigilance for further hurts.

Even in the womb, infants react to pain, tending to move away from painful stimuli. This automatic response persists in the way one might pull one's hand away rapidly from a hot surface and contributes to well-being and survival. However, the newborn baby is relatively helpless and still has a good deal to learn about hurting. His 'hotline' response when hurt is to communicate through intense, characteristic crying that frequently involves his whole body. In 'good enough' circumstances the caregiver plays her part in this biologically programmed 'duet' by tuning into her child, working out what is causing his distress and alleviating it swiftly. Acknowledging and responding to pain forms an active part of 'the dance of attunement and attachment' (see Figure 14) that leads to the development of healthy self-awareness.

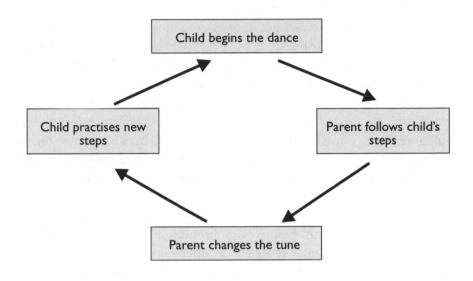

Figure 14: The dance of attunement and attachment

Over time parents become increasingly skilled at anticipating and recognising hurts and babies learn how to seek and accept comfort more effectively. Thus parents' initial responses to the discomfort of wet or soiled nappies, the cramps of an empty belly, muscle aches from remaining in one position, or heat and cold, play a major part in helping infants learn about and manage their bodies, including their reactions to painful experiences. Moreover, alongside their psychological input, caregivers provide infants' immature physiological systems with essential information that helps them establish sound 'feedback loops' and sufficient endorphin 'receptor sites' to facilitate future pain relief.

As part of the cycle of biochemical responses to distress there are specific 'biochemical messengers' that trigger the release of pain-relieving hormones known as endorphins. These 'in-house painkillers', as their name suggests, are part of a range of internally generated morphine-based compounds that modulate the emotional pain of separation and helplessness, as well as physical pain. It seems that subjective experience of body-based pain depends on the activation of areas involved with emotion and attention, rather than on specifically designated 'pain centres'. Endorphins, like morphine and heroin, are known to deactivate such areas.

So clearly, if caregivers are not responsive to their babies, cannot alleviate distress, or actively contribute to it, vital experiences of establishing healthy pain feedback loops are missed, especially those involving the orbito-prefrontal cortex (OFC) and anterior cingulate gyrus (ACG). Essential lessons in managing pain may be disrupted or distorted. Instead of 'having the pain sorted' to a greater or lesser extent, the maltreated youngster is left to deal with unresolved pain as best he can. He is likely to fall back on his next line of defence: his capacity to dissociate (shut off) the pain and his normal responses to it. This process involves the overproduction of endorphins and, once established, can be difficult to alter.

Infants cared for in incubators or subjected to painful medical interventions, and youngsters with chronic, painful conditions, such as irritable bowel syndrome, severe eczema or repeated ear infections, that prove difficult to manage or alleviate, may also use dissociation to manage their distress. This process, in turn, interferes with their perceptions of the world as a safe and comfortable place and inhibits or distorts developing attachment relationships, setting up a vicious circle of unresolved emotional pain and discomfort.

The puzzling patterns of pain response seen in many hurt children are readily understandable in terms of their histories of abandonment, neglect and abuse and the evolution of 'trauma feedback loops'. Such youngsters often complain repeatedly about tiny scratches and minor bumps but seem oblivious to more serious cuts, bruises or even breaks. They may not report severe sore throats or earaches, vomit without appearing to wake, or continue to wear tight-fitting shoes without complaint. It can also put them at additional risk of self-harm and in dangerous situations where rapid response to pain is vital.

An awareness of developmental attachment processes and dissociative trauma responses can make sense of many puzzling over- and under-reactions to pain. Without sufficient co-regulation from the parental attachment figure, the child is not only unable to modulate his painful emotions but also his painful bodily sensations. He will remain 'out of sync' with others and himself and will lack the essential capacity to find 'a happy medium' in his body's responses. When pain becomes unbearable he will resort to dissociation: numbing out the hurts, just as he managed the physical hurts of his early childhood in order to survive. However, when the youngster feels 'minor' pain he is likely to experience this as a major hurt: he then 'over-reacts' and may come across as a hypochondriac. Adoptive parents therefore need help to explore ways of interacting with their children that develop healthier feedback loops and foster equilibrium.

Letter to the Lee family

Dear Gill and James

It is clear that Sharon doesn't always seem to recognise pain or respond appropriately. Carrie, on the other hand, tends to 'do hypochondria' for even the slightest bump or scratch. It's likely that both behaviour patterns come from the same experience of not having had their hurts, or needs, recognised and met consistently in their early years, yet they've learned to cope quite differently. The therapeutic parenting approach you will need to take is, however, similar for both.

Try to offer the girls as much empathy as you can muster (or otherwise fake!) for every little hurt, even though it can feel irritatingly 'attention seeking' at times. It can really help to 'decode the language of trauma' here, so that we can reframe these interactions as 'attention needing': since the children are both, in their own ways, telling us 'I need someone to look after me the way it should have been when I was a baby'. You might choose to remind them of this gently, empathising as much as you can and even wishing you'd been there to 'get it right'.

Taking the initiative and responding sympathetically and enthusiastically also gives you more sense of control, as you're choosing to be proactive, rather than being drawn into reacting. It's almost impossible to control or change children's behaviour. However, it can be remarkably simple to select and control your interactions with children, so that as they join 'the dance of attunement' they change their patterns of behaviour too.

Exaggerated demonstrations of care work very well for both patterns of behaviour, so get in copious supplies of creams, plasters and small bandages and start practising your 'magic kiss' and 'rubbing it better' routines. (Don't forget to 'check for healing' next day and then congratulate the girls on their 'good work on healing'.) Remember that kisses and cuddles can be the best medicine and could be particularly significant for Carrie, who often avoids physical contact. Don't be afraid that all this attention to little hurts will make the girls even more demanding: once they've had enough care and attention they'll be able to let go of the unhelpful behaviours and get on with their lives.

It could be very useful for you to wonder outloud 'what is really hurting' Carrie when she's making a big fuss and there's little evidence of any current hurt. Helping children make sense of their actions in terms of their past hurts is an essential part of their healing. You've now learned enough about the neglectful and inconsistent parental care both children received as babies to translate their 'trauma behaviour' for them. Knowing that you know, and that you care, will help Sharon and Carrie feel 'heard' and increasingly to 'listen to themselves', with your ongoing help.

Sharon will need some additional help learning to acknowledge pain and saying 'ow', with you modelling an exaggerated response for her until she begins to make the connections herself. In addition, consider installing baby monitors to help you 'be there' for Sharon if she vomits without waking during the night. Practising shouting for help together would also be valuable here. The message you're aiming for is 'I'll take care of you and give you what you really need'.

Try 'bumping yourself', and asking for help too: to show Sharon what you do when you hurt yourself or feel ill. When possible, work as a team, so that one parent actively takes care of the other. The additional message you are aiming for here is 'we look after ourselves well too'.

In addition you could introduce games with teddies and dolls that involve bandaging, looking after and making better. This allows the girls to get the idea at one step removed, as long as you're around to show them how to give good care. Puppets and pets could be helpful here. I've recently found a book for young children, called *Kiss It Better* by Jan Ormerod, that could be fun and very useful. It is a sticker book with a story that involves finding the right adhesive plasters (provided on the back page) to put on the right body parts of various toys, and could help the girls learn more about their own bodies and see how 'good parents' look after their children. Let me know if you'd like to borrow it.

Good luck and happy healing!

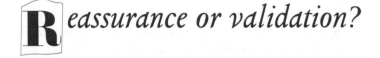eassurance or validation?

Imagine the scene: your adopted child comes home from school upset because someone has teased him for being adopted. Think of occasions when your child has told you she has no friends, is 'bad', unlovable or ugly. Your first response, like that of most caring parents, is to reassure your child that being adopted means they have been 'specially chosen' and are certainly not 'bad, unlovable or ugly'. Similarly you may respond to your child's friendship difficulties with helpful advice about how to get along better with peers. These responses are intended to be helpful and to reassure your child: indeed they may do so at times. However, providing reassurance may have a very different meaning to children who are struggling to make sense of why they were adopted, or to develop a sense of self-worth.

By the time children reach the age of eight years they begin to have a fuller sense of what adoption means. Yes, they may be special to their adoptive parents, yet adoption also means that their birth parents did not keep them with them, or keep them safe. At this stage youngsters are beginning to recognise this and to wonder why they were adopted. Even for the most secure adopted children this can pose a crisis of confidence in who they are and in their relationships with their adoptive parents. How much more difficult this must be for children who have been traumatised by abuse or neglect and who have a very fragile sense of themselves as worthwhile. In these situations reassurance frequently does not work: instead of feeling reassured, the child feels 'unheard'. Your reassurance that you love your child just as much as if he had been born to you is about your feelings and not your child's. It is about your understandable attempts to protect you and your child from pain.

Instead of seeking to reassure your child, it would be better to validate his feelings. For example, give your child 'permission' to talk about what it feels like to live in a family into which he was not born. You may wish to give the child who tells you he is 'bad' opportunities to talk about why he feels he is 'bad' or to empathise with how awful it must be to believe you are unlovable. Remember that giving your child permission to talk about how he feels is not to agree with him: it is to empathise with his difficulties and give him a chance to share these with you.

Your next step may be to wonder outloud (or in conversation with your partner or a good friend) how you can help your child know he is special, lovable, beautiful, even when he does not feel this way. This would be the time to tell your child you know he is lovable and that you will hold onto that belief until he is able to 'own' it himself. This gives him the message that you know he is struggling but, with your help, he can begin to feel better about himself.

Acceptance and validation of feelings, getting alongside your child and holding onto the belief that he can 'do it differently', contribute to an empathetic approach that is actually far more reassuring and actually helps the youngster feel heard and less alone with his feelings. It is a vital step on the road to healing!

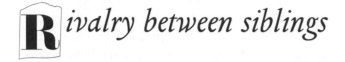ivalry between siblings

Whether two or more youngsters are placed in an adoptive family together, or placed individually into an existing family with children, the issues with which they struggle may be similar. Where children have lived together through abuse and neglect they may have had to compete for scarce caregiving, food, space or toys, or try to care for or protect younger siblings, sometimes to their own disadvantage. Siblings placed from the same family may thus be united by strong trauma bonds that can interfere with the formation of healthier relationships and keep children in old behaviour patterns. In addition, many adopted children are extremely needy, requiring a great deal of patience, attention and love from their parents to heal from their early experiences of abuse and neglect. They struggle to feel special and believe that time and attention given to one sibling means less love for them. Troubled youngsters may resort to aggressive or threatening behaviour towards siblings, or adults, to feel more in control or try to get what they need in 'manipulative' or indirect ways. Dealing with these daily internal battles between siblings can be an immensely daunting task for adopters.

Received wisdom in childcare has been that siblings from the same family are best placed together, since they have already lost so much and should be spared the further loss of family members. Adoptive parents, too, feel that children should be placed together, recognising that a sibling might be the only consistent person in a child's life and that breaking that bond would increase the trauma for both children. Most also feel that siblings will be companions for each other, making the task of parenting easier. In reality many adoptive families find that caring for a sibling group compounds each child's difficulties and makes parenting more complex and stressful. Despite their best efforts to be fair, adopters can feel torn apart by perpetual niggles from their youngsters about 'unfairness' and their resulting hurtful, and sometimes sneaky, interactions. Having to count the number of chips put out on each plate can become mind-numbingly exhausting. Here it is, indeed, a case of 'the total being more than the sum of the parts', where one child's difficult behaviour is likely to trigger dysfunctional patterns in another.

Traumatised children bring into their new families the working models of life they learned in their birth families. They may use these to re-interpret the love of their adopters as abusive, or parents' attention to a sibling as rejection. Siblings may cling tenaciously to shared behaviour patterns and ways of understanding the world, encouraging their brothers and sisters to do so too. Since these shared patterns of thinking and behaving are constant reminders of the past, they can increase children's struggles with feeling secure in new families. In addition, some siblings may show specific behaviour patterns, such as the 'parentified' child's need to take care of younger siblings, which interfere with opportunities to practise being children themselves. Being part of a sibling group can frequently make the task of learning the new 'language of love' more difficult. Hence adoptive parents of sibling groups may not only have to parent each child, but also parent 'a family within a family'. An understanding of these complex issues is essential if parents are to enable their children to feel sufficiently loved and safely contained to let go of their old, unhelpful patterns.

Letter to the Ponting family

Dear Grace and Peter

Justin's behaviour gives us many clues to what he understands about the world, drawn from his early childhood experiences of neglect and, at the very least, witnessing violence at home. In addition he experienced painful medical procedures in his first month of life and several changes in foster care placements before he reached six months.

These experiences would have led to Justin feeling:

- that the pain of continual hunger would never end
- that parents abandon you
- panic that he was helpless and alone
- that he would not be heard when he indicated his needs
- anger that his needs were not being met
- that he was not good enough to be kept safe
- that he was not special to anyone

- that the way to deal with feelings was to become angry and aggressive.

I do understand that Justin has been a difficult child to parent and that he resists parental control. This makes sense when we consider that as a baby Justin learned that it wasn't safe to rely on adults and that being dependent led to being neglected and abandoned. He has felt the need to 'fight his corner' all the way.

I imagine the introduction of Juliet into Justin's life will have re-awakened these early feelings and strengthened his determination to 'do battle'. Justin is scared he's going to be abandoned again and is reverting to the response patterns he developed as a baby. This is most probably why he behaves so badly towards Juliet: he is *afraid* rather than *angry*. Sadly, Justin knows no other way to express feelings except through anger and, as you know, living with an angry child is extremely challeng-ing, especially when they're hurting another child you've brought into your family and you're cast in the unenviable role of 'referee'.

Keeping this in mind, our plan aims to help Justin change the percep-tions, expectation and responses he learned when living with his birth mother, and subsequently in foster care. This means gently challenging his thinking and behaviour, saying for example:

- 'I can see why having a sister might mean you feel we'd love you less. I guess we need more practice together!'
- 'I wonder where you could have learned you weren't special?'

Justin needs to be warmly and regularly congratulated on managing to survive in a scary environment, preferably *before* you deal with any difficult behaviour, so you don't jeopardise his fragile self-esteem. You could say:

- 'I can really understand why you think that if Juliet gets something, you lose.'
- 'Someone must have hurt you a lot when you were a baby, to make you want to get your own back on Juliet like this. I'm so sad for you both.'

However, Justin also needs to know *you* can take control and set firm boundaries when he's 'losing it'. Remind him of the 'zero tolerance on hurting people' in your family we discussed around his aggressive and angry behaviour before exploring ways of helping Justin 'practise' new ways of coping, remembering that actions, especially shared ones, will reinforce your words:

- 'I can help you learn you don't need to swear in this family in order to be heard. Let's practise whispering to each other.'

- 'I don't like to see you hurting like this. At least I can give you both lots of hugs now.'

- 'You were so good at taking care of yourself in your birth family. Now you need help to learn that it's safe for me to take care of *you*. Let me do that for you for now!'

- 'I wonder how I can help you know you're just as special now that Juliet is living here? Here's a hug for my favourite boy!'

- 'I know you find it really hard to know that I love you when I'm giving Juliet attention. Give me ten minutes, then *we* can do something together. You choose!'

- 'You need to practise knowing I can love you even when I'm giving Juliet attention. I've made you a special tape, let's put it on.'

- 'Are you forgetting I'm a parent who can love two children at once?'

- 'I can see old feelings coming. Let's see if we can put them where they belong.'

- 'Boy, you look angry! My guess is you're scared that I don't love you any more. Can we talk about this whilst we jog round the garden?'

- 'Ding, ding, end of Round 1! Contestants to their corners whilst the referee takes a break!'

You could use these kinds of statements in many difficult situations, or even pre-emptively if you anticipate that Justin's going to find something difficult. Some additional useful ones are:

- 'I know it's difficult for you when I give Juliet attention. I'm going to spend a couple of minutes with Juliet now, so you can practise managing those difficult feelings whilst I'm around.'

- 'I'll give you a cuddle now to help you to know I still love you whilst I'm sorting Juliet out'.

- 'I know you find it difficult to share your sweets with Juliet. Won't it be great when you feel good enough about yourself to share?'

Since some of Justin's behaviour at school seems to be connected with feelings of abandonment and not getting his needs met, talking directly to Justin about this could help him make sense of his reactions:

- 'I think you're forgetting I'll still be here when you come home from school.'
- 'I'd find it really difficult to believe that my parents would come back if I had a mum who went out and left me.'

Adding non-verbal messages could help reinforce this. Try slipping a photo of you into Justin's school bag, or popping a short loving note (and a chocolate heart) into his lunch box.

In addition, regular use of cradling with each child at home could help both youngsters feel 'filled up' with the 'good baby and toddler' experiences that were lacking in their birth family. Being physically close to Justin and Juliet as they get in touch with their 'infantile rage' also gives them powerful non-verbal messages of acceptance and comfort that should gradually allow them to let go of their 'life or death' battles with each other for 'scarce resources': your love and safe containment. Making time and space to do this with each child will be challenging but will make family life much less fraught and more enjoyable.

Remember that cradling, as for all these strategies, will not be effective if you're feeling upset or angry. Give yourself time to become calm and feel empathetic and *sad for* the struggles Justin (and Juliet) had, and still have. Be ready to show them you're ready to 'fight their corner' with them now, whilst being 'firm but fair'. Accompany this with the wish (out loud) that you could have been there to take care of both of them when they were babies. The main aim is for you (and not the children) to be in control of the emotional atmosphere in your home.

Go for it and good luck!

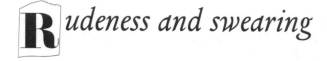Rudeness and swearing

Many adoptive parents live with children who express their feelings in unacceptable ways. One of the hardest of these for many parents is the child who regularly uses disrespectful language, including swearing. This not only causes embarrassment, particularly in public, it also threatens much of what adoptive parents feel is central to family life: the right for all family members to expect respect and consideration from each other.

Of course the adopted child may well have learned a very different set of values. Instead of respect, the abused or neglected child will have learned from experience that he was not worthy of respect and that his needs had little or no value to his caregivers. As a result, the child may fear adult control, seeing this as potentially threatening. Subsequently if he becomes aware that his adoptive parents are readily embarrassed or upset by rudeness this may become a valuable means of covering his fear and of maintaining control within the family.

Repeated rudeness or swearing is likely to create a family environment of anger: a scenario all too familiar to the maltreated child, whose mind and body is likely to have been adaptively 'programmed' to manage and survive an angry and chaotic milieu. Strangely this will feel more familiar, and therefore 'safer', than the calm atmosphere his adoptive parents are trying to create: consequently struggling adopters often get sucked into anger as a way of trying to reduce their child's anti-social behaviours. While understandable this is rarely effective: rather it is likely to exacerbate the behaviours, lead to increasing levels of anger and frustration and decreasing levels of real communication and connection. Others may get caught in a spiral of helpless frustration that equally inhibits effective interactions and reflects their children's hidden desperation, rather than their 'up front' coping strategies.

Parents need to approach these issues with the objective eye of the bemused detective (Columbo or Clousseau can be fun here) in order to pick out the underlying messages in their child's 'difficult' behaviour. For some youngsters swearing and rudeness is quite literally their 'mother tongue': the everyday language of their birth family. They will need lots of practice in the 'foreign country' of their adoptive family to pick up the colloquial expressions in more common usage there. As ever, it is important to remember such children are likely to revert to their 'first language' when upset or tired, long after they've adopted the more acceptable language of their new family.

Alternatively, abusive language is a powerfully direct way of communicating overwhelming feelings, particularly for youngsters who lack self-regulation and emotional literacy. Some youngsters may capitalise on the negative emotions they can induce in caregivers and unconsciously or consciously exploit this to their 'advantage'. Clearly, different constellations of strategies are needed for each child, depending on how it feels to the adopters, as they tune into his outspoken, yet largely unspoken, needs. However, the underlying understanding, interpretation and translation of the language of their youngster's behaviour should underpin all their responses. Thus caregivers should primarily aim to address their child's attempts to communicate and connect, rather than the behaviour itself.

Letter to the Gillespie family

Dear Hazel and Colin

Here are some suggestions for managing Martin's rudeness and swearing. As usual it's important to try to understand why this feels particularly distressing for you and to work out the underlying reasons for Martin's behaviour.

You're not alone in feeling horrified when Martin swears and calls you a 'silly idiot' particularly when you're out in public: swearing and rudeness creates major problems in many adoptive families. Few of us were brought up in families where swearing and rudeness were acceptable means of communicating with our parents and most of us had enough respect to abide by their reasonable rules about 'strong' language. Naturally, when we adopt children we have reasonable expectations that they have similar levels of consideration for us and will be polite and respectful. Instead it often feels that they are hell bent on defying and 'dissing' us. Moreover, the more we try to encourage them to be polite, and the more upset we become when they swear at us, the worse our children's attitude and behaviour seem to become.

Try to begin with the premise that it is not possible to stop children swearing and being rude by reasoned discussion, discipline, anger or punishment. Children who've been traumatised by early abuse and neglect are unlikely to show respect or accept reasonable rules when they move into adoptive families, where there are often very different ways of relating to each other than in their birth families. You'll also need to accept that asking Martin to be polite and explaining the reasons why this is important is unlikely to be effective. It seems that Martin knows in principle what you expect, yet continues to act as if he doesn't care: indeed this seems to strengthen his need to act out the behaviours you are trying to change.

It's important to remember that needing to feel in control is the fundamental reason for Martin's swearing and rudeness. He knows you don't like swearing and is using strong language to try to make you angry and gain an illusory sense of control. It's therefore important for you to try hard not to become angry, or at least not to respond in angry ways to Martin when he's rude. Responding in fun ways is often much more helpful: it not only reduces conflict and adrenalin levels but could also assist Martin to develop healthier brain and nervous system patterns.

Swearing and rudeness can be understood as (unconscious) learned responses. Martin is familiar with swearing because this was the language he was used to hearing in his birth family. We've talked already about how, in situations of stress, traumatised children resort to earlier patterns of behaviour. Rudeness and swearing are therefore Martin's 'first language': the language he still associates with feeling insecure and scared. I know it's very hard, in the face of an abusive verbal onslaught, to see this as indicating that Martin is, at heart, feeling panicky and unsafe. However, it's important that you hold onto this awareness and acknowledge this to Martin in calm, accepting ways.

Having identified the underlying reasons for Martin's behaviour you can then create opportunities for him to practise letting you know he is frightened in different ways. Don't worry if Martin denies feeling fear or insecurity, or tells you he's swearing because you're an awful parent. Your goal isn't to get Martin to agree with you but to maintain emotional control of the situation by reminding yourselves of the reasons for Martin's behaviour and helping him learn a healthier emotional and behavioural language.

Using rude or foul language may also relate to Martin's deepest feelings about himself. Children who have been maltreated don't feel good about themselves and frequently have unrealistic or distorted perceptions of their situation. Feeling intrinsically bad, they tend either to blame themselves for past hurts, or project unacceptable feelings about their birth families onto their adoptive families. As a result of their muddled thinking, their behaviour can appear quite contradictory.

A child who is frequently disrespectful paradoxically sees himself as deserving of abuse or neglect. We see this in the way Martin destroys his own possessions during upsetting outbursts and in the way he 'blows it' after a nice day out with you. His swearing is yet another way he has of letting you know he's feeling 'nasty, dirty and horrible' deep inside. Martin needs you to recognise this for him and help him make sense of his confusing feelings and actions.

Begin by telling Martin you're pleased he's letting you know how awful he's feeling about himself, yet sad he feels that way. You can then hope out loud that he'll begin to feel good enough about himself to use your family's 'language of choice', to avoid so many misunderstandings. You may have to remain Martin's 'external simultaneous translator' ('Jemima Crackit') for some time, especially when he's under pressure. Remember, the more you can 'play' with these situations the better you'll survive them!

'Beating them at their own game' can be a good motto to adopt when tackling verbal abuse and swearing in *older* children who appear 'to do it deliberately' – though hopefully working on this issue *now* will make it a thing of the past for Martin by then.

(For a teenager you could choose to practise the 'language skills' you're learning from your teen when he has friends round to the house. He's likely to be shocked and surprised by this, as his expectation will be that you wouldn't behave unreasonably. Similarly you could use peer pressure by asking your son's friends to explain the meaning of something unpleasant he's said to you. It would be important for the adolescent to get a sense that you're laughing with him, rather than at him, which could send him plummeting into intense shame – and further foul-mouthed outbursts!)

Some shock tactics could still be appropriate (and fun) now, as long as you feel comfortable with them and can sustain your playful approach:

- Suggest you need Martin to be as rude as possible because you'd really like to learn this 'amazing skill', so you can decide whether to use it with his friends and acquaintances. This might be helpful if you don't wish to go all out for a public rendition of Martin's swearing repertoire.

- Another 'fun' approach to Martin's foul-mouthed behaviour would be to act the bemused innocent. Here it's vital to set the right tone: in your body language and facial and verbal expression: avoiding anger, frustration or criticism. Then your response might be any or all of the following:

  ○ 'That's an interesting way to see me!'

  ○ 'I'm not sure I'm physically capable of doing that.'

- 'Oh, thank you for telling me how much you love me!'

- 'I'd really like to hear more of this. Why don't you practise for the next ten minutes while I have a cup of tea, then I'll give you my full attention.' You'll be in a better place to 'hear' Martin after your tea break.

- 'I'm not listening … la, la, la. Let me know when you've finished!' in a singsong voice, whilst sticking your fingers in your ears dramatically and pulling funny faces. Make it clear you're prepared to listen to non-abusive language as soon as Martin is ready.

- Put on the radio to drown out rude comments. After five minutes ask politely, 'Were you trying to say something to me?' Ignoring foul language can be just the right thing in some situations, providing you do so overtly, emphasising that you are choosing not to listen at this point – otherwise Martin is likely to react by 'saying it louder and longer'.

- 'This is Martin-speak for "I love you Mum"', if Martin is rude to you in front of your friends taking the sting out of these remarks and putting you swiftly back in the driving seat.

- 'Hang on, I don't understand the meaning of that. Wait until I get the dictionary or thesaurus.' Discuss other (politer) words he might consider using and suggest you practise these together.

- 'Can I have that in writing please? I need time to think about it.' You could even offer to be Martin's scribe: again putting you firmly back in control of the interaction.

- 'Cows can't cook burgers: that would be cannibalism', when next Martin requests junk food, or 'Cows don't drive. Have you ever seen a driver with an udder and horns?' This might mean you're not able to drive Martin to his friend's house next time he asks. Avoid using this for trips – such as to school – these should remain non-negotiable.

Other effective suggestions to consider are:

- Asking Martin to repeat his words louder, giving him a timescale for this – say, the next five minutes. Use your watch to laboriously time how long he is able to be rude to you and feign disappointment if he's unable to keep up his tirade for as long as you suggested, wondering playfully if he'll be able to manage it next time.

- Mirroring his outspoken language, either louder or softer, every time he calls you names, or repeat as an echo. As always, playfully engaging with deliberately challenging behaviour reduces its impact and gives you back the essential upper hand.

- Acknowledging and genuinely empathising with how bad Martin must be feeling right now. Further rudeness in response could be countered with a gentle but matter-of-fact 'That certainly seems to have hit the mark' that could set him thinking.

- One of you calling the other 'a silly idiot' and then being sent to your room 'in disgrace'. This could be especially helpful if you need a short break from Martin! Subsequently a brief comment to Martin should simply confirm that 'we shouldn't speak like that to anybody!'

- Recording and playing back (at a quiet time of your choosing) one of Martin's swearing outbursts. It's very difficult for children to 'hear' what they sound like when they are out of control. Youngsters are often amazed at how they sound. If handled sensitively this might just motivate Martin to think about the words he's using next time he feels like swearing.

- More pleasantly, and good fun, trying to ask Martin for more 'c' words – providing some yourself. Keep yours as silly-sounding or inappropriate as you can (cantankerous or crustacean for example)! Enjoy yourself here and try to draw Martin into the fun – a friendly tickle or some rough and tumble play could interrupt the pattern further.

- Finding some flattering 'c' or 'f' words to counteract the unflattering ones Martin tends to use and having some fun listing them out loud. Try 'charming, cute, cuddly, creative, crucial, caring' or 'feisty, funny, fantastic, friendly, free-spirited' for starters!

- Sending amusing texts to Martin's phone. He won't be able to resist opening them, so you'll interrupt his flow. Hopefully it'll make him laugh and further defuse his scared or angry feelings.

- Devising an outlandish 'armour' and making an exaggerated play of putting it on, to 'protect you' from the hurtful words. The more ridiculous you look the more effective you could be at changing your negative feelings into positive ones: Martin could well follow suit!

However, the best 'armour' for verbal aggression, as for its physical counterpart, is to act with confidence and refuse to allow yourself to be hurt. Remind yourself that Martin's comments are not directed at you personally: they're part of the 'survival pattern' he learned as a baby, when he felt so unsafe and out of control. The aim of all of your strategies is, therefore, to give Martin ample opportunities to experience parental control in ways that aren't so overwhelming that they trigger even more extreme responses from him. Gradually, by practising that it's OK for you to be in firm, loving control in your family, Martin will be provided with essential 'reprogramming' experiences and will need to resort less to his unhealthy behaviour patterns to remain in control.

As Martin tends to be more openly disrespectful to Hazel it could help him to see Colin 'protecting' her. For example, Colin could go across to Hazel, put his arm round her and say (dramatically!) 'Well, I think you're the greatest mother I've met!' This will challenge Martin's perceptions, without getting you hooked into responding in the ways he expects such as arguments, anger, punishment, being sent away – all of which formed part of his earliest experiences.

Another invaluable strategy is to do something good for each other, or yourself: buy a big bunch of flowers, or a box of chocolates (just for you!), or devise some other treat. This will give Martin the important, non-verbal message that you believe you are special and worthy of better treatment and simultaneously help you to feel better and more valued.

Verbal aggression often leads to physical aggression, since children's behaviour is an attempt to let us know how they're feeling, or thinking. So, try to 'jump the gun' whenever possible by picking up the early signs of hurt and rage and addressing them right away. Saying something like 'I can see this is very hard for you right now' and showing real understanding and empathy through sympathetic body language, including touch, and your caring tone of voice can sometimes be enough to relieve the tension, especially if you're able to wonder out loud what is bothering Martin. You'll usually have a good idea of what is going on; if you're wrong, no doubt he'll set you straight! Either way this creates a 'win–win' situation.

Finding ways of dealing with Martin's underlying distress, be it sadness, terror or rage, in shared ways is also essential. As a baby Martin didn't learn how to calm down or cheer himself up because there wasn't consistent, 'good enough' parenting to help him identify and manage his feelings. If you're able to give him some of these experiences now he'll benefit enormously: he should even learn to regulate his own upsets eventually! Doing something physically strenuous together is particularly valuable, whether it's kicking up leaves, washing the car, making (and eating!) bread or cakes, tickling sessions, or rough and tumble play, dancing wildly or singing crazily at the top of your voices. You know best what would work for you!

Along with this work of helping Martin to practise co-regulation and relinquishing some control of the emotional atmosphere in the family, Martin needs to experience some of the consequences of his behaviour. Always use consequences with masses of empathy, to avoid appearing punitive, and take your time, to put yourselves back in firm but fair control.

I know Martin has difficulty with peers and that you've been working to encourage him to invite friends home to help him develop a friendship circle. While I appreciate that it's important for Martin to have friends you might need to curtail his involvement if he repeatedly swears at you in front of them. Here it's important to remember to be sad that his behaviour has meant he can't invite a friend home for tea and to remind Martin he'll have other opportunities to have friends home when he's shown you he can manage this well. Remind yourselves that these budding friendships won't last long if Martin's behaviour is offensive to his peers – and that he doesn't need the kind of 'friends' who do find it acceptable!

As Martin loves trips to the cinema with you both, perhaps he could miss a trip (or two) to the cinema on Saturdays if he hasn't been able to show you, through his behaviour during the week, that he can manage this safely. Expressing concern that you don't want him banned from the cinema officially should provide the correct level of consequences and empathy for his difficulties. Don't yield to entreaties that he'll 'behave' when you go out, or enter into discussions about whether certain words or behaviours are likely to result in being banned. The former will give Martin the message that he doesn't really need to alter unacceptable behaviours; the latter will deflect the focus of the discussion from your empathetic understanding of Martin's difficulties to one where you are justifying your position. I'm sure you can see how this would immediately put you on the defensive and Martin in the driving seat.

I know you want to show Martin how pleased you are when he's 'been good' but if he 'sabotages' your efforts no one gains, least of all Martin. Keep your praise low key and linked to particular behaviours such as 'good work on helping me clear up. I enjoyed having you around this afternoon', or 'great job! You haven't sworn at me for ten minutes. Come here, I want to give you a hug!'

Many traumatised kids don't really believe they deserve good things, and can't cope with the associated feelings of excitement or pleasure. Expecting something 'bad' to happen next, they 'take control' by doing something 'bad' themselves, which 'proves' they were right all along (that they are 'all bad' and deserve the 'bad' things that happen.) Keeping 'rewards' small and contingent helps you get round this and lets you slip in some positive messages that Martin can handle.

I hope this will give you some ideas for tackling Martin's swearing and rudeness. Remember only to choose strategies with which you feel comfortable and to use them with empathy rather than ridicule. Martin needs to know you understand why he struggles and that you're trying to help him manage life better. This can be a particular challenge when dealing with swearing and rudeness, where it's easy to slip into anger, sarcasm or contempt.

It's also important to have a range of strategies, which you can use 'randomly', since this allows you to alter your responses to Martin in the most helpful way. It will allow you to begin to alter the balance of control in the house and give Martin opportunities to experience that parental control doesn't have to be overwhelming or frightening. On the contrary, you'll be providing a secure structure within which Martin can really begin to feel safely contained and genuinely loved.

Good luck! Don't expect miracles but believe you can make a difference and that by changing what you do, you're helping Martin change for the better too!

Self-regulation (managing arousal)

Children of Matt's age (five years) who have 'good enough' experiences of nurture and structure with their caregivers are beginning to manage their sensory and emotional feelings for themselves. They have had their needs met consistently enough to trust that this will go on happening as and when they need. They have 'got a handle' on some of their feelings and have found healthy enough ways of managing upsets, so that tantrums are becoming things of the past. If things get too much for them they feel they can turn to their caregivers and rely on them for additional comfort and support.

Maltreated children, on the other hand, still lack the fundamental ability to manage their arousal: their physical and emotional feelings often threaten to overwhelm them and they have learned they cannot rely on others to help them when they are distressed. Instead, in order to get by, they have developed unhealthy patterns of relating and of meeting their needs. They have evolved patterns of self-soothing that work up to a point: including rocking, head-banging, poking and picking, repetitive rituals, chattering, being noisy and 'keeping busy'. Some rely on desperately clingy or compliant behaviour to stay close, whilst others use hyperactive or threatening behaviour to feel safe.

Although these were all ways that helped traumatised children survive in maltreating birth families, they are much less appropriate or effective in their adoptive families. Adhering to their behavioural 'first language' gets in the way of good communication and often inhibits the development of healing attachment relationships. The 'first words' traumatised children therefore need to practise with their new parents are the first steps of non-verbal comfort and gesture. As for tiny babies, repeated experiences of having their needs met reliably encourages healthier modulation of arousal and begins to provide an integrated inner structure for the child's perceptions, thinking and behaviour.

Below we explore co-regulation for Matt: in particular how this relates to his prolonged bouts of screaming. (See also 'Emotional outbursts'.)

Letter to the McGrath family

Dear Josie and Freddy

The important 'ingredients' you'll need, to establish real communication through the 'language of love', are comforting physical touch, tender facial expressions, soft voice tones and non-threatening gestures. This is the 'motherese' mums and dads use with babies, almost instinctively. It's less intuitive to do this with five-year-olds, as we expect to relate to them in more 'grown-up' ways. However, I feel sure you're courageous enough to give it a go. Add in as much other 'baby play' as you can, including rocking, singing, dancing around, personal hygiene tasks and feeding, as these will all provide further essential, shared sensory input.

I know Matt finds this nurturing part very hard at times. However, we also know he's able to accept 'permission' from Lucy to join in 'baby games': you can use this subtly to great advantage. At other times you could talk to Matt about how hard he finds it to be little and playful, or to cuddle in with you. Make sense of this for him in terms of his tough time in his birth family and express real sadness you weren't there for him then. Go on to remind him that 'we can practise together right now' and that 'you're never too old for hugs'.

Be ready to acknowledge any resistance as understandable but sad, playfully letting him know he's telling you he needs even more cuddles and hugs! Equally important is the organising structure and safe containment you provide. Here again there's likely to be some active, or passive, resistance, so be prepared and don't show your disappointment or hurt.

Try making a game of 'catching Matt' if he starts moving away, or rubbing his forehead to 'switch on his hug button': but be ready to back off if you feel he really cannot cope with this. Then you can take charge for him: letting him know you can see he's struggling and that you'll save up your cuddles until later. You may find that singing nursery rhymes or reading stories to Lucy (leaving a welcoming space on the other knee for Matt) brings him back, once the pressure is off. Be as low-key and accepting as you can, so as not to panic him or cause him to 'shut down'.

Using these strategies alongside your own ability to self-soothe and manage arousal, you can actively provide co-regulation for Matt. This 'Jemima Crackit' approach also models mature self-regulation for Matt. As you become increasingly familiar with Matt's 'language' it will feel easier to make good choices for him that help him manage his chronic levels of distress and provide him with what he really needs.

Poor arousal and sensory regulation mean Matt frequently faces 'overload', reinforcing his perceptions of the world as hostile and frightening. Sensory integration problems often appear inconsistent: the child may sometimes tolerate things that 'do his head in' at other times. This can be understood in terms of 'total body load': when Matt is already tired or stressed the simplest of experiences may overwhelm him. At these times Matt relies on his 'primitive' survival strategies of 'fight and flight' (such as screaming or controlling-resistance), or 'freeze' (for example withdrawing, slowing his movements, avoiding contact and falling silent).

Let's consider Matt's screaming as a 'flight' response to the need to be cleaned up after soiling. Clearly Matt's already in extreme arousal at this point, so his sensory system is on 'red hot alert': remember how often he feels overheated when distressed. Sadly, just at the moment of greatest need for comfort, Matt is at his most sensitive to further tactile input. He just can't take more touch or closeness.

However difficult it seems, it's important to stay close and provide Matt with sensory input he can manage, so he begins to experience co-regulation with you and learns to modulate his distress. Although it might be tricky to offer cuddles at this stage, wrapping him in a towel could offer comfort Matt can tolerate.

Now create a mantra that focuses you on staying calm and avoid feeling hurt by Matt's rejection of your care. I find gently but firmly repeating aloud that 'it's my job to look after you and keep you safe' helps at times like these. It will not only re-affirm you're doing the right thing, despite Matt's vociferous challenges, but also allow him to 'hear' this.

As in everything, body language and tone of voice are paramount, alongside confidence in your own capabilities. You're speaking directly 'right brain to right brain' to Matt, which is the way mums and babies 'speak' initially and is predominantly non-verbal. However, that means you have to take extra care of what you say, as well as how you say it. 'I know' is a wonderful standby: short, sweet and to the point when said with genuine empathy!

Gradually you should get a sense that Matt is 'coming round' and feeling less highly aroused. Although this may take a great deal of time initially, it should pay long-term dividends, as you'll be 'rewiring' Matt's neural pathways, rewriting his inner 'road maps' of himself, relationships and his world and substituting the 'language of trauma' with the 'body language of love'. This would be the time to pop him in a bath and offer him the nurturing experiences we've already talked about.

It's probably not helpful to say much more until you sense Matt becoming less distressed. At that point he'll begin to be able to 'hear' you more easily. You could then begin to let him know what you think was going on for him and that you know how hard it is for him to feel safe or comfortable at times. Wondering out loud about possible triggers that set him off (good guesswork!) and about what Matt needs (more informed guesswork!) will acknowledge his struggles and hint that things can change. He'll then feel less alone, less helpless and hopeless and more able to connect with you (and with himself) in healthier ways.

Sometimes you may feel so stressed yourselves you need to manage your own arousal levels before trying to help Matt. Don't panic about 'Panicchio': just take time to reach 'the right place' to do a 'good Jemima Crackit job', using your inner 'thermostat' to regulate Matt's overheating and overworking system.

Keep up the good work and look after yourselves as much as you can!

ensory issues

Many children maltreated in their early years struggle to recognise and process sensory information. Whilst 'good enough' parents almost unconsciously provide a variety of manageable and interesting experiences for their babies through all their senses, abused children are frequently exposed to unpredictable or overwhelming sensory input that overloads their developing nervous systems. In addition, neglected youngsters often miss out on vital sensory stimulation during early windows of developmental opportunity, leaving them with poorly functioning systems.

Subtle patterns of behaviour that indicate under- or over-responsiveness in one or more of the sensory pathways can be recognised in toddlers and nursery-age children. For example, some find loud noises unbearable, covering their ears with their hands to reduce stimulation; others 'switch off' temporarily or create their own 'white noise', so that they no longer hear conversations or instructions. These behaviours can appear oppositional but came into being to help youngsters survive their overwhelming and frightening environment. By school age such sensory difficulties may be labelled 'poor attention span', 'hyperactive', 'impulsive', 'difficulties following instructions and sequencing', dyslexia, dyspraxia or dyscalculia. Children may additionally exhibit more general difficulties, such as handling peer relationships, personal space, 'free play' and socio-emotional interactions.

Difficulties with touch are common. Although a physically or sexually abusive family history is often linked to avoidance of touch, or excessive and inappropriate touch, other forms of maltreatment, particularly physical neglect, also have marked effects on children's tactile systems and their ability to accept or seek closeness. In such cases parents must be sensitive to children's sensory difficulties whilst providing them with ample opportunities to experience new sensations, in tolerable, small doses. They must work gently but firmly to break through their children's understandable resistance, to alter their unhealthy patterns of feeling and relating.

Difficulties with lighting and visual displays, unusual or unpleasant smells, lack of body awareness and discomfort from sudden changes in body position (including travel sickness) are other commonly described difficulties that relate to poor early sensory experiences. Parents often find their youngsters' tolerance of their external environment fluctuates with their internal environment and that the compensatory efforts their children develop to cope frequently exhaust them. This additional stress can itself be enough to cause them to 'decompensate' and regress developmentally at times.

As sensory difficulties often contribute to children's relationship and behavioural difficulties, they are referred to in many of the 'worked examples'. Here we discuss briefly Matt's sensory issues in relation to his screaming outbursts. Matt has difficulties with several senses: with the 'feel' of clothing, washing, rain or wind on his face, getting messy, close physical contact (touch), intense sunlight and 'busy visual environments' (vision), loud noises (sound) and sudden movements and coordination (proprioception and kinaesthesia). He also has a peculiar interest in unpleasant odours (smell). HANDLE UK provided expert assessment and guidance for his parents in addressing these difficulties.

Letter to the McGrath family

Dear Josie and Freddy

When you see Matt becoming agitated, wrap him in a small blanket or rough towel and sit as close as he'll allow. Most children gain more comfort from contact with these kinds of fabrics than from soft ones. This relates to the experience of deeper touch, which is calming to the nervous system, rather than light touch that is exciting or alerting. It also provides clear, safe containment for Matt when he's beginning to feel 'out of control' and will give him opportunities to calm down sooner, with your support.

Simultaneously, try to avoid further distress at times of heightened sensitivity by drawing the curtains, keeping the lighting low and reducing other visual input to a minimum. Turn the TV off! Do your best to keep auditory distractions down and perhaps put on a CD of calming music as soothing 'white noise'. Beware too of odours: you could use a blend of essential oils (like lavender) you know Matt is comfortable with, as the olfactory equivalent! Gentle rocking and something crunchy to chew or firm to suck on would provide additional soothing input.

Additionally, provide Matt with something soft and squeezable to stroke or hold (his 'fidget toy'). Gradually add some deep pressure touch, whether it's through pressing down firmly on Matt's shoulders or creating a 'boyburger-sandwich', with two large cushions as the 'bun', as he begins to 'let you in'.

Trust your judgement on this: you know Matt better than anyone and are 'on the spot'. Keep reminding yourself that whilst any, or all, of these suggestions could help, it's your presence that is the most important feature of the soothing interactions (providing sufficient co-regulatory experiences that eventually lead to self-regulation). Just as babies need someone close to feel secure and comfortable, so Matt desperately needs your closeness, however much he resists this initially. Be mindful, too, that Matt's sensory tolerance may fluctuate dramatically: then you'll avoid the pitfall of thinking 'he's doing it deliberately'.

A direct result of Matt's poor early attachment experiences is the disorganised nature of his sensori-motor system. Not having received the 'right' messages at the 'right time' about touch, taste, smell, sound, sight or movement, Matt remains over- (or under-) sensitive to many sensory experiences, often depending on general stress and fatigue levels. We see this in his responses to sunlight, wind, the feel of the shower, fidgeting with clothing, his rigid movements and his affinity for foul-smelling materials. He also has poor awareness of internal sensations, such as hunger and pain. The latter may contribute to his attempts to hurt himself.

Since lack of neural organisation is closely associated with poor modulation of arousal (self-regulation), working on managing Matt's sensory 'load' will not only help him feel more comfortable in the short term but also help his systems become organised and more 'in control' in the longer term: so the more 'good baby and toddler' times you can have together, the better. Snuggles, stories and opportunities for bottle-feeding can be very important here. Action songs and lullabies, controlled rough and tumble play and quiet times, soft cuddlies and big, ride-on toys, inside times and outside times are also invaluable to provide variety of input and improve Matt's sensory tolerance and arousal levels.

We can discuss enriching Matt's 'sensory diet' and managing his other sensory integration difficulties when next we meet, but remember it's your presence and support that will really help him 'digest and absorb' and feel more comfortable!

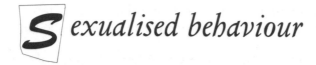 exualised behaviour

Many adoptive parents expect some sexual acting out from newly placed, older children. However, few are fully prepared for the diversity, intensity and bizarre nature of some of the behaviours: nor do they necessarily anticipate these behaviours in younger children, or from youngsters who have not previously been reported as displaying problems. In some cases this is reflected in the lack of openness and accuracy in case histories and in the support services available to children and their substitute families.

Despite discussions during the assessment and preparation phases, sexualised behaviour is a particularly difficult issue for most parents to feel comfortable about. In children it often feels like 'the hidden extra' no one is quite able to deal with, despite the vast growth in knowledge in the area. It seems to be a subject everyone claims to know something about but where there may be little shared knowledge, agreement or collaborative working. It is also an issue that seems to have a greater impact on male, rather than on female, caregivers. Perhaps there is a 'collective guilt' resulting from the belief that sexual abusers are predominantly male, inadvertently compounded by the prevailing ethos of 'safe-care'. This can place adoptive dads in an invidious position that, in turn, can pose additional difficulties within families.

Far more than neglected children, youngsters who have been sexually abused have experienced some degree of closeness, touch and non-verbal communication. Since the abuse involved another person, they have also learned something about relationships and where they fit in. However, the messages which they received are confused and confusing, providing them with highly distorted 'road maps' of the world. Nor do these interactions provide adequate co-regulation; instead they tend to raise arousal levels to unbearable levels. As a result they are likely to dissociate themselves from the experience, shutting themselves in an empty, isolated space inside their heads where they cannot be touched.

Since the majority of sexual abuse occurs within the intimacy of families it is in subsequent close family situations most problems occur. When the abuser was also the child's caregiver, it placed the child in an intolerable double bind that made him especially vulnerable to physical and emotional dysregulation, disorganised attachments and dissociative behaviours. Sexualised behaviour, including masturbation, may be the only ways he knows of self-soothing and managing his pervasive distress.

Where, in addition, there has been overt neglect and multiple caregiving, the opportunities for abuse at the hands of relatives and acquaintances increase. Subsequent sexualised behaviours may then appear in broader arenas. Moreover, for sexual abuse to occur there is likely to have been some level of covert emotional neglect in the main caregiving relationship that failed to protect the child. The picture of sexualised behaviour in adopted children is therefore highly complex. Perhaps the one thing that is most predictable is that whatever is least expected, or most dreaded, by adoptive parents is often the very thing that occurs. New parents must therefore prepare themselves to expect the unexpected. Whilst this may seem a confusing paradigm it is nothing compared to the confusing messages previously received by the sexually abused child.

To begin with, youngsters' understanding of love is derived from their earliest experiences: sexual abuse projected as 'love' teaches them that this is how love is expressed. This may be particularly relevant where children have experienced some aspects of the sexual abuse as pleasurable, where they were told it made them 'special' or if treats, including attention, were used to 'normalise' the behaviour. Not only does this increase the chances of children showing sexualised behaviours in new family relationships, they may also perceive adoptive parents' attempts to ignore or inhibit their behaviour as signs that they are not loved or lovable. Caregivers lacking confidence to provide essential healthy experiences of closeness may walk a tightrope between over-reacting and ignoring the behaviour. In neither of these scenarios are children likely to learn new, healthier patterns of relating and interacting.

Moreover, sexually abused youngsters are likely to have internalised other very powerful and destructive messages from their abuser. They were probably made to feel worthless and experienced helplessness and lack of personal space, boundaries and trust. They may have seen contempt, disdain, disgust or even hatred in the perpetrator's eyes, from which they will derive self-loathing and shame that further disempower and isolate them. It may drive them into 'shame-rage', where they are more likely to victimise others, or into 'superkid' mode, turning their powerlessness into 'pseudo-omnipotent' beliefs and the desire to control. They may swing between the two extremes of under- or over-arousal and reaction, depending on their perceptions of their current circumstances. Caregivers must be able to provide exaggerated, firm but fair boundaries on a long-term, consistent basis, to enable youngsters to begin to feel safely contained and valued for themselves.

Over and above this, violated children may tend to engage in unconsciously flirtatious behaviour, open or prolonged self-stimulation or instigate sexualised activities with younger children. Many parents have been raised to believe that children and sex do not mix and that 'nice children don't do that'. Even when adopters accept such behaviour, they may remain anxious about the impact it will have on other children, relatives, friends or the wider community. Whilst they must be highly vigilant for sexualised approaches and victimising behaviour and help their children to know when it is appropriate to masturbate, they must avoid shaming their children or appearing to reject them.

Since love, trust and boundaries are fundamental issues for abused children, they become prominent issues for adoptive parents too. Caregivers should receive the care, confidence and structured supports that enable them to feel safe and sure in relating to their troubled children. Whilst they cannot afford to risk being accused of abuse by a distressed child, they cannot afford *not* to listen and respond to the child's behavioural language: these two-way communications, inevitably, are primarily non-verbal exchanges involving intimacy and touch. These are risky issues for adoptive families but ones that must be faced, with the support of other professionals, if sexually abused children are not to remain at serious risk, to themselves or others, throughout their lives.

Letter to the Warne family

Dear Sam and Elaine

It's understandable that Mic and Sara's sexualised behaviour is causing you distress and you often feel at a loss. Although the children have different patterns of acting out, they both lack boundaries and awareness of 'what is normal'. As a starting point, therefore, you should aim to provide consistent and repeated messages about the behaviours that are acceptable from Mic and Sara. These messages need to be specific, saying what your child can do as well as what he can't do. You could adopt a mantra along the lines 'in this family our private parts are always private' that establishes a sound structure without you appearing critical or rejecting, since both children are easily shamed and would not then be able to 'hear' what you have to say. When Mic tries to touch your breast in ways that makes you uncomfortable, let him know that 'in this family children don't touch breasts: we can hold hands'.

It's probably best not to try to ignore Mic's 'in your face' sexualised language, as it's so frequent and insistent. Try to understand this as his 'first language', the language of trauma he learned in babyhood and then start to wonder out loud what you think he really wants to say. If rude words or actions feel like they're intended to shock, show him they don't! On my last visit I responded to every 'bum' uttered with a word that rhymed – so Mic knew I was listening while remaining in control of where the 'conversation' went. He soon let it go!

The 'bum in your face' behaviour can also be 'heard' by letting Mic know that 'in this family we don't "do bums"' whilst suggesting what's really bothering him. Your best guess will probably be spot on! 'Everything feels back to front' or 'You don't want to look me in the face right now' might be fair (and polite) interpretations to throw in. Again, being playful can defuse 'rude' or confrontational situations and put you back in safe charge of the interaction.

You'll need to draw very clear distinctions between sexual behaviour and loving behaviour and demonstrate how you show love in your family. Again these need to be specific and clear. Be sad for the children that they were given such muddled messages in the past and let them know you intend to help them practise learning your family's way. Remind them repeatedly it's not their fault they were treated so badly and given such confusing messages. At the same time let them know they can take responsibility (with your support) for making changes and learning about real love.

In addition, aim to set aside times when talking about the children's sexual experiences is acceptable, so Mic doesn't need to do this at inappropriate times, or act it out so much. Sara will also need help to look at what happened to her but may need more time before she's able to face this without 'shutting down'. In both cases the children will cope, and 'hear' better if you provide some comforting physical contact and the 'sessions' are kept short.

You'll often find these conversations cropping up when you're out walking, or focusing on another activity, such as messy play or cooking. Driving the car, with the children safely strapped in the back seat, also provides opportunities for 'little chats' that can feel more relaxed and less intimidating. As Sara finds eye contact difficult this could be very effective, whilst you could use your rear mirror to good effect to observe her reactions.

Mic's sexualised behaviour with young and vulnerable children is particularly worrying. This is a zero tolerance area: Mic must not be allowed to be in situations where he can hurt other youngsters. Fortunately your other children are older, capable of looking after themselves, and of letting you know what's going on.

Mic needs to hear how hurtful and frightening to other children his actions can be and that they are definitely not acceptable. You could say: 'It's my job to keep you safe, to make sure you don't get hurt and that you don't hurt others.' Once 'he knows that you know' and understand, he may need to 'tell you' less through acting out. (This is more likely to be effective than asking him to remember what it felt like to be abused, at this stage, as he isn't in real touch with his feelings.)

As you now know, getting angry, upset or ignoring the behaviour will have the opposite effect: Mic will have to work hard to 'say it louder' with increased 'bad' behaviour. At the moment what he most needs is to start being able to acknowledge what he's doing (tell him rather than ask him!); to know that you believe he can change; and to begin to believe you can help. You'll need to give Mic the message that you intend to do everything you can to help him. Remind Mic as often as possible that no one deserves to be treated the way he and Sara were treated; indirectly this could help him recognise that other children do not deserve to be abused either.

Try not to be tempted to ask Mic why he does what he does, as this will probably elicit grunts or 'don't knows'. This would probably be true right now, as it is likely he enters a dissociative state before he begins the abusive behaviour. In time he will be able to make more sense of this, as we help him to get in touch with his feelings and with his early history. Similarly, attempting to get Mic to put himself in the shoes of the children he victimises would probably be counter-productive until he becomes more fully self-aware. You could, however, begin to wonder out loud how he and Sara must have felt as small, helpless children in their birth family and whether those 'little child' feelings are still there.

Linking what Mic is doing now with his early experiences will help him begin to make more sense of his confusion and his actions now, not as an excuse but as a way of helping him to let go of this behaviour. Be careful to emphasise that you know it wasn't Mic's fault when he was abused and that he isn't a 'bad boy'. Although he'll probably go on holding very negative beliefs about himself for some time yet, your positive messages will gradually begin to have some credence too.

Helping Mic look at what was going on, and how he was feeling, just before he hurt or frightened another child could be very useful. Give him a lot of help here, for example, 'I was wondering whether you were feeling upset (angry, lonely) because I was really busy today with redecorating'. You know him well enough to trust your intuition here! The odd time you aren't spot on Mic will probably let you know anyway, which could be very useful.

Now here comes the hard bit! It seems to me that in the short term the only real way to make sure Mic cannot act on his sexualised impulses is to keep him close to you at all times (obviously not whilst he's in school!), or to keep him away from social events completely until you feel you can trust him (this should always be your decision not his.) Although Sara also needs your close presence and guidance, she may not need this level of supervision and it would be hard to keep both children on such a short rein.

If you opt to go on an outing as a family, for example, you would need to work together to make certain Mic doesn't stray more than two metres from your sides, at any time. This sounds tough, perhaps even punitive, but the consequences for all of you (and Mic in particular) of his continuing to practise his abusive behaviour are likely to prove far harder and more punitive. Saying 'I love you too much to let you hurt yourself/other people' will give Mic the 'right message'. If you feel it would be easier for one of you to stay at home with Mic, that would be a good choice too.

I also need to mention the sexualised behaviour that Mic and Sara display together. I know you're vigilant and try hard to keep the children supervised as much as possible. This is a great way of giving them messages that you're working hard to keep them safe. You could also consider using baby monitors as 'additional eyes and ears'. Be open about this to counteract the pervasive secrecy that formed part of their birth family life.

I know you may be worried the children could interpret the monitors as you not trusting them. However, I feel it's more likely to give them messages that you're doing everything you can to keep them safe, especially if you tell them openly of your plans. You could remind them that it's your job to keep everybody safe. Tell Mic and Sara they deserve this and that you're going to help them practise feeling safe, right now.

Turning to Sara's tendency to masturbate excessively in her bedroom and to 'flirt' with strangers she meets. Since you can't be there every moment of the day your older children could help you by letting you know what's going on. Your approach should then be open and matter of fact: supportive and understanding yet clear that 'flirty' behaviour is not the best way 'to make friends' or get on with grown-ups.

Next, give Sara clear guidelines about when it is OK to 'play with herself': perhaps in her room, on her own, with the door shut. Point out gently that your older daughter sometimes can't sleep when Sara masturbates at night. You'll need to take great care not to give Sara messages that what she does is 'not nice', which would confirm her image of herself as 'dirty' and 'bad'. Similarly acknowledging that 'all children do that sometimes' could help Sara feel less 'crazy and mixed up' and more heard and understood. You could then begin to help Sara make connections between what happened in the past and what is happening now.

At the same time, keep in mind that 'bedroom conditions' of being alone could in some ways replicate those of the original abuse: where Sara was most likely to feel isolated and alone. In addition, as Sara tends to be obsessive, repeatedly making herself red-faced and sore through masturbating, she's unlikely to derive much real comfort from her behaviour. So be prepared to offer her some attractive alternatives during the day, either immediately, or after she has spent a few minutes alone. 'Let's go for a walk together' or 'maybe we could paint a picture' could fill the emotional (and time) gap her masturbating seems to fill and give you some 'close, talking time'.

At night, your approach to giving 'unlimited attention' needs to be a little different, as it's conventionally a time of 'separation'. Try 'filling Sara up', before she goes to bed, with extra-special baths, bedtime routines and stories. Perhaps you could buy a soft, cuddly, 'beany baby' for Sara to hold and stroke, to help her feel you're still with her and to provide healthier self-soothing. Tapes (with earphones) of you singing, reading or giving short, loving messages could also help.

Remember that Sara needs almost endless practice, during the day, of being heard and getting her real needs met, so that she can manage bedtimes better. It would a good idea to focus frequently on 'good baby and toddler' experiences: activities that allow her to experience lots of baby care and play, with you as prime instigator. Shared stories, lovingly prepared bubble baths, cuddles with warm towels, action rhymes involving fingers and toes, games of animal snap, being pushed on swings whilst you sing: the list is endless. I'm sure you'll come up with better ones! Over time, these will give Sara comforting alternatives to rely on, rather than on self-stimulation or ineffective self-soothing.

I know these measures might put extra strain on you now but I believe it will pay off quite quickly and be of great benefit in the longer term. Essentially, I feel that you can't afford *not* to take some powerful steps like this to make sure both children find safer ways of relating and can remain with your family permanently. Whilst not wishing to alarm you, the potential for Mic to become an abuser in adulthood, without your help now, is sizeable.

Take some time to think about what feels best for you before you decide on your plan of action. In the meantime, working on helping the children feel safer and closer to you emotionally will help. The family cradling we discussed could be useful here. And remember to take care of yourselves!

Taking, borrowing, stealing?

Stealing, like lying, is an issue that frequently carries a huge emotional charge.[1] Adults raised within stable homes to be respectful to others and their property may have unconscious beliefs that those who 'take things' or 'lie' are destined for a life of crime. Hence living with a child who does take things can bring fear and shame to adoptive family members as well as challenging their fundamental expectations of the innocence of children and the safety and sanctity of their own homes.

Maltreated children have highly distorted views of the world and of themselves. If they have been neglected or abused they may quite understandably feel that their innocence, and their lives, have been taken from them. Their personal space has repeatedly been invaded and their boundaries are 'all over the place': not having been treated with the respect they need and deserve, they have not learned to respect themselves or others. Birth family members may also have engaged in criminal activity, providing confusing role models for their children. Moreover many children who experienced physical neglect may have learned to take things for themselves from an early age: often foraging in bins or 'borrowing' from their classmates at school.

When children move from their birth families and are placed in adoptive homes they frequently interpret this as 'having been taken, or stolen away' by the very people who are offering them safety and love. It may be better to believe one has been 'stolen' than to feel one has been 'given away'. Although youngsters may be able to acknowledge the hurts they experienced at the hands of their birth families there is often a part of them that hotly denies this and holds idealised images of the 'good parent' and 'bad child'. Without this youngsters may well have succumbed to an overwhelming sense of helplessness and grief. Instead, by unconsciously creating more positive scenarios ('If only I could be good my mum would take me back and love me') children can maintain some sense of hope and belonging, relieve their deep hurts and gain a semblance of control over their lives.

Thus, in the 'language of trauma', stealing takes on very different meanings for hurt children that is reflected in their expectations and behaviours. It is essential that caregivers receive complete and accurate histories of their children and are provided with the 'lexicon' to help them make best sense of their child's current thinking and actions. In addition, exploration of the childhood experiences that formed their own current beliefs and patterns of parenting can provide caregivers with the extra insights they may require to live with children for whom stealing has become an established pattern.

Letter to the Warne family

Dear Elaine and Sam

During our last meeting we discussed some of the meanings behind Ceri's persistent stealing at home. Understanding why Ceri takes your things, and those of the older boys, is a big step towards helping him change. I thought it would help to put our thoughts into a written list, so you can refresh your memories when you feel the need.

- It's vital you recognise that it's not your fault that Ceri steals and that there are lots of ways of managing the problem. It is, however, your responsibility to be understanding, to make the problems clear to Ceri and to do what you can to keep temptation to a minimum; it's Ceri's to accept responsibility for his actions, and to live with any consequences.

- Ceri is telling us through his behaviour about his difficult feelings, including fear, jealousy, sadness and anger. Since these are still very muddled in his head he uses his 'mother tongue', the language of trauma, to communicate with you. As this behaviour became hard-wired into his brain as a baby, he often slips back into 'stealing as communication' when things get tough.

- Since Ceri missed out on early parental help with sorting out and making sense of his feelings, both emotional and physical, his muddles persist. When he feels excited those feelings inside get confused with feeling sad or scared or hungry. Over time he has worked out (unconsciously) that doing something (in this case taking your things) covers up that 'yukky feeling' for a while. As yet Ceri has no other effective ways of managing overwhelming feelings or of letting you know he needs some help with them.

- Ceri didn't receive enough loving care, including good nourishment, as a baby and toddler. Now, particularly when he feels alone, he experiences 'emptiness' and takes what he can from where he can to feel 'filled up'. Sadly this still doesn't make him feel that he has 'enough'.

- The fact that Ceri takes things from your birth sons suggests that he has particular issues with them relating to belonging. It's hard for an adopted child to feel secure in his 'new' family. Not having had 'enough' good parenting at the right time makes sharing extremely difficult. This feeling is often exaggerated where there are children born to their adopters, who are perceived as being 'more entitled' and 'getting more than their fair share'.

- At a very early age Ceri had to fend for himself because no one else was emotionally or physically available to take good care of him or provide him with the predictability and security he needed. Feeling so 'out of control' forced him to try to take control wherever possible. Creating situations by stealing that puts him centre stage, with grown adults rushing round in circles after him, can feel empowering, even when it may also mean getting told off or punished. It's a hard pattern to give up when it truly feels as if life depends on it!

- Since getting your attention in this way gives Ceri what he needs, albeit in distorted ways, it's become a firmly established pattern. There's probably some element of deliberateness in Ceri's behaviour now, which you're picking up on. Naturally this makes you more anxious and frustrated and your responses could become more punitive. This in turn keeps you in negative feedback loops and perpetuates the negative cycle of actions and interactions.

- From the start Ceri's birth mother gave him messages that he was a 'bad baby' for being hungry, or crying, or needing her love. He has taken these messages to heart and truly believes he is 'bad'. Bad people do bad things. When Ceri is found out or confronted this confirms his negative self-image and he's flooded with 'bad' feelings he then tries to push away. This makes sense of why he seems 'not to care' when you try to talk to him about his behaviour: it's too painful and scary to care so he 'switches off' (dissociates)!

- Furthermore, his deep-seated sense of badness makes Ceri feel you'll eventually send him away. The anxiety of waiting for 'lightning to strike twice' is so great he takes things in the unconscious belief this will happen sooner rather than later. Again this gives him some illusion of safety and control.

- Having been treated with little respect as a baby, Ceri has very little self-worth. It's therefore difficult for him to set real value on anything else. Other people's material objects can become imbued with inflated value, which once they are 'his' lose any intrinsic worth. This makes sense of Ceri's tendency to take things and then hide them, throw them away or destroy them.

- Ceri's thinking often gets stuck at toddler level: seeing is wanting, which is then equated with having. This contributes further to his apparent disregard for other people's private possessions.

- Ceri's stealing may be symbolic of how he still feels about being 'stolen away' from his birth mother, as he puts it. That he tries to cover up with 'lies' also suggests he feels he's 'living a lie' and perhaps belongs back with his birth mum. No wonder he tends to take things from you, (Mum). There could also be an element of symbolism in Ceri 'mis-taking' things, given that he feels he is 'one big mistake'.

These are confusing and complex concepts, so no wonder you've been having such a hard time. However, they also reflect quite accurately the confusion and complexity of Ceri's distorted thinking and show us the way forward. This means that, before tackling Ceri's behaviour directly, you'll need to help him work out 'what's going on now and what went on then'. Although this will inevitably take time, understanding and commitment, this is your best starting point to help Ceri 'sort things out in his head' and begin to express himself more openly and honestly.

Ceri needs to feel consistently and predictably filled up with love: that's the way youngsters learn to feel secure and valued. This isn't as easy to do with a 12-year-old boy as it is with a baby or toddler but it's essential if you are to fill those developmental gaps sufficiently. It'll help to think of Ceri as a teenage toddler who sometimes needs the encouragement, support, limits and opportunities to be playful on which toddlers thrive. These include repeated tangible reminders that you're thinking about him and care about him until trust in you 'always being there for him' becomes embedded in his heart.

You could try leaving little messages for Ceri to find when you are not around. This would help him to feel more 'filled up' and less isolated and needy. Why not create some 'hug IOUs' to hide in unexpected spots or send them as short text messages or images? The new watch you had planned for Ceri could also be a regular and timely reminder of your continuing presence, especially if you have it engraved with your names.

Sweet items are very much associated with love: breast and formula milk are loaded with sugars. Tiny chocolate hearts slipped under the pillow, or ready to be 'nibbled' by his electronic mouse, could be just the thing to raise a smile and give him that 'warm fuzzy' feeling which may help him feel good enough about himself not to steal. Don't worry about being over-indulgent. Remember your summer job in the chocolate factory? You soon went off chocolate big time. Seemingly unlimited access to something craved can reduce its attraction and introduces some choice: to 'take it or leave it'. Hopefully this will become a reality for Ceri eventually.

You've found that telling Ceri to 'go to your room and calm down' doesn't work: it's all too frequently followed by sneaking into somebody else's room and taking something of theirs. This is the way Ceri has evolved to manage 'big feelings': he certainly seems to be getting a lot of practice! However, his behaviour tends to have 'big repercussions' too. Now you understand more clearly why Ceri acts this way you can begin to practise new ways of dealing with feelings.

Ceri needs to hear repeatedly that no child deserves to be treated badly and that you know it's never the child's fault when they're mistreated. Try to tease out the essential difference between it being OK to feel how he feels but not OK to hurt himself or other people as a result. Gently retelling Ceri's real-life story will help clarify his muddles. You could wonder whether Ceri believes the policeman 'took him away' from his birth mother. Letting him know you understand that a child who feels they may have been 'stolen' may in turn 'steal' will help him to make sense of his behaviour.

In your pet cockatoo you have an ideal way to explore some difficult issues. Ceri's very fond of him and readily identifies with his 'ugly/naughty' side, although he struggles with dealing with this ambivalence in relation to himself ('I love you even when you misbehave') and his birth mum ('she did her best to love you but she couldn't get it right'). By putting the focus at one step removed from Ceri himself he's more likely to be able to think clearly about the implications. This 'mental rehearsal' forms the basis for establishing new pathways of awareness and communication between you. Try also to avoid using the words 'good' and 'bad' in this context as they are imbued with such strong value judgements that they do not allow for the 'big grey area' of tolerable ambiguity in between.

As well as being Ceri's 'sounding box', hearing and amplifying his thoughts and actions into speech, you'll need to be the 'loving safe container' for him. Being neglected and abused means being denied opportunities to feel loved and safe (nurture), with firm, unambiguous boundaries (structure). This applies as much to actions as to feelings and sensations. Nothing is scarier for young children than having no reliable way of predicting situations or the people around them. This is a big issue for Ceri and he certainly lets you know repeatedly just how much he's in need of strong, clear limits.

Symbolically Ceri oversteps the known boundaries whenever he goes into your bedroom or takes other people's things. At a very deep level he knows that taking others' possessions isn't right but he persists in doing so, letting you know 'volubly' that his boundaries are 'all over the place'; just as deep down he's desperate for you to take control and help him set limits on his behaviour. However, he'll only be able to contemplate this when you're able to put his actions into words and give them meaning.

Whilst we would expect a 12-year-old to have a good idea about boundaries and need only occasional, subtle reminders and appeals to their 'better nature', Ceri needs you to show him in exaggerated ways what this means. You'll need to be 'Jemima Crackit', his external conscience, until he can trust himself better not to take your things. Providing reasonable, non-punitive consequences and 'being sad for' Ceri rather than 'mad at' form an integral part of the 'Panicchio habilitation' package.

Start by exploring what steps you could take to prevent putting temptation in Ceri's way. If you have a secure place to keep your money and jewellery then get into the habit of using it at all times and encourage your older children to do the same (a bum bag for your purse may be a very useful investment here). With practice this will become second nature and will avoid some of the bad feeling about the invasion of personal space and demands for retribution from siblings who believe there shouldn't be 'one law for us, another for Ceri'.

Next be creative and design some 'hug cheques' to leave in places where you previously kept money. You could also slip some of them in with your cash. These could 'promise to pay the bearer on demand' a certain number of hugs. Hopefully this will help Ceri feel he's still in your hearts and thoughts even when you're not around, reducing his need to take things sneakily. You might put up reminders around the house asking 'have you cashed in yet?' or 'time for a pay out?' to act as shared, coded reminders to Ceri.

You'll need to be careful not to blame yourself (or the other children) if Ceri takes advantage of any short lapses in vigilance on your part, as he inevitably will. No 'recovery programme' expects immediate success without some backsliding: you'll all feel better if your expectations don't lead to early disappointment. You're aiming for gradual and realistic progress towards increased trust and trustworthiness.

As part of Ceri's habitual behaviour is now driven by the effect he has on you, your best weapon could be to change your response. If, for example, you don't put your purse away and cash 'disappears', avoid becoming angry and accusatory. Instead express mild disappointment in yourself that you weren't able to prevent Ceri taking advantage and then come up with suitable consequences for him, such as repaying the missing sum with interest. This can be equated with high bank charges for unplanned overdrafts and can be seen to be firm but fair. Use the 'extra' to do something enjoyable for yourselves.

Whatever you do, be careful not to put yourselves in a situation where Ceri never receives any pocket money because it's all 'owed'. This could trigger his feelings of emptiness and abandonment and lead to rebound stealing. It would also mean that Ceri wouldn't be able to practise managing his money well.

Why not introduce 'home service', a scheme analogous to community service involving paying back in kind? Make a list of jobs that can offset items taken and which will also make you feel better about the unpleasant incidents. Not having to clean my bathroom myself was worth a good deal! Be confident that Ceri will do his bit. If he's initially unwilling, try saying 'thanks for your help. I know you'll do a good job' with genuine feeling in anticipation of a good result. It can work little miracles!

Other tangible, 'natural' consequences you could introduce could include limiting 'extras'. As Ceri has problems with food, avoid any limits relating to diet. However, treats, outings, magazines or even time spent on the PC or watching TV could be presented as 'necessary cut-backs due to unexpected cash flow problems' or as 'golden opportunities' for Ceri to do some thinking. Remember, the art of effective 'consequencing' is to be 'sad for' not 'mad at' the child. Even a single hint of 'I told you so' can turn a valuable learning opportunity into an experience of anger, punishment and rejection.

Practise together, maybe with your older boys, what you could say in such circumstances. Such comments as: 'what a pity. I know you were looking forward to (...)', or 'I know. I was hoping to do (...) today too' can be useful. However, it's not so much what you say as the way you say it: Ceri is highly skilled at picking up on non-verbal communications. Although it's hard, you'll find that acting matter of factly and with empathy even when you're feeling cross could be convincing not only to Ceri but to yourself as well!

Try to give yourself time to 'get it together' before you address an incident of 'stealing' with Ceri. You may be 'lucky' and discover items missing whilst Ceri is at school. This would give you plenty of time to work through your inevitable anger and frustration, through unrealistic fantasies of 'revenge' to a point where you can have some fun planning your (reasoned) response. This puts you back in healthy charge of a situation where timing can be crucial.

I'm sure you'll have some great fun ideas yourselves for tackling Ceri's stealing. One strategy you could try is to dress up in a Sherlock Holmes hat and pipe and carry the biggest magnifying glass you can find. Be as 'hammy' as you like as you 'search for clues': speaking your thoughts out loud as you 'work it out'. Why not 'grill' the dogs and the bird as possible 'suspects' or 'witnesses' to add to the ludicrousness of your behaviour?

I know that as fair and reasonable people you've struggled in the past to tackle Ceri about his stealing without absolute proof. There have also been long arguments when he's persistently denied any wrongdoing, even when the truth is 'staring you in the face'. So there's little point quizzing Ceri, trying to get him to 'own up' or explain why he did what he did. As the grown-ups you can 'own' the knowledge yourself matter-of-factly and help Ceri accept this for himself. This has the advantage of not having to demonstrate 'guilt beyond all reasonable doubt': instead you can judge the situation on the balance of probabilities. This should sidestep the fatuous lies and sullen silences you're likely to meet through confrontation. The less practice Ceri gets at these the better! Don't worry unduly about 'getting it wrong': you'll 'get it right' most of the time. Use times when you don't as opportunities for Ceri to see it's not the end of the world to make mistakes and then apologise graciously.

You can also explore with Ceri why you think he acted the way he did when he did: you know him so well you'll be able to work it out. Share your interpretation with Ceri, with as much empathy as you can summon. Demonstrating you can be trusted to deal with things insightfully and fair-mindedly will encourage Ceri to internalise the concept of trust in you, which will gradually be reflected in his increasing truthfulness and trustworthiness.

Not only will you have to guard against your own over-reaction to gain and retain emotional control of these situations, you'll need to be seen to 'have the judgement of Solomon' in also being understanding to your outraged teenagers. Quite naturally they're going to feel peeved at having things go missing and will want 'retribution'. In the past you have tried to mediate in such circumstances, which has left you feeling you've let everybody down. Perhaps now is the time to allow your teens to 'take the law into their own hands' *just a little*.

'Pay back' for your older sons could take a slightly different angle from yours. Alan and Rod are securely attached youngsters with good levels of social, emotional and cognitive understanding, yet it's unfair to expect them to act like fully mature adults. You could consider encouraging 'peer pay back time' instead, along the lines of the victim support scheme. This could include allowing them to vent their feelings directly to Ceri.

First talk to the boys about how they feel about Ceri taking and messing with their things, acknowledging their feelings and validating them as natural and understandable. Next, explain to them how you intend to handle Ceri's stealing from yourselves in the future: emphasising understanding the meaning behind Ceri's actions and the value of setting boundaries and installing realistic consequences.

Once you're confident they're on your wavelength ask them how they'd deal with this sort of thing in school or in the street, when you're not there to 'police' the situation. Now give them your blessing to take similar action at home, on the strict understanding that no one gets hurt and there's no damage to property. Let Alan and Rod know you believe they can handle this well and that it will help Ceri learn from his mistakes.

Used occasionally the 'shock and surprise' element here could certainly set Ceri thinking. Be prepared to do some sensitive 'out loud thinking' with him if necessary. You'll need to take a watchful back seat, ready to offer tacit support to 'the victims of crime' whilst overtly acknowledging how Ceri must feel as a result. You could say 'I'm really sorry you've had such a hard time from Alan and Rod. I wonder what it was that made them react that way?' in a gently knowing tone. Follow this by wondering 'what needs to change for us all here?' This gives Ceri the message you'll do what you can to help him and that you expect him to work at it too. If you feel the boys' response needs toning down, keep it between yourselves: in public you must present a united front.

You could also suggest that the boys consider going into Ceri's room and doing something really easily spotted and silly, as a gentle but salient reminder of how it feels to have somebody 'messing with your things'. Encourage them to be very obvious in, for example, moving items around and leaving giant fingerprints, or adding some highly conspicuous items to Ceri's belongings. Draw the line at their taking things from his room or causing damage. Strange, amusing or enigmatic messages could also be left for Ceri to find and make sense of.

For boundaries to seem 'firm but fair' children also need to practise making choices and living with the consequences. Pocket money could be a prime target here for Ceri. However much you don't want him to 'waste his money' he needs age-appropriate practice at finding out for himself what is and is not really worth it. This is bound up with Ceri's distorted sense of self-worth and will need a sensitive approach and a good deal of practice.

Making mistakes is the downside of making choices but is an inevitable and integral part of 'the learning curve'. Your goal is to remain empathic, to avoid 'rescuing' Ceri from his mistakes and to resist saying 'I told you so', or 'you should have...'. It can be painful and frustrating to watch a child you love get hurt through his distorted thinking and actions. Conversely, it's supportive to introduce the idea that you have to make mistakes if you're to learn and grow: transforming them into valuable opportunities to practise 'getting things wrong and putting things right'. Try to make some all too obvious mistakes yourself, exaggerating your reactions and talking to yourself whilst you work things out.

When you feel he's ready, Ceri could also gain valuable practice in taking good care of your money. Invite him to go to the local shop and make some simple purchases for you. This implies an increasing level of trust and responsibility to which he may rise. Try to give him almost the right money, so there's only a small amount of change and less room for 'mistakes'. Be pleased for Ceri if he's up to the task; show sadness if he messes up and suggest he needs 'more practice'.

All this will draw on your reserves of energy, patience and love. Make sure you don't 'over-draw' on these reserves and go 'into the red': that could be dangerous. The best way to 'stay in the black' is to replenish yourselves on a regular basis. It's so easy to slip into the habit of putting the children first. Laudable although this may seem, it's unrealistic. You are the most important figures in your family and you need to be able to function well under challenging circumstances. So make sure you look after yourselves and each other!

Note

1. While lying has not been addressed as a separate issue, it is a repeated theme (see 'Dissociative states' and 'Terrible shame'). In terms of the 'language of trauma', lying is best understood as a child's attempt to create a 'coherent story' from disjointed or shame-laden memories. This can relate directly to his lack of early 'object' permanence and constancy: a sense of 'who, me?' or 'not me', rather than a conscious attempt to deceive initially.

Terrible shame

Terror drives some individuals onto the attack; others turn tail and run. A third group becomes rooted to the spot, frozen in their tracks and unable to respond. So it is with shame. Some respond by becoming enraged, fixing the potential 'shamer' with a steely stare. Others disengage to such an extent that they appear transfixed, unable to make eye contact, or 'go off in a sulk'.

Whilst a little anxiety or fear puts children on their metal, giving them the edge in unfamiliar or challenging situations, so a modicum of guilt can galvanise them into changing their behaviour or making amends. However, if fear becomes too great it 'tips them over the edge' and they panic: running around without focus, talking too much, comfort eating or rushing for the bathroom. Here the brain prioritises action over calm, reasoned thought. The more this has occurred in children's pasts, the more likely it is to recur, even in non-threatening circumstances.

The neurobiological reaction to embarrassment or guilt has a similar nervous-energising effect, often with parallel reductions in 'thinking power'. However, once the degree of discomfort or self-loathing becomes too great the whole body system shuts down, inner and outer connections are lost and there is little 'brain space' for verbal language and reasoning.

Early maltreatment establishes a poor self-image that primes children to try to escape from the harsh judgement of others and self by seeking invisibility. They cut off, and simultaneously feel cut off, from the world. This pattern of shutting down may begin in the womb in response to perceived threat and involves primitive reflexes. Many aspects of developmental maturity can thus be compromised by hardwiring of very early adverse experience.

Helping traumatised children to tolerate unfamiliarity, change, 'being seen' and being themselves demands high degrees of awareness and subtlety from caregivers. Non-verbal, body language speaks louder than words: where even a mildly irritated glance or gentle criticism could strike shame into a child's heart. So it is primarily through the unspoken, healing language of the senses in the 'dance of attunement and attachment' that broken connections can be re-established and new connections made.

Sharing 'the blame' and working on 'the problem' together are powerful transformers of shame. Children need no longer feel worthless outcasts, as they are drawn back into the warmth of their caregivers' hearts, facing 'the truth' for themselves and accepting greater responsibility for their actions. With time they can begin thinking things through and contemplate making, and surviving, what previously felt like 'fatal' mistakes.

Parents need to be vigilant for tell-tale signs of toxic shame (such as avoiding eye contact and withdrawing or, conversely, intense eye contact and 'in your face' aggression/denial) in order to draw their child back into the 'comfort zone'. Through 'co-regulation' of unbearably high or low arousal and 'co-reconstruction' of parent–child attachments and events, both present and past, (see also pp.234–5) parents enable their children to feel increasingly real, in touch and 'joined up'.

*T*hink toddler think (T3)

Many of the challenges for adoptive families revolve around issues of control, within the home and within the classroom. Control, and the healthy reclaiming of parental authority, is therefore a major focus of developmental reparenting. However, it often feels difficult to 'do' control in ways that feel nurturing and responsive, so that 'the nurture' is not swallowed up by 'the structure'. Conversely it can be tempting to 'go soft on boundaries', in attempts to nurture closeness and self-esteem. 'Think toddler think' (T3) can help adopters find the right balance for their children.

For example, the adoptive parents of nine-year-old Jasmine spoke with affection mixed with irritation, of their daughter's 'laziness', recounting how she would not wash herself, or her hair. Checking with previous carers, they ascertained that Jasmine had been able to achieve reasonable levels of self-care and cleanliness, yet was 'choosing' not to do so in her new home. The adopters' expectations that Jasmine should keep herself clean were not unreasonable for her age, especially as they were concerned about potentially detrimental comments from her school friends. Was this a control issue, with Jasmine 'trying to wind them up', and engaging in negative attention-seeking behaviours or something deeper?

Jasmine came from a large family, where physical and emotional neglect were the norm and where older family members regularly intimidated younger ones. Her behaviour made good sense in terms of her past: the 'language of trauma' she chose was unconsciously letting her new parents know she needed to go back and 'fill in the baby gaps' in her life.

Adults frequently fail to give children the credit they deserve for communicating, through the language of behaviour, exactly what went wrong and what needs to be put right. In this case it was clear Jasmine's poor early nurturing experiences had left big gaps in her behavioural repertoire. When she was a baby there had been no one to cuddle her, wash her, stroke her hair, or give her messages that she was worth taking care of, consistently. Essentially Jasmine didn't 'get' self-care, nor did she receive the encouragement or opportunities to practise these essential skills for herself. However, on moving into her foster family it seems that she had somehow learned these personal hygiene skills. Why then did she 'choose' not to do so in her adoptive family?

Things children learn in their earliest years readily become hardwired: they become etched into their brain circuits and behaviour patterns. Those that come later do so to a lesser degree and are more vulnerable to lapses under stress: children naturally revert to more primitive neural pathways and responses. Everyone 'decompensates' at times, when tired, or stressed out: then we may wish that someone else would take over and 'do it for us'. This seemed to fit for Jasmine: T3 allowed her adopters to view the issue more empathically and explore how neither the adopters nor Jasmine had had sufficient reciprocal practice of taking care of or being cared for in Jasmine's early years. In effect there was an experiential void for the adoptive parents that exactly matched Jasmine's own experiential void of not having had the chance to be raised by 'good enough' parents. Here was the perfect, natural opportunity for them to practise these things together!

Clearly there were empathic, respectful ways of side-stepping Jasmine's 'inappropriate' attempts to get her needs met. For example, her parents might have considered saying 'you're welcome to have a story once you've been in the bath' or bought some girly bubble bath, to which they pinned amusing messages such as 'use me and see what happens!'. However, it is often more appropriate to think in terms of 'filling developmental gaps' and seizing some heaven-sent opportunities for hands-on caregiving by transforming the problem and emphasising the affectionate, nurturing elements the adopters already displayed. It also acknowledges a fundamental principle of developmental reparenting: that of not asking children to do something of which they are not developmentally capable at that moment.

Work began by helping the adoptive parents get in touch with their feelings of sadness for Jasmine, by imagining how she must have felt being left hungry, cold and dirty for long periods and how she might have coped with being teased at school for being 'smelly'. Next Jasmine's experiences were explored in terms of abandonment, rejection and shame and how this might be echoed in the present, if Jasmine's deep need to be looked after was not acknowledged, or she was again exposed to the candid comments of her peers.

T3 was then used to consider what Jasmine's parents might expect a toddler (or baby) to need help with, in order to keep clean and feel good. It was suggested that they might empathise directly with Jasmine, saying 'I know how hard this is for you right now' and wonder out loud how 'baby Jasmine' would have felt about being dirty, smelly and uncomfortable. The adopters could continue by saying how much they wished they had been there, to give Jasmine the care she needed and deserved, leading naturally into 'Well, good job we have the chance to do it now.' Additionally they might say 'We didn't get the chance to look after you back then, so we need lots of practice too.' The essential message is of genuine empathy for Jasmine's hurts and of real willingness to help her. In this way issues of control are avoided, since the adults chose to do what their child's behaviour was 'asking' them to do, while retaining the option not to, when they did not feel good about doing so due to time or energy considerations.

T3 can also be used effectively in classroom situations. For example Joe, aged six, had experienced devastating neglect and abuse in his large, chaotic birth family. He also had an extremely interrupted school history: as a consequence staff were struggling to manage his troubling behaviour in class. The school staff, like Joe's adoptive parents, were committed and supportive. After exploring some of Joe's difficulties (including sitting still, playing appropriately, following instructions and relating to peers) with them, T3 allowed everyone to 'see' Joe differently: as a child who had not had sufficient opportunities to learn self-calming techniques, or to play, who was hypervigilant and easily panicked.

Some sensory input, appropriate for very young children, was discussed, alongside ways of avoiding 'triggering' Joe into higher arousal. It was proposed that Joe should attend school for half days only, in the nursery section, with his adoptive parents' agreement. If difficulties persisted, further 'progress backwards' could be considered. For example, Joe might benefit more from staying at home with his parents for some time, so that he could take in enough nurture and security to increase his developmental readiness to cope with the challenges of the wider world of school. Here it would be essential that his adoptive parents were provided with sufficient community supports and 'mini-breaks' to remain nurturing and live to tell the tale!

Theoretically, T3 allows children to move developmentally from dependence towards independence: just as toddlers automatically move from the comfort of an available 'secure base' towards increasing exploration (with the occasional reassuring look back) until their 'secure base' becomes part of their internal 'route map of the world'. It therefore represents progression rather than regression, since traumatised youngsters unconsciously 'regress' at times, as they seek to 'fill in the gaps', often in inappropriate ways. For hurt children, T3 offers powerful ways for adoptive parents to get in touch with their youngsters' 'hurt inner child', the panic-ridden kid, hidden deep inside even the most well-defended 'tough guy'.

Armed with T3 and a clear picture of their children's pasts, adoptive parents can support them through distressing times when they re-experience the body states and states of mind of their traumatic early years. Simulta-neously parents can begin replacing negative early messages (such as 'you're bad, you don't deserve good care') with positive actions that give new messages ('you are worth it, I care about you enough to do this'). 'Redoing the baby stuff' alters the mind–body connections that threaten to ruin young-sters' lives and those of their adoptive families. It enables parents and children to access safely those disconnected, or denied, hurt baby parts, join kids up and change their distorted perceptions, expectations and belief systems. Once filled up, these very young part-selves are no longer needy and demanding: feeling more secure, connected and contained, they can take their place in children's increasingly coherent narratives.

Since toddler socialisation goes hand in hand with increasing exploration, issues of shame are also relevant to T3. Once infants become mobile they get into all sorts of 'trouble' of which they have no conception. A major task for parents at this stage is to keep their toddlers safe by setting boundaries, and introducing the concept of 'no!' 'Good enough' parents do this through the use of 'short, sharp shocks of shame': when their toddler may be literally pros-trated by shame and loss of energising connections with caregivers. This sequence must immediately be followed by 'interactive repair', when wise adults move towards their children and reconnect with them, through touch, body language, eye contact and reassuring voice tones. Gradually youngsters learn about the people and the rules that keep them safe. They can explore their widening world with relative impunity, trusting in their caregivers' capacity to take good care of them.

Neglected and abused toddlers frequently suffer overwhelming levels of shame and disconnection without sufficient repair. Since these are unbearable states, children learn to 'bypass' shame (through shame-rage) or cover their shame by 'being good' in attempts to hide their 'badness'. Toxic shame has devastating, long-lasting effects on children's lives, since it so fundamentally affects their self-image, self-worth and self–other connections. Thus T3 gives adoptive parents another chance to address toxic shame and re-establish two-way connections with their youngsters. Gradually this can begin to transform children's views of themselves and their world. By refusing to allow their children to reject them and by providing comfort, nurture and support at earlier developmental levels, parents facilitate the essential neurobiological 'rewiring', without which youngsters will be unable to move into healthier, more mature relationships and behaviours.

In the final analysis, T3 is about choice: about increasing adopters' choices of how to live with their hurt children and about increasing youngsters' choices and opportunities for healing. T3 will not cure all ills and it will not be the right choice for all occasions, all of the time. However, when it feels right, it could be just the right choice for parents and children to fill in the gaps and to grow closer and more whole. Beyond the courage and determination to change perceptions, expectations and responses, both parents and children need support and lots of practice in order to grow in confidence and in themselves. They will also need understanding and the strength of their community networks around them: a challenge for every member of society.

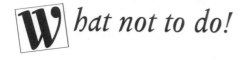# **W**hat not to do!

Shouting and yelling at children or other family members

A noisy atmosphere can replicate children's early life experiences and encourages them to 'tune out'. Instead, parents should try to speak in normal voice tones. When asking children to do something, they should use calm but firm tones; when reprimanding youngsters it may be better to employ even quieter tones.

Hitting or threatening

Again this may replicate children's early experiences, alongside giving messages that aggression is acceptable. Expecting children not to hit out is unlikely to succeed if parents use aggression as a way of dealing with difficult situations. Hurt youngsters need to be led by example to learn alternative ways of managing anger.

Threats can also make youngsters anxious and agitated and interfere with learning new skills, through triggering defence mechanisms. It is likely to increase rather than decrease difficult behaviour: angry children will become angrier, dissociative children more 'tuned out' and 'switched off'.

Being inconsistent

Inconsistency confuses children, reinforcing beliefs that their world is chaotic and making it harder for them to learn right from wrong. It does not allow children to practise discriminating between acceptable and unacceptable behaviours.

Parents need to be consistent in letting their children know what is acceptable and unacceptable in their behaviour, whilst varying their choice of strategies. This reduces the chance that youngsters, by predicting their parents' responses, can stay in control, which would interfere with the helpful messages parents wish to give and undermine their emphasis on promoting a positive emotional atmosphere.

Doing everything for children

Doing too much for children trains them not to think, not to problem solve and not to be appropriately independent. Getting parents to think for them is a strategy children may employ to defend against change.

Instead parents can use natural or logical consequences for behaviour: requiring youngsters to think, remember and be attentive. Handled with empathy, this also reduces children's tendency to be angry at parents when things go wrong.

Children need to practise doing things for themselves and to help with family routines, within the limits of their current capacity. This creates a sense of family connection and achievement and simultaneously increases their ability to think for themselves and to develop self-worth. However, parents should remain mindful of the need to treat children in accordance with their emotional rather than their chronological age (see T3).

Constant reminders

Again these encourage children not to think for themselves and can make them feel you lack faith in their capabilities, further reducing their self-esteem.

Instead parents should minimise the reminders they give to their youngsters and allow them to learn from their mistakes, remembering to give appropriate praise when children manage tasks without reminders.

Warning about the consequences of behaviour

This is similar to constant reminders, with similar consequences for youngsters. Parents can help children practise making choices by allowing them to face the (safe, limited) consequences of their behaviour and being sad for them, rather than saying 'I told you so!'

Forgetting to praise children when they behave well

It is easy to notice difficult behaviour and to overlook times when children are behaving well. However, paying more attention to negative behaviour than to positives reduces the likelihood that children will behave well in future. Instead parents should acknowledge and praise the positive behaviour and work towards transforming negative behaviours into positive ones.

Limiting time spent with children

In today's busy world it is all too easy to avoid spending time with children, particularly troubling ones. Maltreated children may ask for the latest designer goods when what they really need is time, attention and love. Spending half an hour every day (at least) giving youngsters some undivided attention gives them important messages that they are loved and worthy of nurture. Housework can always wait until tomorrow: children's emotional well-being cannot.

Missing opportunities to have fun

Parenting is one of the hardest jobs that adults undertake. It is a 24/7 activity: there are no holidays and it requires the multi-tasking brainpower of a genius. Difficult it is: yet this does not mean that it always has to be serious!

Successful parents build times for fun and relaxation into their parenting routines. They look for opportunities to laugh with their children, to play with them and to relax and chill out with them. This could be problematic if youngsters seem hell-bent on making family life conflict-ridden and stressful. Yet it is still possible – if not essential – to create some fun times.

Parents need to be in charge of the emotional atmosphere in their homes, by making sure they build good times into their family routine, whatever their children's behaviour.

Feeling like 'the wrong parents'

Troubled children need confident parents who can claim them, despite their rejecting or hurtful behaviours. Parents sometimes need reminding that they are just the right mums and dads for their youngsters, so that they can keep going through the hard times.

Putting everybody else first

Children need to see that their caregivers take good care of themselves too. Encouraging self-awareness and self-respect in hurt youngsters is an essential counter-balance to the negative messages they received in their early lives.

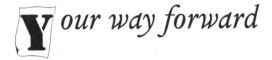

Your way forward

Final reflections

We sincerely hope you have found some of the suggestions in this book helpful, whether you are a professional working with adoptive families and wanting an understanding of the issues that often arise, or if you yourself are undertaking a journey through adoptive family life and want to make sense of your child's difficult behaviours. We recognise that what we are proposing might seem like a Herculean task: and it certainly does require a significant change in the way you think about your child and the way to manage his behaviour. However, while we recognise that change is difficult for everyone and that it takes time and practice to alter instinctive ways of thinking and relating we also believe that not to change is even more time consuming.

You have no doubt read this book because you have been struggling with some aspect(s) of your child's behaviour; the methods you have tried have been ineffective and possibly counterproductive. This means you have expended a great deal of energy to little effect.

We firmly believe that what we are proposing will be more time efficient and effective. You only have to compare the time and energy expended in shouting at your child for even five minutes with saying calmly 'I can see how hard this is for you' to recognise the truth of this statement.

We have often been asked how long one needs to continue with developmental reparenting for it to have an impact. While we believe you will begin to see change within six months, if not sooner, we also believe that developmental reparenting should be seen as a way of interacting that is 'for life'. Why return to patterns of interacting that are emotionally draining and ineffective when you have begun to embrace one that can have a profound impact on the way you view yourself, your children and the world around you?

And finally can we leave you with these thoughts:

- good luck in the task you have set yourself
- have fun as you begin this journey of discovery and repair with your child
- look after yourself and your adult relationships
- accept all the *good* help and support you can get – it's a positive move, not a sign of 'failure' or of not being 'good enough'
- recognise that you are the most valuable resource that your child has in his journey to emotional health.

References, recommended reading and resources

References and selected additional reading (mostly for adults)

Amen, D. (2002) *Healing the Hardware of the Soul*. New York and London: The Free Press.

Archer, C. (1999a) *First Steps in Parenting the Child Who Hurts: Tiddlers and Toddlers*. London: Jessica Kingsley Publishers.

Archer, C. (1999b) *Next Steps in Parenting the Child Who Hurts: Tykes and Teens*. London: Jessica Kingsley Publishers.

Archer, C. (2004) 'Substance misuse, attachment disorganization and adoptive families'. In R. Phillips (ed.) *Children Exposed to Parental Substance Abuse*. London: BAAF.

Archer, C. and Burnell, A. (eds) (2003) *Trauma, Attachment and Family Permanence: Fear Can Stop You Loving*. London: Jessica Kingsley Publishers.

Archer, C. and Gordon, C. (2004) 'Parent mentoring: an innovative approach to adoption support'. *Journal of Adoption and Fostering 28*, 4, 27–38.

Acredolo, L. and Goodwyn, S. (1996) *Baby Signs*. London: Hodder and Stoughton.

Ayres, A.J. (1994) *Sensory Integration and the Child*. Los Angeles, CA: Western Psychological Services.

Balbernie, R. (2001) 'Circuits and circumstance: the neurobiological consequences of early attachment experiences and how they shape later behaviour'. *Journal of Child Psychotherapy 27*, 3, 237–55.

Baron-Cohen, S. (1999) *Mindblindness: An Essay in Autism and Theory of Mind*. London: A Bradford Book (MIT Press).

Becker-Weidman, A. and Shell, D. (eds) (2005) *Creating Capacity for Attachment*. Oklahoma, OK: Wood N Barnes Publishing.

Borysenko, J. and Borysenko, M. (1994) *The Power of the Mind to Heal*. Carson, CA: Hay House Inc.

Bowlby, J. (1969) *Attachment* (Volume I of *Attachment and Loss*). London: Hogarth Press.

Bowlby, J. (1973) *Separation: Anxiety and Anger* (Volume II of *Attachment and Loss*). London: Hogarth Press.

Bowlby, J. (1988) *A Secure Base*. London: Routledge.

Braun, B. (1988) 'The BASK (behavior, affect, sensation, knowledge) model of dissociation'. *Dissociation 1*, 1, 4–23.

Caldwell, C. (ed.) (1997) *Getting in Touch: The Guide to New Body-Centred Therapies*. Wheaton, IL: Quest Books.

Carter, R. (2000) *Mapping the Mind*. London: Phoenix (Orion Books Ltd).

Cole, A. and Cole, L. (2002) *Bod's Way*. London: Contender Books.

De Casper, A. and Fifer, W. (1980) 'Of human bonding: newborns prefer their mothers' voices'. *Science 208*, 1174–6.

Dement, W. (2001) *The Promise of Sleep*. London: Pan Books.

Eliot, L. (2000) *What's Going on in There?* New York: Bantam Books.

Ferber, R. (1986) *Solve Your Child's Sleep Problems.* London and New York: A Fireside Book, Simon and Schuster.

Field, T. (1985) *The Psychobiology of Attachment and Separation.* London: Academic Press Inc (London) Ltd.

Fonagy, P. (2002) 'Multiple voices versus meta-cognition: an attachment theory perspective'. In V. Sinason (ed.) *Attachment, Trauma and Multiplicity.* Hove: Brunner-Routledge.

Gerhardt, S. (2004) *Why Love Matters: How Affection Shapes a Baby's Brain.* Hove: Brunner-Routledge.

Gluckman, P. and Hanson, M. (2005) *The Fetal Matrix: Evolution, Development and Disease.* Cambridge: Cambridge University Press.

Gordon, C. (2003) 'Hands-on help'. In C. Archer and A. Burnell (eds) *Trauma, Attachment and Family Permanence: Fear Can Stop You Loving.* London: Jessica Kingsley Publishers.

Gordon, C. (2003) 'Holding the Fort'. In C. Archer and A. Burnell (eds) *Trauma, Attachment and Family Permanence: Fear Can Stop You Loving.* London: Jessica Kingsley Publishers.

Hart, A. and Lucock, B. (2004) *Developing Adoption Support and Therapy: New Approaches for Practice.* London: Jessica Kingsley Publishers.

Heath, A. and Bainbridge, N. (2000) *Baby Massage: The Calming Power of Touch.* London: Dorling Kindersley.

Heller, S. (2003) *Too Loud, Too Bright, Too Fast, Too Tight.* New York: Quill (HarperCollins Publishers, Inc.).

Howe, D. (1996) *Attachment Theory for Social Work Practice.* London: British Agencies for Adoption and Fostering.

Howe, D. (2005) *Child Abuse and Neglect.* Basingstoke: Palgrave Macmillan.

Hughes, D. (1997) *Facilitating Developmental Attachment: The Road to Emotional Recovery and Behavioral Change in Foster and Adopted Children.* Northvale, NJ: Jason Aronson Inc.

Hughes, D. (1998) *Building the Bonds of Attachment: Awakening Love in Deeply Troubled Children.* Northvale, NJ: Jason Aronson Inc.

Hughes, D. (2003) 'Psychological interventions for the spectrum of attachment disorders and intrafamilial trauma'. *Attachment and Human Development 5,* 3 271–9.

Jernberg, A. and Booth, P. (2001) *Theraplay* (2nd edition). San Francisco, CA: John Wiley and Sons Inc.

Keating, K. (1992) *The Complete Tiny Book of Hugs.* London: Harper Collins Publishers.

Keck, G. and Kupecky, R. (1995) *Adopting the Hurt Child.* Colorado Springs, CO: Pinon Press.

Keck, G. and Kupecky, R. (2002) *Parenting the Hurt Child.* Colorado Springs, CO: Pinon Press.

Kellie-Smith, G. (2003) 'Difficulty with learning or learning to be difficult?' In C. Archer and A. Burnell (eds) *Trauma, Attachment and Family Permanence: Fear Can Stop You Loving.* London: Jessica Kingsley Publishers.

Ledoux, J. (1999) *The Emotional Brain.* London: Phoenix, Orion Books Ltd.

Levy, T. (ed) (2000) *Handbook of Attachment Interventions.* London and New York: Academic Press.

Levy, T. and Orlans, M. (1998) *Attachment, Trauma and Healing.* Washington, DC: Child Welfare League of America Press.

Lyons-Ruth, K., Bronfman, E. and Atwood, G. (1999) 'A relationship diathesis model of hostile-helpless states of mind: expressions in mother–infant interaction'. In J. Solomon and C. George (eds) *Attachment Disorganization.* New York and London: Bantam Books.

MacFarlane, J. (1975) 'Olfaction in the development of social preference in the human newborn'. In M. Hofer (ed.) *Foundation Symposium: Parent-Infant Interaction.* Amsterdam: Elsevier.

Mollon, P. (1998) *Remembering Trauma: A Psychotherapist's Guide to Memory and Illusion.* Chichester: John Wiley.

Niec-Oszywa, A. (2001) *Boost Your Child's Immune System The Natural Way*. New South Wales: Allen and Unwin.

Nielson, C. (2000) *The Tao of Babies*. London: Ebury Press.

Pert, C. (1999) *Molecules of Emotion, the Science of Mind-Body Medicine*. New York: Touchstone.

Perry, B.D. (1999) 'The memories of states: how the brain stores and retrieves traumatic experience'. In J. Goodwin and R. Attias (eds) *Splintered Reflections. Images of the Body in Trauma*. New York: Basic Books.

Perry, B.D. (2000) *The Neuroarcheology of Childhood Maltreatment: The Neurodevelopmental Costs of Adverse Childhood Events*. The ChildTrauma Academy. http://www.childtrauma.org

Perry, B.D., Pollard, R., Blakley, T., Baker, W. and Vigilante, D. (1995) 'Childhood trauma, the neurobiology of adaptation, and "use-dependent" development of the brain: how states become traits'. *Journal of Infant Mental Health 16*, 4, 271–91.

Portwood, M. (1999) *Developmental Dyspraxia* (2nd edition). London: David Fulton Publishers.

PPIAS (Parent to Parent Information on Adoption Services) (1993) *Parent Assertiveness with Consequences and Empathy Handbook* (out of print). Northamptonshire: PPIAS.

Putnam, F. (1997) *Dissociation in Children and Adolescents: A Developmental Perspective*. New York: Guilford Press.

Rutter, M. and English and Romanian Adoptees Study Team (1998) 'Developmental catch-up, and deficit, following adoption after severe global early privation'. *Journal of Child Psychological Psychiatry 39*, 465–76.

Sachs, P. (1996) *Take Care of Yourself*. London: Penguin Books.

Schore, A. (1994) *Affect Regulation and the Origin of the Self*. Hillsdale, USA: Lawrence Earlbaum Associates.

Schore, A. (2001a) 'Effects of a secure attachment on right brain development, affect regulation, and infant mental health.' *Infant Mental Health Journal 22*, 7–67.

Schore, A. (2001b) 'The effects of early relational trauma on right brain development, affect regulation, and infant mental health'. *Infant Mental Health Journal 22*, 201–69.

Siegel, D. (1999) *The Developing Mind: Toward a Neurobiology of Interpersonal Experience*. New York: Guilford Press.

Shirar, L. (1996) *Dissociative Children: Bridging the Inner and Outer Worlds*. New York and London: W.W. Norton and Co.

Solomon, J. and George, C. (1999) 'The place of disorganization in attachment theory'. In J. Solomon and C. George (eds) *Attachment Disorganization*. New York: Guilford Press.

Tisserand, M. (1990) *Aromatherapy for Women*. London: Thorsons.

Van der Kolk, B. (1996a) 'The body keeps the score'. In B. van der Kolk, A. McFarlane and L. Weisaeth (eds) *Traumatic Stress: The Effects of Overwhelming Experience on Mind, Body and Society*. New York: Guilford Press.

Van der Kolk, B. (1996b) 'Trauma and memory'. In B. van der Kolk, A. McFarlane and L. Weisaeth (eds) *Traumatic Stress: The Effects of Overwhelming Experience on Mind, Body and Society*. New York: Guilford Press.

Van der Kolk, B. (1996c) 'The complexity of adaptation to trauma: self-regulation, stimulus discrimination and characterological development. In B. van der Kolk, A. McFarlane and L. Weisaeth (eds) *Traumatic Stress: The Effects of Overwhelming Experience on Mind, Body and Society*. New York: Guilford Press.

Vaughan, J. (2003a) 'The drama of adoption'. In C. Archer and A. Burnell (eds) *Trauma, Attachment and Family Permanence: Fear Can Stop You Loving*. London: Jessica Kingsley Publishers.

Vaughan, J. (2003b) 'The drama unfolds'. In C. Archer and A. Burnell (eds) *Trauma, Attachment and Family Permanence: Fear Can Stop You Loving*. London: Jessica Kingsley Publishers.

Waites, E. (1993) *Trauma and Survival*. New York: WW Norton and Company Inc.

Waites, E. (1997) *Memory Quest.* New York: WW Norton and Company Inc.

Watkins, J. and Watkins, H. (1997) *Ego States, Theory and Therapy.* New York: Norton and Co.

Winnicott, D. (1971) *Playing and Reality.* New York: Basic Books.

Winnicott, D. (1984) *Deprivation and Delinquency.* London: Routledge.

Books to read with young children (of all ages!)

Althea (illus. Cory, F.) (2003) *Dyslexia.* Essex: Happy Cat Books Ltd.

Bradman, T. and Winter, S. (2001) *Nicky and the Twins.* London: Diamond Books.

Carle, E. (1982) *The Bad-tempered Ladybird.* London: Picture Puffin.

Carle, E. (2000) *The Very Hungry Caterpillar.* London: Picture Puffin.

Carle, E. (2000) *The Mixed-up Chameleon.* London: Picture Puffin.

Carle, E. (2000) *The Very Quiet Cricket.* London: Picture Puffin.

Cole, B. (1997) *The Bad Good Manners Book.* London: Puffin Books.

Cole, B. (2001) *Hair In Funny Places.* London: Red Fox.

Cole, B. (2001) *The Smelly Book.* London: Red Fox.

Cole, B. (2003) *The Slimy Book.* London: Red Fox.

Cole, B. (2004) *Mummy Never Told Me.* London: Red Fox.

Cole, B. (2004) *The Trouble With Mum.* London: Egmont Books Ltd.

Cole, B. (2004) *The Trouble With Dad.* London: Egmont Books Ltd.

Cole, B. (2004) *The Trouble With Gran.* London: Egmont Books Ltd.

Cole, B. (2004) *The Trouble With Grandad.* London: Egmont Books Ltd.

Cole, B. (2004) *Bad Habits!* London: Puffin Books.

Corentin, P. (2001) *Splosh!* London: Andersen Press.

Craft, R. (illus. Blegvad, E.) (1976) *The Winter Bear.* London: Picture Lions.

Dahl, R. (2001) *Revolting Rhymes.* London: Puffin Books.

Dahl, R. (2001) *Dirty Beasts.* London: Puffin Books.

Dahl, R. (2001) *The BFG.* London: Puffin Books.

Dahl, R. (2001) *James and the Giant Peach.* London: Puffin Books.

Dahl, R. (2004) *The Magic Finger.* London: Puffin Books.

Dahl, R. (2004) *Matilda.* London: Puffin Books.

Donaldson, J. (illus. Scheffler, A.) (1999) *The Gruffalo.* London: MacMillan Children's Books.

Donaldson, J. (illus. Scheffler, A.) (2004) *The Gruffalo's Child.* London: MacMillan Children's Books.

Donaldson, J. (illus. Monks, L.) (2004) *Sharing A Shell.* London: MacMillan Children's Books.

Duncan Edwards, P. (2002) *Rude Mule.* London: MacMillan Books.

Edwards, D. (illus. Hughes, S.) (2002) *My Naughty Little Sister.* London: Egmont Books Ltd.

Edwards, D. (illus. Hughes, S.) (2002) *My Naughty Little Sister's Friends.* London: Egmont Books Ltd.

Edwards, D. (illus. Hughes, S.) (2002) *My Naughty Little Sister and Bad Harry.* London: Egmont Books Ltd.

Edwards, D. (illus. Hughes, S.) (2002) *When My Naughty Little Sister Was Good.* London: Egmont Books Ltd.

Edwards, R. (1999) *Copy Me, Copycub.* London: Frances Lincoln.

Freeman, L. and Deach, C. (1986) *Loving Touches.* Seattle, WA: Parenting Press, Inc.

Freeman, L. and Deach, C. (1993) *It's my Body.* Seattle, WA: Parenting Press, Inc.

Gil, E. (1983) *Outgrowing the Pain*. New York: Dell Publishing.

Goldsack, G. (2001) *My Mum is Great*. Bath: Parragon.

Goldsack, G. (2001) *My Dad is Great*. Bath: Parragon.

Goldsack, G. (2001) *My Grandma is Great*. Bath: Parragon.

Goldsack, G. (2001) *My Grandad is Great*. Bath: Parragon.

Hewitt, S. (1996) *Feeling... Angry*. London: Franklin Watts.

Langley, J. *Missing*. London: Frances Lincoln.

Lear, E. (illus. Oxenbury, H.) *The Quangle Wangle's Hat*. London: Mammoth.

McKinley, P. *Elephants Don't Do Ballet*. London: Frances Lincoln.

Milne, A.A. (2000) *Winnie the Pooh*. London: Methuen.

Milne, A.A. (2000) *The House at Pooh Corner*. London: Methuen.

Milne, A.A. (2000) *Now We Are Six*. London: Methuen.

Milne, A.A. (2000) *When We Were Very Young*. London: Methuen.

Moss, M. (2003) *I Forgot to Say I Love You*. London: MacMillan Publishers Ltd.

Oram, H. and Varley, S. (2001) *Badger's Bad Mood*. London: Diamond Books.

Ormerod, J. (2003) *Kiss It Better*. London: Walker Books.

Rayner, C. (1986) *The Getting Better Book*. London: Piccolo Books.

Ross,T. (1999) *Don't Do That!* London: Red Fox.

Ross,T. (2001) (Little Princess Series) *I Want to Be*. London: Collins Picture Books.

Ross,T. (2001) (Little Princess Series) *I Want a Sister*. London: Collins Picture Books.

Ross, T. (2002) (Little Princess Series) *I want my Dummy*. London: Collins Picture Books.

Ross,T. (2001) (Little Princess Series) *I Want my Dinner*. London: Collins Picture Books.

Ross,T. (2001) (Little Princess Series) *I Don't Want to Go to Hospital*. London: Collins Picture Books.

Roxbee Cox, P. (illus. McCafferty, J.) (2004) *Don't Be a Bully, Billy: A Cautionary Tale*. London: Usborne Publishing Ltd.

Roxbee Cox, P. (illus. McCafferty, J.) (2004) *Don't Tell Lies, Lucy: A Cautionary Tale*. London: Usborne Publishing Ltd.

Roxbee Cox, P. (illus. McCafferty, J.) (2004) *Give That Back, Jack: A Cautionary Tale*. London: Usborne Publishing Ltd.

Sendak, M. (2000) *Where the Wild Things Are*. London: Red Fox.

Snunit, M. (1998) *The Soul Bird*. London: Robinson.

Snunit, M. (1998) *Come and Hug Me*. London: Robinson.

Usborne Pocket Science. *What Makes You Ill?* Usborne Pocket Science (internet linked: www.usborne.com).

Usborne Pocket Science. *Where Do Babies Come From?* Usborne Pocket Science (internet linked:www.usborne.com).

Usborne Pocket Science. *What's Inside You?* Usborne Pocket Science (internet linked: www.usborne.com).

Usborne Pocket Science. *Why Do People Eat?* Usborne Pocket Science (internet linked:www.usborne.com).

Usborne Pocket Science. *How Do Animals Talk?* Usborne Pocket Science (internet linked:www.usborne.com).

Usborne Pocket Science. *Why Is Night Dark?* Usborne Pocket Science (internet linked:www.usborne.com).

Usborne Pocket Science. *Why Are People Different?* Usborne Pocket Science (internet linked:www. usborne.com).

Vachss, A. (1993) *Another Chance to Get It Right.* Milwaukie, OR: Dark Horse Publishing Inc.

Williams, M. (2000) *The Original Velveteen Rabbit.* London: Picture Mammoth.

Willis, J. (2002) *What Do You Want To Be, Brian?* London: Andersen Press.

Wilson, P. (1996) *The Little Book of Calm.* London: Penguin Books.

Wilson, P. (1999) *The Little Book of Sleep.* London: Penguin Books.

Wilson, P. (1999) *The Little Book of Hope.* London: Penguin Books.

Also any audio- and videotapes and CDs (including some of above titles) of rhymes or crazy fun music that parents can put on and 'go mad' for and with their children.

Parenting resources

Adoption UK (formerly PPIAS): 46 The Green, South Bar Street, Banbury OX16 9AB. Tel. 01295 752241; Helpline 0870 7700 450 (11am–4pm Monday to Friday) www.adoptionuk.org

Brain Gym: www.braingym.org.uk

Developmental Integration Technique (DIT): www.developmentalintegration.co.uk

Family Futures Consortium Ltd: 35 Britannia Row, London N1 8QH. Tel. 0207 354 4161; www.familyfutures.co.uk

Holding Families Together, Caroline Archer: caroarcher@ntlworld.com

Holistic Approach to NeuroDevelopmental and Learning Efficiency (HANDLE): www.handle.org

Listen to Learn (AIT) Centre: Tel. 01694 724975

National Light and Sound Therapy Centre (Auditory Integration Training (AIT): www.light-and-sound.co.uk

Parent Network for the Post Institutionalised Child (PNPIC): www.pnpic.org

PNPIC/PARC (Parents of Adopted Romanian Children): Marion Connolly, 53 Castlelands, Balbriggan, Dublin, RoI. Tel. 0035 31841 1530; e-mail: parcireland@eir.com.net

Index